reining in the state

reining in
the state

Civil Society and Congress in
the Vietnam and Watergate Eras

Katherine A. Scott

 University Press of Kansas

Published by the
University Press of
Kansas (Lawrence,
Kansas 66045), which
was organized by
the Kansas Board
of Regents and is
operated and funded
by Emporia State
University, Fort Hays
State University,
Kansas State
University, Pittsburg
State University, the
University of Kansas,
and Wichita State
University

© 2013

by the University Press of Kansas

All rights reserved

Library of Congress Cataloging-in-Publication Data

Scott, Katherine A. (Katherine Anne)

Reining in the state : civil society and Congress in the Vietnam and
Watergate eras / Katherine A. Scott.

pages cm

Includes bibliographical references and index.

ISBN 978-0-7006-1897-2 (alk. paper)

1. Executive power—United States. 2. Transparency in
government—United States. 3. Separation of powers—United
States. 4. Civil society—United States. 5. United States—Politics and
government—1969–1974. I. Title.

JK585.S36 2013

352.23′5097309046—DC23

2012042382

British Library Cataloguing in Publication Data is available.

Printed in the United States of America

10 9 8 7 6 5 4 3 2 1

The paper used in this publication is recycled and contains
30 percent postconsumer waste. It is acid free and meets
the minimum requirements of the American National Standard
for Permanence of Paper for Printed Library Materials z39.48-1992.

For M. R. and P. R.

Contents

Acknowledgments, ix

Introduction, 1

1   "Recruiting an Army": Russ Wiggins Demands Transparency, 10

2   "What's Going On in the Black Community?": Ramsey Clark
    Investigates Civil Disorder, 33

3   "A Communist behind Every Bush": The Army Spies on
    Civilians, 51

4   Senator Sam, or How Liberals Learned to Stop Worrying and
    Love a Southern Segregationist, 67

5   It's "Poppycock": Congress Challenges Executive Privilege, 95

6   An "Effective Servant of the Public's Right to Know":
    Representative Moorhead Revises FOIA, 122

7   "Tempers Change, Times Change, Public Attitudes Change":
    Passing FISA, 150

Epilogue, 179

Notes, 187

Bibliography, 219

Index, 229

Acknowledgments

My parents, Mike and LeOla, have a knack for making adventures out of the simplest things. When I was a kid, one of our favorite "destinations" was the University Bookstore in Seattle. This book is dedicated to my parents who instilled in me a love of learning and a lifelong appreciation for reading. To my mom, my cheerleader, who encouraged me to be whatever I wanted to be including: jockey, barrel-racer, three-day event rider, Washington State senate page, snowboarder, and finally, historian. To my dad, for whom history and learning, reading and writing, have been lifelong passions, I hope this book will make you proud.

This project began as a master's thesis at the University of New Mexico, and many people have guided and shaped its development. David Farber, Richard Immerman, and Beth Bailey offered counsel, friendship, and perfectly timed encouragement when the road to completing this project seemed unbearably long. David's exacting standards made this a much, much better product and me a better writer. For his support, I am grateful. David Greenberg provided sage advice on the dissertation. In Temple University's History Department I found a stimulating intellectual environment and friends who made the lonely archival work endurable, including Ryan Edgington, Michele Louro, Holger Löwendorf, Drew McKevitt, Abby Perkiss, Kelly Shannon, Wendy Wong, Jay Wyatt, and David Zierler. I fondly remember many writing and brainstorming sessions with Abby at Chestnut Hill Coffee Co.

In writing this book I wanted to tell a story about political actors, often overlooked, who shaped events. I am grateful to those who took time to sit down and talk with me about their experiences including Larry Baskir, Aryeh Neier, Charlie Peters, Chris Pyle, John Shattuck, and Mel Wulf.

For the past three years I have closely observed the political and legislative process as a historian in the U.S. Senate Historical Office. To my Senate colleagues, especially Don Ritchie and Betty Koed who offered constructive feedback on the manuscript, I thank you. Special thanks to

Albin Kowalewski, of the House Historian's Office, for helping me locate sources and for his advice on several chapters of the manuscript.

I am indebted to a number of institutions for providing financial support for this project including the Lyndon B. Johnson Library, the Gerald R. Ford Library, the Seeley G. Mudd Manuscript Library at Princeton University, and the Center for Force and Diplomacy and the College of Liberal Arts at Temple University.

Mike Briggs at the University Press of Kansas has enthusiastically supported this project from the beginning. The reviewers, David Barrett and Loch Johnson, provided thoughtful comments, saved me from some errors, and encouraged me to think more broadly about the implications of this story. Their suggestions made this a better book.

Twelve years ago I met Yvan Charpentier in a dumpy bar in the U District. *Quelle chance!* Yvan's unique perspective of the United States and his astute observations about its political culture have made for lively conversation over the years. While he diligently advanced his own career he kept the home fires burning, did the household chores, cared for and entertained little Clara, so that I might focus on writing. He did it (mostly) without complaint. His cheerful "How much more time do you need?" prompted me to work harder so that we could all go have fun together. No one (except me) is more impatient to see this book published. In the words of Francis Cabrel: *Je t'aimais, je t'aime, et je t'aimerai. Gros bisous* to Clara and baby Zane; here's to our many adventures to come.

reining in the state

Introduction

On Saturday, June 11, 1977, John Shattuck, a young attorney with the American Civil Liberties Union (ACLU), parked his car at Marygrove College in Detroit, Michigan. He entered the auditorium, winding his way through the crowd to the folding table on the side. Shattuck pulled dozens of pamphlets and brochures from his worn leather briefcase including one published by the House Government Operations Committee titled, "Litigation under the Freedom of Information Act" and placed them in neat piles on the table. He glanced at his watch and as if on cue, an organizer for the Michigan Coalition to End Government Spying appeared behind the podium to introduce the attorney from Washington, D.C. People quickly took their seats as Shattuck, speaking in his booming baritone, began a talk that he had given dozens of times before. The ACLU's campaign to educate victims of government surveillance, he explained, was a nationwide effort to help citizens understand their basic constitutional rights. Using new laws like the Privacy Act and the Freedom of Information Act (FOIA), those who suspected they had been targets of secret government spy operations could obtain copies of their "dossiers" from government agencies. If they secured evidence that their rights had been violated, Shattuck assured them that the ACLU would provide free legal advice to those wishing to pursue lawsuits against government agencies. A few in the audience scribbled on notepads. After concluding his remarks, he moved off stage, making way for the next speaker, U.S. Congressman John Conyers.[1]

In 1977, the House Committee on Government Operations published the first of its kind citizen's guide on how to request records from federal agencies. Nearly 50,000 copies of this guide were distributed by men like Shattuck to American citizens from 1977 to 1986. Members of Congress, the House Committee on Government Operations, and other federal agencies distributed thousands more. Shattuck attended dozens of conferences like this one in the late 1970s. As an attorney for the ACLU he was part of an army of activists battling to rein in the state. They suc-

"There's Something Wrong About This"

"THERE'S SOMETHING WRONG ABOUT THIS" — A 1971 Herblock Cartoon, copyright by *The Herb Block Foundation*

ceeded in transforming the American state from one that operated with few checks and balances regarding government intrusion into privacy, to one that was inherently more transparent. Their movement had a lasting impact on the nation's most powerful institutions and shaped American political culture well into the twenty-first century.

This book is a history of the movement to rein in the state during the 1970s. It chronicles the efforts of a group of unheralded heroes who battled to reinvigorate judicial, legislative, and civic oversight of the executive branch to prevent abuses by government agencies in the future. The cast of characters includes Russ Wiggins, editor of the *Washington Post*, who organized a journalist campaign for government transparency; John

Moss, a representative from California, who called the public's attention to government censorship during the Cold War; U.S. Army Captain Christopher Pyle, who blew the whistle on the army's secret domestic surveillance programs; Aryeh Neier, the director of the ACLU, who created a legal strategy to increase judicial oversight of executive branch security measures; Senator Sam Ervin, a civil libertarian, who demanded greater congressional oversight of the executive branch; and Morton Halperin, a former National Security Council (NSC) staff member, who called attention to the gross constitutional violations of the nation's top security agencies. During the 1970s, these reformers stood apart from the radical left and the anti-government right. Rather than overthrow or demolish American political institutions, they sought to bring the American state in line with democratic practice. Like their early twentieth-century forbearers, they believed in the power of good government. Informed by 1960s culture, they sought to invigorate participatory democracy.

These reformers responded to an era of unprecedented growth of the federal government since 1932. Nothing better exemplified that growth than the vast expansion of the national security state. In the immediate aftermath of World War II, federal officials centralized foreign policymaking within the executive branch to ensure that intelligence gathering and sharing were more systematically integrated into the American state. The National Security Act of 1947 established the Central Intelligence Agency (CIA) and the NSC and unified the armed services under one administrative office within the new Department of Defense. These capacities greatly enhanced the power of the president to conduct foreign policy.[2] In particular, Cold War–era presidential administrations, sometimes but not always working closely with Congress, further expanded the national security state with new agencies and departments. Before the mid-1970s, democratic oversight of this burgeoning bureaucracy, whether by congressional hearings, mass media investigations, or public interest groups, was inconsistent, at best.

During the 1960s and early 1970s American presidents Lyndon B. Johnson and Richard M. Nixon responded to an era of social change movements, radical politics, and urban disorders by expanding the federal government's domestic surveillance capacities. Using new computer and data bank technologies, federal agencies watched, wiretapped, and spied on broad segments of the American population. By the mid-1970s the Departments of the Army and Justice alone maintained some 400 data banks containing nearly 200 million files on individuals and organizations in the United States, capacities that rivaled the Federal Bureau of Investigation (FBI) (in 1970 the U.S. population totaled some 203 million). Rarely did elected and appointed officials and career civil servants worry how the implementation of these programs might undermine civil liberties. Few possessed a profound appreciation for constitutional law. They were, for the most part, technocrats with a powerful trust in the use of technology and institutional capacity to solve social problems. A few cautioned against such broad domestic surveillance operations, fearing the breakdown of constitutional authority in the process. But even they assumed the programs would be temporary, though necessary, evils—measures that officials would discontinue after tempers cooled and social order returned. While scholars have developed a rich literature that explores the growth of the FBI's domestic response to urban unrest and civil disorder in the 1960s, few have explained the central role the Department of Justice and the Department of Defense played in domestic security operations, especially in the 1960s era.[3]

The state's domestic spy operations and the tumultuous politics of the 1960s created fertile ground for reformers to challenge the power and reach of the national security state. The turbulent events of the late 1960s—the increasingly unpopular war in Vietnam, the limitations of the War on Poverty, the assassinations of Robert Kennedy and Martin Luther King, Jr., the urban riots and campus protests throughout the decade—seriously undermined the U.S. public's belief in the competency of national political figures and government institutions to solve the nation's problems. The citizenry's alienation also fostered a wave of individual and organizational efforts to rein in state power. When whistle-blowers pulled back the curtain on secret domestic surveillance programs in the early 1970s, neo-progressives led the campaign to halt these programs.

Activists such as Christopher Pyle, Aryeh Neier, and Morton Halperin partnered with editors and journalists Russ Wiggins, Charlie Peters, and Seymour Hersh, who demanded greater transparency of government agencies. Beginning with Franklin Roosevelt's censorship policies during World War II, presidential administrations regularly restricted or censored the news during the Cold War era. Frustrated journalists and editors demanded better access to information at the local, state, and federal levels. Editors and journalists organized a right to know movement through their professional organizations, such as Sigma Delta Chi and the American Society of Newspaper Editors (ASNE). Spurred on by the censorship policies of both Democratic and Republican presidential administrations, and in particular, the Johnson administration's "credibility gap" over its Vietnam War policy, journalists revived a kind of investigative journalism that had lain dormant for decades. The mainstream media created new forms, both in print and television, through which journalists could publicize their exposés. NBC's *First Tuesday,* CBS's *60 Minutes,* and the *Washington Monthly* offered forums for journalists to publish in-depth stories about the nation's most powerful people and institutions.

Investigative reports of civil liberties abuses by national security agencies spurred neo-progressives and members of Congress to rein in executive power. While scholars have detailed efforts by the legislative branch to rein in the state following the Watergate scandal, their work has overlooked congressional efforts to challenge executive privilege, wiretapping, and surveillance and to protect First Amendment rights and individual privacy—efforts made long before Watergate became headline news.[4] Beginning in the 1950s and working closely with organizations such as the ASNE, the ACLU, Common Cause, and the Center for National Security Studies, members of Congress devoted their committee and staff resources to better understanding the burgeoning power of the executive branch, particularly on national security issues.

In the twenty years before Watergate, activists relied on a loose coalition of elected officials, Republicans and Democrats, conservatives and liberals, senators and members of the House of Representatives, to strengthen their calls for national security reform: Donald Rumsfeld (R-IL), Barry Goldwater, Jr. (R-CA), and William Moorhead (D-PA), and Senators Ervin, Edward Kennedy (D-MA), Walter Mondale (D-MN), Chuck Percy (R-IL), Frank Church (D-ID), Mike Mansfield (D-MT), and William Fulbright (D-AR). But few federal lawmakers had done more to investigate and reform the state's control over public information than California Democrat John Moss, chairman of a House Government Operations subcommittee and the father of the FOIA. After conducting dozens of hearings, consulting closely with media organizations and right to know advocates, and publishing thousands of pages of reports, Moss earned bipartisan support in the House and Senate for his legislative efforts. In 1966 President Lyndon Johnson signed the FOIA, legally defining the public's right to know and providing Americans with new tools to request government information. In the Senate, conservative Democrat Sam Ervin of North Carolina investigated issues related to the presidential aggrandizement of power, including executive privilege, wiretaps and black bag jobs, surveillance, and the right to privacy.

Activists' demands for greater transparency and accountability in the executive branch appealed broadly to members of both parties. Conservatives denounced the burgeoning power of the executive branch as a violation of the separation of powers and as evidence of a tyrannical executive. They pointed to Soviet-style totalitarianism as an example of state power run amok. Senator Ervin called the right to dissent one of the founding principles of the United States and a keystone of American democracy. The state must impose law and order, conservatives insisted, while also protecting the fundamental tenets of American democracy—especially the right to privacy.

Like conservatives, liberals opposed state domestic spy programs on constitutional grounds. But their objections were not rooted in a fundamental aversion to state power. Though they charged national security managers with blatant disregard for American constitutional rights—dissent, freedom of association, personal privacy—they worried more about how unchecked state power undermined American democracy. The state's natural tendency toward secrecy, they argued, deprived citizens of their fundamental right to know what their government was doing. Liberals wanted to protect legitimate national security institutions such as the FBI and CIA by making these agencies more transparent and accountable to the public. Though conservatives and liberals differed in their philosophical approach to solving the nation's problems and in their understanding of the role of government in everyday life, they all agreed that the army had no business spying on civilians.

By uniting this loose coalition of allies, reformers won major legislative victories and landmark judicial decisions throughout the 1970s. Beginning with the 1966 signing of the FOIA, the movement reached its apex in 1978 with the passage of the Foreign Intelligence Surveillance Act (FISA). Contrary to recent works that have identified the 1970s as the first decade of "diminishing democracy" when Americans withdrew from national associations that had organized sociopolitical life for nearly two centuries, civic activism flourished throughout the decade.[5] Public advocacy groups proliferated in the 1960s and 1970s, largely because of the institutional failures of the state. Activists worked with public advocacy groups to create new organizations dedicated to educating the public and lobbying elected officials to enact legislative reform. Believing that policy change would come only through the imposition of new legal and institutional structures, they sought to ignite public debate and shape public discourse. Through conferences, letters-to-the-editor campaigns, and congressional hearings and investigations, they coordinated a strategy to educate the public to the abuses of the national security state. Through the process of discourse and debate, reformers gained public and congressional support for sweeping policy changes, including the FOIA (1966), its revisions in 1974, the Privacy Act of 1974, the Government in the Sunshine Act of 1976, resolutions creating permanent intelligence oversight committees in the House and Senate, and the FISA (1978).

Reformers, investigative journalists, and "good government" activists reshaped powerful institutions in the 1970s, though until now they have received little attention by historians. To explain the politics of the era we must explore how civil society developed new capacities to force change even as street protests and radical politics diminished. Though recent works have done much to broaden our understanding of the role individuals, organizations, and associations have played in leveraging political power at the local, state, and national levels, the role of civil society in American political development remains under-explored.[6]

This is a story not only of efforts to stop repressive government power. It is also a story of how these reformers' efforts, ironically, had the long-term effect of legitimating the national security state. Activists instituted policy reforms to strengthen oversight of the federal government among its three branches. They developed new state capacities to manage constitutional checks and balances: bureaucracies within bureaucracies to process FOIA requests, new congressional committees to oversee domestic and foreign intelligence programs, and a new national security court to oversee requests for wiretaps. To restrain the federal government's domestic security programs, reformers strengthened and enlarged the state, simultaneously legitimating and normalizing domestic security programs.[7] Reformers built up the state in order to restrain state power.

This book traces the growth of this movement from a small but vocal coterie of the nation's most powerful news editors and journalists in the 1950s, to its apex with the passage of the FISA in 1978. While the movement is best defined by activists' trust in "good government," reformers' motivations changed over time. In the 1950s and early 1960s, they demanded greater transparency from government. The state's response to civil unrest and disorder in the mid-1960s prompted activists to reiterate the people's right to protest. These constitutional violations led neo-progressives to demand broader protections by reinvigorating checks and balances throughout the 1970s. Chapter 1 examines the roots of the right to know movement when journalists, editors, and publishers responded to government censorship policies. Their campaign prompted some Americans, and a key ally in Congress, Representative John Moss of California, to demand greater transparency in government and culminated with the passage of the first federal law requiring the disclosure of information. Chapters 2 and 3 trace the state's response to urban revolts, mass protests, and rising crime, focusing on the secret programs developed within the Department of Justice and the Department of Defense to gather information about rioters and dissidents across the nation.

When a counterintelligence officer blew the whistle on the U.S. Army's domestic surveillance program, reformers had evidence of domestic spying that they had long suspected—but could not confirm. Chapter 4 explores how one officer's story united liberals and conservatives to demand an end to the executive branch's unchecked domestic surveillance programs. In the late 1960s and early 1970s, advocacy groups like the ACLU sought to rein in national security policy from the bench. In the words of Aryeh Neier, the ACLU's executive director and an architect of its civil litigation program, the organization hoped "to stop political surveillance of dissenters," and to compel the government, through the courts, "to reveal information that it tries to keep secret."[8] Chapter 5 explores the judicial and legislative strategies pursued by reformers.

When the Watergate story broke, reformers argued that the scandal was further evidence of the need to rein in the state. Indeed, Watergate proved a watershed event, which prompted broad debate in the public sphere about the problems of executive power and the need for greater transparency in domestic security policy and more careful oversight of the activities of various agencies—especially the FBI and CIA—within the national security state. Chapter 6 explores how, in the wake of Watergate, Congress enhanced citizens' ability to access government information, revising the FOIA to grant the public and the media more powerful tools of discovery. The Privacy Act created a new mechanism for citizens to petition the government for access to their individual records and to dispute the material held therein. Reformers hailed these laws as major victories for the American people.

The Senate Watergate investigation revealed that the executive branch had misused intelligence agencies and capacities, sometimes for political gain, and chapter 7 explores the congressional response to these revelations, placing the creation of permanent congressional intelligence oversight committees in the context of a longer reform effort. Reformers also successfully passed a law to restrict wiretapping and surveillance of American citizens on home soil, the FISA.

The battle to rein in state power did not begin or end in the 1970s, but this successful movement offers a lens through which we can better understand the parameters of the same struggle today. The concentration of power within the executive branch, one of the defining features of the federal government in the twentieth century, has ignited fierce public debate on the left and right. Though the executive branch continues to have extraordinary powers, particularly in the conduct of foreign relations and national security, this study suggests that state power is, after all, historically contingent. In the 1970s reformers envisioned how a nation of empowered citizen activists could prevent government abuse in the future. They promoted a set of principles that define political debate today: that the people have a "right to know," that transparency strengthens democracy, and that the state cannot be allowed to accumulate unchecked powers without impinging upon the rights of its citizens.

CHAPTER ONE

"Recruiting an Army"
Russ Wiggins Demands Transparency

John Finney, science correspondent for the New York Times, *fumed. In February he received a polite letter from the U.S. Navy in response to his query. Yes, the navy had recently provided two scientists with a grant to study giraffes in Africa. The recipients of the award, the navy spokesman explained, would examine giraffes' capacity to lift their heads swiftly from the ground to the air without blacking out. The navy had received criticism for funding the study. Critics had asked the obvious question: why send researchers to Africa when they could study giraffes at the local zoo? Given that taxpayer money funded the project, Finney assumed that receiving a copy of the report would be a simple matter. The navy promised to send Finney a copy of the report as soon as it was complete. Months passed. When he opened the* Post *on October 28 to find a front-page story by Nate Haseltine describing the study's conclusion, he was incensed. Not only had he been out-scooped by Haseltine, but it seemed clear that the navy had never intended to give him the report.[1] Reporters like Finney were always up against the government's monopoly on information.*

Russell "Russ" Wiggins had closely observed Senator Joseph McCarthy's meteoric rise to national prominence. As managing editor of the *Washington Post and Times-Herald*, he regularly approved front-page stories featuring the senator's allegations. He knew, as did many of his colleagues, that those allegations had been at times misleading or downright false. Though Wiggins abhorred the Wisconsin senator's tactics, McCarthy's charges were news, in the most basic definition of the word. Like other editors, Wiggins assured himself that his audience would ferret out the truth. He surely agreed with a *New York Times* editorial explaining the uneasy relationship many news editors had with McCarthy: "It is difficult, if not impossible, to ignore charges by Senator McCarthy just because they are usually proved exaggerated or false. The remedy lies with the reader."[2]

In 1953, as chairman of the Senate Permanent Subcommittee on Investigations, McCarthy targeted several high-profile government agencies for investigation, including the State Department and the U.S. Information Agency. When he announced plans to investigate the U.S. Army Signal Corps in the fall, Wiggins felt certain that the senator had gone too far. Indeed, the tables quickly turned on McCarthy when the army accused him and his assistant, Roy Cohn, of seeking preferential treatment for committee staff member and army private G. David Schine. Broadcast on national television, millions of Americans followed the Army-McCarthy hearings.

President Dwight Eisenhower shared the public's interest in the Army-McCarthy investigation. Initially, the senator's strident anticommunism and his committee's work had strengthened the Republican Party. Though the president privately expressed concern about McCarthy's tactics, publicly he maintained a cordial, if distant, relationship with the senator, until McCarthy's attacks on the army forced the president's hand. Eisenhower could not tolerate the senator's assault on the organization in which he had spent his adult life. Though he had at times cooperated with McCarthy and his investigations, Eisenhower ended that cooperation when the committee demanded access to high-level White House documents and threatened to subpoena top White House aides. The president wrote a letter to Secretary of Defense Charles Wilson asserting the president's absolute right of executive privilege.[3]

John Adams of the U.S. Army read aloud the president's letter to the Senate subcommittee on May 17, 1954: "to maintain the proper separation of powers between Executive and Legislative Branches of the Government," the president had instructed members of the executive branch "not to testify to any such conversations or communications or to produce any such documents or reproductions . . . regardless of who would benefit by such disclosures." McCarthy's opponents immediately cheered the White House position. Editors at the *Times* applauded the president's letter, asserting that "the [Sub] committee [on Investigations] has no more right to know the details of what went on in these inner Administration counsels than the Administration would have the right to know what went on in an executive session of a committee of Congress."[4] Though the media would normally oppose the withholding of information, in this case, McCarthy's opponents hoped the episode signaled an end to the senator's celebrity status.

As a newspaperman, Russ Wiggins found the president's claim of executive privilege bittersweet. Surely it undermined McCarthy's power. The president's assertion of executive privilege, however, posed a challenge to the news business. As chairman of the American Society of Newspaper Editors (ASNE), Wiggins stood at the forefront of a small but vocal right to know movement. What the movement lacked in size (less than 1,000 members nationwide), it made up for with disproportionate access to the corridors of public opinion. By the mid-1950s Wiggins and his organization counted a few members of Congress among their allies. After repeated clashes with the executive branch—first with Harry Truman's administration over the management of loyalty programs, and later because of Eisenhower's assertion of "executive privilege"—some elected officials began to publicly criticize the opacity of the executive branch. In the House, John E. Moss, Jr., from California's third district, became journalism's most influential ally. A Democrat, Moss was politically motivated to criticize the Eisenhower administration, but the congressman also firmly believed in the immutable right of the public to know what its elected officials, and by extension, its government, were doing. In the context of the Cold War, these right to know activists argued that freedom of information was one of the defining characteristics of a free, open, and democratic society.

As chairman of the Subcommittee on Government Information of the House Government Operations Committee, Moss worked doggedly to make the issue of transparency and the public's right to know a political issue as well as an issue of public policy. From 1955 to 1966 the Moss committee investigations produced seventeen volumes of hearings and fourteen volumes of reports.[5] The transparency campaign began to bear fruit by the mid-1960s, thanks in no small part to American involvement in Vietnam. Harnessing the power of a concerned and increasingly vocal polity who demanded access to information about government actions and decision-making processes, Moss and a bipartisan coalition of congressional allies successfully passed legislation to force government transparency. The Freedom of Information Act of 1966 codified the new transparency regime. Its supporters hoped that it would bring down the "paper curtain" which had come to symbolize the government's control of information.

Russ Wiggins got his start in Washington in 1933 as a correspondent for the St. Paul, Minnesota, *Dispatch Pioneer Press*. The New Deal era was an exciting time to be in the nation's capital and Wiggins worked hard, rising to the position of managing editor at age thirty-five. It was during a

Russell J. Wiggins, managing editor, *Washington Post and Times-Herald* (Raymond H. Fogler Library, University of Maine)

stint in the army during the war that Wiggins met Phil Graham, who later became owner and publisher of the *Washington Post.* This relationship, perhaps more than any other, would define Wiggins's professional career in the years to come. After the war, Wiggins worked briefly as assistant to the editor at the *New York Times,* but it wasn't long before Graham invited him to Washington to serve as managing editor of the *Post.* He quickly became an influential member of ASNE, a hub of professional activism in the 1950s.

Given his long career in Washington, Wiggins was accustomed to censorship. Since World War II, editors and journalists had adjusted to the executive branch's tendency to withhold information in the name of protecting "national security." Reporters came to refer to these varying degrees of censorship as the "paper curtain"—the barrier the White House and executive-level departments and agencies erected to prevent inquisitive reporters from gaining access to information. In the postwar years, President Harry Truman was the first to issue new standards for the dissemination of information. In September 1951 Truman issued Executive Order 10290, establishing "minimum standards" of classification of information "designed to protect the national security against unauthorized disclosure."[6] The order was intended, in the words of one journalist, to "keep secret or restricted information out of the hands of spies." In practice, the measure allowed the executive branch to withhold information from anyone in the name of national security. The press and the president's political opponents criticized the measure. Associated Press editors, at their annual meeting, denounced it as "a dangerous instrument of news suppression" and challenged the president to find a balance between "the sometimes conflicting claims of complete information and absolute security." Despite the efforts of local, state, and federal officials to "conceal public information," the editors resolved "we have full confidence in the power of American newspapers to defeat [censorship] if every editor does his part." Robert McCormick, prominent conservative and the editor/publisher of the *Chicago Daily Tribune*, declared in a public radio address in 1951 that Truman's order was "designed to keep the American people from knowing what their government is doing." He suggested that the administration's news policy was a method for "seal[ing] away" any information that reflected unfavorably on the administration or its friends. McCormick issued a call to arms: "This is what freedom of the press means to you. You will enjoy it only so long as you defend it and fight for it."[7]

No one knew better than President Truman's White House press secretary, Joseph Short, how much the media detested restrictive information policies. At a briefing following the announcement of the president's executive order, Short attempted to defend it, noting that the White House had consulted with the ASNE before drafting the order. Short's explanations did nothing to calm the gaggle of angry reporters. What should they do, they demanded to know, if they feel information has been unnecessarily classified? Short suggested, "go to the information officer of the agency involved, and, if he declines to act, carry the matter to the department head." And in the event that meeting produced no results? Short conceded, "I can only stick my neck out and say—come and see me about it."[8]

Historically, the relationship between the White House and the press had been a contested one. But the testy exchange at the press conference suggested that White House correspondents were growing increasingly impatient with the government's monopoly on information. Truman's executive order galvanized a coordinated effort among editors and reporters to challenge government secrecy. In the early 1950s print news editors and journalists had two large professional organizations through which they could lobby their cause, Sigma Delta Chi, the association for journalism professionals, and ASNE.

To better challenge censorship policies, ASNE formed the Freedom of Information committee and elected James Pope, editor of the Kentucky *Louisville-Courier Journal*, as chairman. A recipient of the Society of Professional Journalism's highest honor for extraordinary contribution to the profession in 1952, Pope was well respected by his peers. Pope believed "that when the people rule, they have a right to know all their Government does" and was a committed advocate of government transparency. Shining a light on local, state, and federal government seemed a herculean task that would require an army of dedicated activists. To fight censorship, Pope encouraged journalists to arouse public opinion: "If you tell the people in the paper and report that someone is keeping news from them, then you are recruiting the army that can do the job."[9]

Pope and his colleagues carefully drew parallels between the "tightening down of news barriers" at home and the censorship exercised by totalitarian regimes behind the Iron Curtain. This was precisely the message that freedom of information advocates took to the gathering of the Associated Press Managing Editors Association (APME) in late September 1951. V. M. Newton, chairman of the APME news production committee, urged attendees to "join together as allies and make a joint fight in behalf of the highest principles of freedom of the press." Speakers expressed concern about the ten-year jail sentence handed down to one of their own, the Associated Press's bureau chief in Prague, William N. Oatis, who had been arrested in May 1951 and subjected to torture, before confessing to espionage. According to Turner Catledge, executive managing editor of the *New York Times*, the case highlighted the challenges American journalists faced when reporting from behind the Iron Curtain. Regularly, journalists compared the battles fought by American soldiers against the armies of tyranny: press freedom was "being blocked off now by more camouflage, more barbed wire and red tape entanglements, than any army of freedom ever encountered in the trenches." Drawing a parallel with the Oatis case, Kent Cooper, AP executive director, expressed his "alarm" at the American government's efforts to "cover up mistakes in public office." Russ Wiggins suggested that Truman's executive order granted civil servants the legal justification to cover up their own wrongdoing. "Many crimes," Wiggins asserted, "have been committed in the name of security." He urged "courageous" editors to "find means of circumventing" the government's paper curtain.[10]

With American soldiers fighting in Korea, even the most vocal advocates for the freedom of information recognized the state's need for secrecy in matters of national security, but journalists opposed being "spoon-fed information carefully selected" by bureaucrats. Some argued, "If we are to hear only the good news, we shall know little of what's going on in Korea. . . . the American people have the right to know the whole story. Whose war is this, anyway?" Drew Pearson of the *Post* complained that the Truman administration held fewer press conferences than its predecessor. Some found it ironic that the man who rose to national prominence as chairman of the Senate's Special Committee to Investigate the National Defense Program was now restricting the flow of information from the executive to the legislative branch. Critics warned that the president's executive order and censorship policies might facilitate corruption: "Recalling some of the war contracts let during the last war, it is obvious what kind of information these bur[eau]crats will mark 'secret' and seal away."[11]

Journalists and editors who compared U.S. information policies with those of totalitarian Communist states did so at their own risk. Anticommunism in the United States, driven in part by the Truman administration's policies, and in part by Senator Joe McCarthy, shaped American political discourse. Challenging government information policies—particularly those related to national security—made reformers vulnerable to claims that they aided Communist enemies. One editorial explained this tenuous position: "We don't want to aid the enemy . . . no one, least of all the correspondents, wants to violate security." Instead, newspapermen made their demands in the context of First Amendment rights, which they argued protected the citizens' right to know and the right to free association. Activists made the case that the democratic adherence to the Bill of Rights distinguished the United States from its Cold War enemies. As Kent Cooper explained, the right to know is a right that cannot be forced on America's allies "whose conceptions of press freedom are not like ours," but these freedoms should be encouraged for "it is the well-informed peoples who will be free."[12]

Though they had the ability to shape public opinion, freedom of information advocates lacked hard evidence that government agencies consistently and intentionally limited the people's "right to know." Partly in response to journalist and editor requests for advice as to how to gain greater access to information at the local, state, and federal level of government, ASNE commissioned a comprehensive study of existing policies. The Freedom of Information Committee selected Harold Cross, counsel for the *New York Herald Tribune* and lecturer on libel at Columbia University, to complete the study. Cross produced an exhaustive study of information policies at the local, state, and federal level titled *The People's Right to Know*. The ASNE hailed the book as a guide for the "working newspaper man" who sees the "need for full information about increasingly complex government." The book offered advice for the legal profession where "few . . . have specialized in any degree in the laws affecting access to public information." Members of Congress might also be interested to know "that their colleagues in the executive branch of the national government have been according themselves extensive immunity from the public gaze." *A People's Right to Know*, the ASNE hoped, would provide ammunition for the "unfocused protests against news suppression" to take on the "firm, confident character of a true resistance movement."[13]

The movement had many promising leaders and a growing "army" of activists. But it lacked an ally with access to the levers of political power. John Emerson Moss, Jr., a Democrat from northern California, would become the right to know movement's greatest advocate. Little in his political or personal record made him a natural proponent of the public's "right to know." Moss was born in Hiawatha, Utah, on April 13, 1913. His father, John Sr., worked in the coal mines. His mother, Orta, cared for the family's five children. When John Jr. suffered from chronic respiratory ailments not uncommon in coal mining communities, Orta convinced her husband to bring the family west in 1923, where they settled in Sacramento. Only three years later, in April 1927, John's mother passed away suddenly from blood poisoning. John's father "went to pieces" and disappeared, returning to visit his children only intermittently over the next few years. Orta's sisters took John and his siblings under their wings.[14]

As the country descended into the Great Depression, John Jr. helped support the family by working after school at Sacramento's largest drugstore, Central Drug. While working behind the counter as a soda jerk, he had ample opportunity to listen as locals talked about the news, their worries, their hopes and dreams. He voraciously devoured local newspapers.[15] While he planned a career in medicine, Moss attended Sacramento City College after graduating high school where he found his intellectual home. His interests drifted away from pre-med science courses toward government. Under the tutelage of several faculty members, including historian Herman Leader and Dr. John Harold Swan, who later became dean of the McGeorge School of Law, he joined the Young Democrats. After working on several local and statewide campaigns, including Culbert Olson's successful bid for governor in 1938, the Democratic State

Central Committee elected Moss secretary of education. He rose quickly through the state party ranks, eventually becoming Sacramento County's Democratic Central Committee Secretary. He also coordinated Frank Buck's successful campaigns for a seat in the U.S. House of Representatives in 1940 and 1942.[16]

Initially rejected by the military for medical ailments, including early onset arthritis, Moss joined the war effort in 1943 when draft boards began to relax their medical standards for want of men. He performed personnel work for the navy in San Francisco. During his two years in the service Moss distinguished himself only in the number of times that he angered and irritated his superiors. His refusal to follow orders, his obstinacy, and his insatiable demands for explanations as to why tasks had to be carried out in a certain way infuriated his superior officers. Perhaps more than any other life experience, Moss's time in the navy helped shape a coherent political philosophy. The military's insistence on "unquestioning conformity," Moss later recalled, seemed incompatible with a "self-governing society" where individuals have a right to question authority and a "right to know" what their government is doing.[17]

In February 1945, with a medical discharge in hand, Moss hurried back to Sacramento where he opened an appliance store. For three years he struggled to keep his independent family-owned business afloat. Eager to get back to politics he decided to run for the California state assembly in 1948. Moss and his wife, Jean, funded his campaign out of their own pockets. He won his seat and served in the state assembly from 1949 to 1952, when he ran for a seat in the U.S. House of Representatives. Again financing his own campaign, Moss eked out a victory, besting his opponent by only 3 percentage points—or 5,200 votes.[18]

The 1952 election offered the GOP a resounding national victory, handing Republicans control of both chambers of Congress and the White House for the first time in twenty years. Moss was one of a handful of Democratic freshman who took the oath in the House of Representatives at the beginning of the 83rd Congress. But if the young congressman was daunted by his minority status, he didn't show it. Taking lessons from his years in the California statehouse, he introduced himself to every committee chairman and tried to get to know them.[19]

Moss's first committee assignment was with the relatively obscure Post Office and Civil Service Committee, but the assignment propelled the young Californian down a path to becoming the nation's most vocal right to know advocate. Only a few weeks into the session, the committee chair, Republican Edward Reese of Kansas, appealed to the Civil

John Emerson Moss, member of the U.S. House of Representatives, 1953–1978 (John E. Moss Papers, Department of Special Collections and University Archives, The Library, California State University, Sacramento)

Service Commission for documents relating to the Truman administration's dismissal of federal employees, including postal workers, who were known to be Communists. The inquiry was politically motivated: Reese hoped the files would reveal that the White House had done nothing to prevent Communists from working in government agencies. Moss, on the other hand, believed that the president had done all he could to bar Communists from serving in the federal government and thought the files would prove it. The Civil Service Commission, much to the frustration of both members, refused to supply the House committee with key documents.[20]

In 1954 President Eisenhower invoked "executive privilege," directing his closest advisors not to disclose the details of White House meetings to congressional committees. Many liberals cheered the president's decision, believing that it would weaken Senator Joe McCarthy's power on Capitol Hill, and thereby that of the Republican Party. When Democrats regained the majority in the House in 1955, however, political considerations drove them to challenge the president on the issue of transparency. William Dawson of Illinois, chairman of the Committee on Government Operations, selected Moss to chair a special subcommittee and tasked him with investigating allegations that the executive branch intentionally withheld information from the media, Congress, and the general public. Dawson insisted that "if the pertinent and necessary information on governmental activities is denied the public, the result is a weakening of the democratic process and the ultimate atrophy of our form of government."[21] Moss threw himself into his work, spending hours each day poring over materials in his office and at home.

A quick study and an astute politician, Moss came to understand that clashes over access to information had defined the relationship between the legislative and executive branches since the nation's founding. In 1792, when the House created a committee to investigate the military blunders of General Arthur St. Clair, President George Washington and his cabinet at first refused to comply with House demands for persons and papers, though Washington later acquiesced. The Eisenhower assertion of executive privilege worried journalists and editors because it expanded this concept to include virtually any topic discussed in the West Wing.[22]

Though he recognized the history of the issue, Moss had little information about the extent of the problem. Did the executive branch systematically deny the press or Congress access to information? Moss contacted the ASNE, who provided the congressman with the Freedom of Information committee's annual reports. The ASNE reports collectively painted a bleak picture of an obtuse government determined to distribute only information that painted the respective agency or department in the best light. Moss wanted to know: How did the departments and agencies within the sprawling executive branch interpret the president's "executive privilege" claim? How did they respond, generally, to requests for information related to the functioning of the government? To answer these questions, Moss instructed his congressional staff to prepare a questionnaire for government agencies about their information policies: How many work in these branches? How are they funded? What percentage of time do individuals spend answering requests for information compared with time spent preparing information for press releases?[23] Moss's staff distributed the questionnaire throughout the executive branch, including to agencies such as the U.S. Navy, Army, and Marines.

On November 7, 1955, Moss gaveled to order his first "hearing" on freedom of information, announcing that the committee sought an answer to a simple question: Does "the public ha[ve] available all information about the day-to-day operations of the Federal Government"?[24] Moss invited the most prominent voices in the field of journalism to testify. Russ Wiggins kicked off the discussion, commending the committee for collecting statistics from executive agencies, which he thought proved what journalists knew all along—that the government did not have a uniform information distribution policy. Each agency handled information requests differently, if they considered them at all. It was just the kind of evidence that Wiggins and his group of journalist activists needed to strengthen their calls for transparency.[25]

Wiggins focused his statement on the roots of the government's information policy. From his perspective, the decline of open government paralleled the expansion of government. But he also believed that the policies of federal agencies to withhold information as the rule, rather than the exception, reflected a bureaucratic culture with a "declining faith in the wisdom of the people which is an aspect of this generation's counterrevolution against free institutions." National security issues, which had steadily increased since World War I, further restricted the flow of information from the government to the people. Wiggins conceded that living "in a world where we must be prepared to resist aggression" required some secrecy. "Most editors have accepted the necessity for secrecy of the kind established" by presidential executive orders, Wiggins insisted, even though the details of those restrictions might be "objectionable." Wiggins called secrecy "infectious and contagious," offering myriad examples of cases where bureaucrats had overclassified materials, not for security purposes, but for political ones.[26]

Considered to be the nation's foremost legal expert on right to know issues, Harold Cross encouraged lawmakers to draft legislation granting citizens a legal right to request and inspect "federal nonjudicial record[s]." Congress, he politely charged, had been derelict in its constitutional duties, neither enforcing existing statutes nor enacting new legislation to provide citizens with access to documents relating to the "dynamic, dramatic expansion of government activities." "On the face of the law as it stands," Cross explained, "a vast area of Federal public business is none of the public's business except as officialdom is disposed to be gracious." Absent legislation, the courts had been "bereft of authority" and had stood "aside as a band of silent men." Cross forewarned, "Until the time arrives when the freedom to obtain information receives the same majestic consideration as the freedom to print or utter information, Congress is the primary source of relief."[27]

Advocates of greater transparency followed the testimony of Wiggins and Cross. V. M. Newton, Jr., the managing editor of the *Tampa Morning Tribune* and the chairman of Sigma Delta Chi, described "the 'paper curtain' draped securely over the release of news in the executive branch." Newton claimed some departments practiced outright censorship, others were guided by the "arrogance" of "public servants" who jealously guarded information, while yet others practiced "propaganda" and exhibited "favoritism, intimidation, and revenge" in the release of government information. Newton charged that the legislative branch was no better, noting that committees "held 3,105 meetings in 1953" and 44 percent of those were "secret meetings with the press and the public barred." Keeping abreast of more than 2,000 executive-level agencies and departments made a journalist's task impossible, and the press had come to rely "in good faith" on the "proclamations, reports, and propaganda issued by Government." The growth of government and the parallel rise in the opacity of institutions, according to Newton, perverted the democratic process, leaving the American public with little information with which to assess the operations of their elected and appointed officials and the daily procedures of their government. A little secrecy in government, Newton concluded, was impossible. Secrecy spread like cancer, infecting every cell of the American government. "We can no more have a little secret government than we can have a little freedom, a little justice, or a little morality."[28]

The issue of government transparency was a small-town problem, too. Guy Easterly, the owner-publisher of a weekly newspaper in small town La Follette, Tennessee, explained that "no longer are the people of the many small communities across the Nation isolated from their Government, as they once were." He estimated that La Follette residents came into regular contact with ten or twelve separate government agencies such as the Atomic Energy Commission at Oak Ridge, the Internal Revenue Department, the Tennessee Valley Authority, the FBI, and the Bureau of Mines. Journalists at his newspaper reported on state, county, and municipal governments, but consistently found the federal government to be the least transparent at every level.[29]

Syndicated columnist Joseph Alsop, Jr., compared U.S. information policies with those behind the Iron Curtain. Alsop charged the U.S. government with investigating and intimidating the "newspaperman who ventures to publish what he regards as a life-and-death fact of considerable national importance." A journalist who dared seek out information the government wanted kept secret, according to Alsop, was subject to "having his wires tapped," an extrademocratic procedure "done in the sacred name of security."[30]

James Reston, Washington correspondent for the *New York Times*, described how national security agencies deliberately frustrated journalists who wanted information. The CIA, for example, employed news management experts to complicate journalists' efforts to report on the agency. "Trained in the tradition of probing under and trying to get the news," the journalist of the Cold War era faced an embarrassing dilemma with the agency: "Is [he] going to tell the truth" or is he "going to mislead the American people by putting out something put out by the Government which he knows not to be true"? Reston said that the CIA posed a "growing problem" for the free press and beseeched the Moss committee to investigate the agency.[31]

Radio and television news organizations, explained Theodore Koop, director of Columbia Broadcasting Service, faced unique challenges from "Government officials [who] refuse or fail to recognize this comparatively new media of radio and television." Speaker of the House Sam Rayburn, for example, allowed only "reporters with pencil and papers" to cover committee hearings.[32] Wade Nichols, editor and publisher of *Redbook Magazine*, explained that though magazine journalists did not report on the "fast-breaking news of the moment," they, too, suffered from restricted access to information. To evaluate a government program over time, Nichols explained, his writers often requested access to government archives, requests that were nearly always denied. Nichols encouraged the committee to push for legislative remedies because, he argued, the executive branch would never voluntarily change its policies.[33]

When the committee reconvened after lunch, Moss proposed an open discussion among lawmakers and experts. Republican Representative Clare Hoffman of Michigan charged journalists with failing to accurately report the news. Because they did not adhere to journalistic standards, Hoffman insisted, journalists did not deserve greater access to information. James Pope of the Kentucky *Louisville-Courier Journal* reminded the congressman that the First Amendment protected the right of free speech even if that speech was inaccurate, and "as a member of Congress, there is very little that you can do about it." Should a new law granting freedom of information, Hoffman retorted, be extended to even the "notorious liar?" Newton responded with a fiery reply. Would Hoffman be in "favor of a limitation, by law if necessary, forbidding a candidate for Congress who repeatedly lies to his constituents from trying to get elected to office?" No, Hoffman replied, but the constituents could punish him by not returning him to office. Newton replied, "We have the same restraint if we repeatedly lie to our people. They quit taking our paper."[34]

Moss attempted to steer the conversation back to the issues at hand. To legislate a "right to know," Congress would have to define its consti-

tutional "right to information." From where did it come? Representative William Dawson believed that the legislative branch's power of the
purse granted it the constitutional right to know how and where the executive branch spent that money. The House directed the Government
Operations Committee, parent of the Moss subcommittee, for example,
to "follow appropriated funds," which, Dawson concluded, "carries with
it the right to get information—any information that those agencies
possess—in order that Congress might determine whether or not they
are efficiently and economically administering the agency according to
the legislation establishing it." Therefore, Congress had a constitutional
right to know. Dawson further argued that the executive branch had historically extended executive privilege to cabinet secretaries, even though
"only the President can claim privilege of a communication between
the two." Eisenhower's letter to Senator McCarthy's committee in 1953
had asserted that the secretary of defense could claim executive privilege
against the McCarthy inquiry, rather than the president asserting that
right for himself.[35]

At the end of the day, Moss was convinced that the "right to know"
must be legally defined. He recognized the challenge of striking a balance
between the executive branch's need to protect national security with the
media's claims that the public had a "right to know" about the actions
of its government. It was a complicated matter that would require careful study and further inquiry. Committee staff conveyed these concerns
when they composed the final report, which they submitted to Speaker
Rayburn on July 27, 1956. Absent legislation, the report noted, executive
departments and agencies had followed their own rules. "It is now incumbent upon Congress to bring order out of the present chaos." "Departments and agencies which generate governmental information all are
created by Congress," wrote Moss's staff, and "derive their powers from
Congress and are subject to such limitation as Congress may impose."
Absent legislation the executive branch could, and likely would, continue
to obstruct the free flow of information.[36]

The report emphasized that a defining feature of free societies was the
free exchange of information about the workings of government. "The
inherent right of people to control their government rests solidly on the
foundation of information." The staff's report further stated, "The Iron
Curtain countries of today, the dictators of recent history. . . . In each
case the ruling group grasped control because of the lack of information to the people." Neither Hitler nor Stalin could have maintained their
power over their people without controlling the flow of information to

the public. The report juxtaposed these autocratic governments with the words of James Madison, a principal author of the U.S. Constitution: "A people who mean to be their own governors must arm themselves with the power knowledge gives. A popular government without popular information or the means of acquiring it is but a prologue to a farce or a tragedy or perhaps both." The message could not have been clearer: one of the distinctive features in a free and open society was the public's right to information, its right to know. By undermining that right, the U.S. government came dangerously close to imitating the despots and autocrats that the U.S. government adamantly and publicly opposed.[37]

Not everyone on the committee agreed with the report's conclusions. Congressman Clare Hoffman appended a supplementary statement. He argued that the Constitution "imposes upon the President a duty or grants to him authority" that no one individual or group, including Congress, the general public, or the press, could compel him to disclose information. Hoffman insisted that the executive branch had the right to consider requests for information on a case-by-case basis and in the context of the particular moment.[38]

When Moss eventually retired from the House he was known among his colleagues as a rather "dull" and "plodding" man. He earned that reputation, at least in part, because of his dogged approach to the issue of open government. Among his freedom of information allies Moss was known as a tenacious bulldog.[39] Encouraged by media activists like Wiggins, who declared in his 1956 book *Freedom or Secrecy* that government opacity was pushing the nation "farther and farther away from the concept of a free people that is the master and not the servant of its government," Moss offered an amendment to the 1789 "housekeeping statute" that granted federal agencies the power to keep and file records. The Moss bill, which became law in 1958, added one sentence to the original statute, forbidding federal agencies from withholding records and information from the public.[40] It was a small triumph for the bulldog: a largely toothless bill that lacked enforcement mechanisms. But it was a crack in the otherwise impenetrable wall of the executive branch.

When President John F. Kennedy took the oath of office on January 20, 1961, Republicans challenged Moss to hold the new administration to the same standards of openness that the congressman had demanded of the Eisenhower administration. The *Chicago Tribune* encouraged the "self-anointed guardian of the public's right to know" to demand task force reports on government operations prepared for the president-elect. The paper charged that Moss was more likely to make members of his subcommittee "guardians of the Democratic right to suppress" than he was to enforce right to know principles with the new Democratic administration.[41] His critics had a point. Moss had been politically as well as ideologically motivated to challenge the Eisenhower administration's information policies. Moss announced in April 1961 that his committee would "follow the same procedures we employed with the Republican Administration in an effort to win acceptance of the critical need for a fully informed public."[42] Indeed, the new administration seemed reluctant to embrace transparency. In 1961, Deputy Assistant Secretary of State for Public Affairs Carl Rowan dismissed newsmen's calls for greater transparency as a "self-deception" driven by those who wanted "to make a buck." A former reporter for the *Minneapolis Star and Tribune*, Rowan stated, "Many of the newsmen with whom I deal are far more concerned about their reputations than about how well-informed the American public is."[43]

In late October 1962 the United States and the Soviet Union squared off over the placement of Soviet nuclear warheads in Cuba, only 90 miles off the coast of the Florida. The whole world watched as the superpowers reached a new level of brinksmanship. President Kennedy approved a naval blockade of Cuba. For thirteen long and tense days the administration negotiated with the Soviets, demanding the removal of missiles from Cuba, all the while enforcing strict news censorship policies including denying television and print media access to the Guantanamo base and the U.S. fleet (a privilege newsmen had enjoyed during World War II). On October 28, the two nations reached an agreement. The Soviets would dismantle the missiles in Cuba, in exchange for the removal of Jupiter missiles from Turkey and a U.S. pledge not to invade the island nation.[44]

When the crisis was over Arthur Sylvester, assistant secretary of defense for public affairs, admitted that the administration had purposefully misled the press in an effort to stop "leaks," which might have jeopardized diplomacy. When journalists at a press conference complained about the lack of information, Sylvester defended the administration's news policy. "The results, in my opinion, justify the methods we used," he said, because the "news flowing from actions taken by the Government is part of the weaponry."[45] One journalist reported, "Mr. Sylvester said that it was the inherent right of a government 'to lie to save itself.'"[46] One editorial reflected the position of many in the news business, claiming that "'management' or 'control' of the news" amounted to "censorship" by another name.[47] Appearing at his first news conference following the crisis, the president offered "no apologies" for what the head of the National Association of Broadcasters called the suppression of news in the Cuban crisis. Kennedy said he would support changing the Defense Department's restrictive news policy when the "public interest isn't being met."[48]

The following year news organizations complained to the Moss committee that U.S. State Department officials "were attempting to control stories filed by U.S. correspondents covering the war between North and South Vietnam." The subcommittee opened hearings in mid-1963, and state department officials revealed they had issued a "press guidance" statement to U.S. diplomats in Saigon. The directive had advised that while "news stories which criticize the [Ngo Dinh] Diem government could not be 'forbidden,' . . . newsmen should be advised that trifling or thoughtless criticism of the Diem government" would not be favorable to U.S. interests. The State Department advised diplomats not to bring journalists "on military activities of the type that are likely to result in undesirable stories." When he released his subcommittee's report on Vietnam, Moss strongly condemned the State Department's practice of "hiding the facts from the American public" about U.S. policy in South Vietnam.[49]

Its Vietnam inquiry notwithstanding, the Moss committee did not demonstrate the same enthusiasm for critiquing the Kennedy administration's information policies. When the administration detonated a series of atomic bombs in the Pacific Ocean in July 1962, Moss blamed the media for failing to report on the atomic tests, not the administration for trying to keep them secret.[50] Careful observers noted that the committee did not take the same aggressive stance with the Kennedy administration, but instead took "constructive" looks at administration policy to "avoid the impression that it will conduct an investigation."[51]

Following Kennedy's assassination and President Lyndon Johnson's commitment of U.S. ground forces to Vietnam, Congress began slowly to demand access to information about the situation on the ground in Vietnam. Increasingly frustrated by the Johnson administration's lack of transparency in defining U.S. goals in Southeast Asia, journalists on the ground in Vietnam aggressively pursued leads to help inform their readers back home. Their reporting, based on leads they gathered from official and nonofficial sources who often spoke on condition of anonymity, suggested a growing "credibility gap" between the administration's assessment of the war and the facts on the ground. In 1965 a CBS public opinion poll found that when asked about the "truthfulness of official U.S. announcements of American casualties and other Vietnam war information" only 15 percent of those polled believed the government was "always" truthful while 67 percent believed it was "sometimes truthful."[52]

The national media shared the suspicions of the general public, and in 1966 Saul Pett of the *Los Angeles Times,* attacked what he called a pattern of "double-talk" in Washington. President Eisenhower had lied about the U-2 plane shot down over the Soviet Union, and President Kennedy had lied about U.S. support for the Bay of Pigs invasion. The Johnson administration, according to Pett, adopted a new level of deception with the American public about the war in Vietnam. Though the "president is almost never lacking in announcements," wrote Pett, the White House put tight restrictions on the information that could be included in those many news releases. Pett cited Defense Secretary Robert McNamara's repeated statements about U.S. "progress" in Southeast Asia as a case in point. "How, asks the reporter, can you call our losses 'light' when a whole company was wiped out? You can, the government says, when a whole battalion was involved. But was a battalion involved? the reporter asks. The question goes round and round." At the very least, reporters like Pett noted that in the Johnson White House, there are some who are "passionately secretive about innocuous details," who express indignation "when transparent political motives are suggested," and who like to "give reporters the feeling that everywhere in government 'Big Brother' is watching."[53] Though the Democrats controlled both chambers of Congress, even members of the president's own party expressed exasperation about their lack of information on the war in Vietnam. Senator Wayne Morse of Oregon (one of only two senators to vote against the Gulf of Tonkin Resolution in 1964) called it "shocking" that the administration continued to "misrepresent to the American people" the facts about the war in Vietnam.[54]

For all these reasons, congressional support for legislation to define the people's right to know intensified in the mid-1960s. In the House, fifteen congressmen introduced separate, nearly identical, bills to enhance government transparency. At least half of those sponsors were Republicans, including rising stars Donald Rumsfeld of Illinois and Robert Griffin of Michigan, both members of the Moss committee.

The Johnson administration adamantly opposed all "freedom of information" bills, and Moss invited the administration to explain its opposition to the legislation. Norbert Schlei, assistant attorney general from the Justice Department's Office of Legal Counsel, insisted that any bill that defined the public's right to know "would contravene the separation of powers doctrine and would be unconstitutional."⁵⁵ President Johnson, like other chief executives before him, was keen to protect executive privilege. The administration opposed any bill that would "shift to the judicial branch a constitutional prerogative of the Executive." The administration granted that Congress had a right to information, but the White House opposed a one-size-fits-all bill that would apply to all executive agencies alike. The issue of access to information was "too complicated, too ever changing to be covered by a closed system of rules." Schlei concluded that "there is quite widespread opposition within the executive branch" to treat the problem "in one package as is attempted here."⁵⁶

During his tenure as chairman of the Government Operations subcommittee, Moss had gone toe-to-toe with three presidential administrations on this issue. Each had offered similar arguments. Moss suggested to Schlei that the White House had misinterpreted the purpose of the legislation, which was not to undermine executive privilege but reaffirm the public's right to information. If the White House found pending legislation objectionable, Moss offered to write a bill that would address its concerns while providing greater access to information. Schlei responded that though the administration had "devoted many hours to working on that kind of approach," the Justice Department had not yet reached a point where it could "come forward" with a proposal. Schlei promised to continue to look into the issues and to report recommendations back to the committee at a time when the information "will still be relevant and helpful." Moss did little to hide his frustration and chided Schlei for failing to provide "a more constructive statement" from the administration. Congress, Moss insisted, had not "been impetuous here. Ten years in moving a piece of legislation is a rather long period of time." To which Schlei conceded: "Yes; it is, sir."⁵⁷

For all his equivocating, Schlei had, in fact, acknowledged in his opening statement that Congress's constitutional responsibility to oversee the national budget granted it the right to some measure of information. It was an inconsistency that Donald Rumsfeld could not let pass. The administration, Rumsfeld argued, had taken two seemingly contradictory positions, on the one hand arguing that the legislation was "not only unconstitutional but impossible," while on the other hand indicating that "Congress does have the legislative authority [to require] disclosure of certain types of information." Moss reminded Schlei that the bill was an effort to grant the public access to information, not to protect congressional rights to information; as a co-equal branch of government, that type of legislation was unnecessary. As Moss had often argued in the past, the ongoing growth of government required that the public have greater access to information, not only to be "kept informed," but to assure Americans were "not exposed to propaganda."[58] Robert Griffin questioned whether executive privilege could reasonably be derived from the Constitution. "Executive privilege is not necessarily accepted by all members of this subcommittee," he argued. Rumsfeld claimed that all information "is in the public interest . . . that is the only reason we are having this hearing." He later recalled that his "support of the bill came down to one long-held belief: Good judgments require accurate information."[59] The White House position, that the problem was too big to address with legislation, seemed an inadequate response to lawmakers. In light of the nation's escalating involvement in the Vietnam War, it struck many as an untenable position.

Rather than support one of the more than a dozen pending freedom of information bills in the House, the Moss committee unanimously approved Senate bill S. 1160, authored by Senator Edward Long of Missouri. Long's bill required that the executive branch make "matters of official record" available to the general public. Any person could demand access to government information for any reason. The bill also included some concessions to the administration, providing nine exemptions for information relating to national security and defense, trade secrets, and personnel and medical files. For the first time in the nation's history, executive agencies would be required to assume the burden of proof for the withholding of information from the public. The bill specifically forbade the executive branch from withholding information from the legislative branch.[60]

Protecting the "steady flow of information," Moss argued, was vital to the "lifeblood of the democratic system," one of the features distinguishing the "free world" from those nations behind the Iron Curtain.[61] Congress was not alone in trying to force the administration's hand. Letters from the public supporting transparency reminded the Johnson White House that some Americans strongly disagreed with his opposition to the legislation. Arthur Jaeger, a college student from Staten Island, New York, wrote President Johnson in August 1965 demanding that the president defend his position. "As a college student and a member of the 1968 electorate," Jaeger wrote, "I would like to know your reasons for opposing the [Freedom of Information bill]." He continued, "the public has a right to know what is going on, and the government has the responsibility of informing us of its actions." He stated, "I personally feel that the voter should be cognizant of the actions of its elected officials," and that included knowing "not only the good but also the bad."[62] Jaeger's letter expressed a growing frustration among some Americans, particularly those who were of draft age, that their government seemed distant, big, and unaccountable. In a carefully worded response, the Department of Justice's Office of Legal Counsel, Lee C. White, explained that the administration supported the "principle of the purpose of freedom of information" but opposed a legislative solution that proposed to solve "important and intricate problem[s]" by "substituting a simple word-formula." Such legislation, asserted the White House, would result in "less rather than greater availability of information." White defended the president's use of executive privilege, noting that Johnson "invoked" the privilege "as sparingly as possible" after carefully "reviewing all of the circumstances" and determining "that nondisclosure of information is absolutely necessary in the public interest."[63] The president's response could hardly have reassured the young Jaeger.

Despite White House opposition, the House passed the Senate bill unanimously. Congress and the White House faced off over the FOIA bill. Meeting with Moss and his counsel, Attorney General Nicholas Katzenbach declared the president would not sign the bill. Moss offered Katzenbach a compromise. Moss would consider inserting the administration's language in the final House committee's legislative history report, if members of his committee would accept it. This was not a minor concession. Legislative histories provided roadmaps for researchers and lawmakers who sought to understand and interpret the law. Allowing the administration to insert its reservations and disagreements into the legislative history meant that critics of the law might find ways to loosely interpret and apply it. Moss received much criticism for this concession, but as his counsel, Benny Kass, later recalled, Moss wanted the president to sign the bill. The law would stand as written, but the House committee report, including wording composed by the Justice Department, granted executive branch officials more freedom to interpret FOIA's exemptions. Kass later recalled, "We believed the clear language of the law could override any negative comments in the House report. If the statute is clear, you don't look to the legislative history." Since Congress had adjourned after passing the bill, the president could still pocket veto the measure, thereby denying Congress the opportunity to override the veto. Not willing to take that chance, Moss spoke with leading FOI advocates, including Russ Wiggins at the *Post*, encouraging them to call, wire, and write the president, urging that he sign the legislation.[64]

A lugubrious President Johnson signed the bill on July 4, 1966, though not at a public ceremony. In the midst of waging an increasingly unpopular war in Southeast Asia and battling crime and disorder in the nation's streets, the last thing the White House needed was a flood of FOIA requests. For those who worked on behalf of the legislation there was cause to celebrate. The Freedom of Information Committee of Sigma Delta Chi heralded the law as a great triumph in the history of journalism. One astute observer called the passage of FOIA a "watershed event" that "reversed the philosophy of releasing Government information." Others cautioned that without an administrative "watchdog" the flow of information was likely to be hindered by "executive powers," especially in areas of national security.[65] To his constituents back in Michigan, House Minority Leader Gerald Ford championed the people's right to know and warned of the "mushrooming growth of Government secrecy." He had strongly supported the bill and credited Republican support for its passage as evidence of his party's firm belief in "the right of the public to essential information." Though the bill would not solve all problems of government secrecy, Ford believed the 1966 FOIA would be "a great improvement over present policies."[66]

Indeed, Republicans and Democrats in Congress could be proud of their achievements in the 89th Congress, which included sweeping legislation to insure government transparency, hearings on the U.S. war in Vietnam, and efforts to combat civil unrest in the United States. Not satisfied with one legislative victory, Moss turned his subcommittee toward a new issue, one that his staff had uncovered over the course of investigating executive branch transparency laws: government invasions of privacy including wiretapping, letter opening, and other forms of surveillance. It was an easy fit for the Moss committee staff. After all, the issues were related. Both issues suggested that the bigger government became, the less responsive it was to the basic constitutional principles outlined by the founders. In 1966 the Moss committee launched a series of investigations into the government's invasion of privacy. And this issue, perhaps more than any other, would ignite fierce opposition from the executive branch.

CHAPTER TWO

"What's Going On in the Black Community?"

Ramsey Clark Investigates Civil Disorder

The soldiers came out of the trucks prepared, as their officers had instructed, for insurrection. In their pockets were situation maps plotting power plants, radio and television stations, and federal armories. These locations were likely targets, they were told. Protect them first. Detroit, America's one-time "arsenal of democracy," looked like a war zone. Smoke billowed out of storefronts; cars lay helplessly overturned in the streets. In the distance, gunfire sounded. But where were the revolutionaries? The guerillas and insurgents? The ones who wanted to overthrow the government?

The soldiers' situation maps, it turned out, were useless. The rioters were not threatening power plants or attacking federal armories. The six o'clock news later revealed that the real action was at the liquor, appliance, and furniture stores. This wasn't a war after all. It seemed the looters, arsonists, and vandals were trying to tell the nation something. But what, America's government officials desperately wanted to know, were they trying to say?[1]

The summer of 1967 burned hot and violent. Urban rioting in more than seventy American cities prompted one journalist to dub it the "summer of bloodshed and pillage." Watching the cities smolder on the evening news, Americans worried that the nation was descending into a state of lawlessness. The Republican Coordinating Committee proclaimed a national crisis. Americans, asserted the committee, were being denied the "most basic of civil rights," to be "safe on the streets and in their homes from riots and violence." President Lyndon Johnson's "man on the ground" in Detroit predicted that other U.S. cities were likely to burn that summer.[2]

Wars on the streets of American cities bore a striking resemblance, in the minds of some Americans, to the war being waged in the villages of Vietnam. James Reston observed that, "next to finding a solution to the war in Vietnam, the war in the cities at home is the most important issue before the nation."[3] During this time of political demonstrations, rising street crime, and urban disorder, the nation's top law enforcement officer, Attorney General Ramsey Clark, found himself a lightning rod for furious public criticism. Critics saw him as "something of an old-fashioned liberal in a time of increasing anxiety." Clark's "consistent concern for civil liberties," argued one prominent elected official, made him "psychologically unsuited to the job of law enforcement."[4] One astute observer claimed that Clark's weak position on issues of "law and order"—an increasingly critical political issue in the late 1960s—"made his opponents' flesh crawl."[5] The mass media portrayed Clark as unable and unwilling to combat urban disorder. Political partisans fueled this attack and castigated Clark and the entire Johnson administration, not only for failing to quell the riots more quickly and more forcefully, but also for failing to foresee them. Conservatives in both parties believed that the government needed far greater power in order to squash the radicals and agitators who, they argued, planned, instigated, and led the riots—and other acts of public disorder.

Partisanship aside, Attorney General Clark thought that his critics were at least partially right; the Justice Department did not have the right tools to predict and prepare for urban disorder. And he believed that he had a duty to find those tools, because he knew that the Justice Department lacked the institutional resources to combat such riots. In the wake of violent upheavals in Detroit, Michigan, and Newark, New Jersey, in the summer of 1967, Clark reevaluated the intelligence capacities of the Justice Department. Clark believed that the administration's inadequate response to urban disorder stemmed, in no small part, from a lack of quality intelligence about "what's going on in the black community."[6] An able administrator, Clark conceived of a new unit within the Justice Department, the Interdivisional Information Unit (IDIU), to enable the state more accurately to predict where and when civil disturbances—specifically urban upheaval—might occur. One Justice Department official later recalled the IDIU was the answer to the Justice Department's "concern that local police did not have 'any useful intelligence or knowledge about ghettos [and] about black communities in the big cities.'"[7] In the late 1960s the IDIU legitimized the surreptitious intelligence-gathering activities of various federal, state, and local agencies. Clark reasoned, as did many of his colleagues, that if bureaucrats had access to more data—intelligence about those who rioted and where and when—the state could more readily anticipate urban unrest and communicate more efficiently and effectively to local and state law enforcement tasked with maintaining law and order. In the context of urban upheaval, these methods targeted black ghetto inhabitants. An ardent proponent of individual rights, Clark recognized that powerful state interests could abuse such an apparatus. By housing the intelligence clearinghouse under his direct watch, Clark believed he could protect civil liberties while tackling wars in the streets. As a further precaution, in 1967, Clark personally banned the use of all wiretapping and electronic surveillance at the federal level.

Dissatisfied with Clark's leadership of the Justice Department and the Johnson administration's general response to lawlessness, Congress passed the Omnibus Crime Control and Safe Streets Act of 1968. Seeking to empower local and state law enforcement officers to fight crime, conservatives, led by Senator John McClellan of Arkansas, inserted a provision (otherwise known as Title III) to legalize wiretapping and electronic surveillance. Title III vastly expanded the power of the state to intrude—legally—into the private lives of individuals, in the name of law and order. Under the Omnibus Act the IDIU acquired extraordinary new capacities, connected to a vast network of local and state intelligence operations. When Richard Nixon took power in January 1969, he would authorize his administration to use these new capacities with almost no limits.

When Ramsey Clark joined President John F. Kennedy's administration in 1961, no one would have predicted his dramatic fall in public approval only six years later. Everyone knew him as the son of Tom Clark, an associate justice of the Supreme Court, and Harry S. Truman's former attorney general.[8] For a tall, lanky youth that most people identified as "low key," young Ramsey Clark moved fast. Even before graduating high school in 1945, he rushed to join the marine corps. After serving on missions to Moscow, Budapest, Vienna, and Berlin, he was demobilized and returned home to study law and history at the University of Texas. He graduated in only two years. After marrying Georgia Welch, his UT sweetheart, Clark moved the family to Chicago where he earned a master's degree in history and a law degree at the University of Chicago. Two years later, Clark joined his father's practice in Dallas where he worked for ten years as a corporate lawyer.[9]

Through his father's contacts in Washington (it was House Speaker Sam Rayburn who passed Ramsey's name along to Attorney General Robert Kennedy), Clark joined President John F. Kennedy's administration. Though his connections secured his position, Clark proved to

Ramsey Clark (Mudd
Manuscript Library,
Department of Rare Books
and Special Collections,
Princeton University
Library)

be a skilled administrator. Only thirty-four years old, Clark headed the
Lands Division, the least glamorous of all the Justice Department posts.[10]
"Ram" (as his wife, Georgia, liked to call him) didn't mind. Clark threw
himself into his work, quickly earning a reputation in the beltway as a
"penny-pinching administrator and an unruffled solid thinker." Clark
was a "natural New Frontiersman," moving quickly into the attorney
general's inner circle of advisors.[11] He proved such an able and trustwor-
thy team player that Robert Kennedy selected him as the administration's
"man on the ground" during the most explosive of the early civil rights
standoffs in the South; first, at the University of Mississippi in 1962, and
later during the Birmingham, Alabama, riots in 1963. Throughout the
tumultuous summer of 1963, Clark remained Kennedy's informal contact
with southern officials, offering advice on how schools could be peace-
fully desegregated. These events proved transformative for Clark; he became a committed advocate for racial equality.[12] He maintained this role
into the Johnson administration.

Even as the White House focused its efforts on engineering peaceful settlements to racial standoffs in the South, northern cities began to
smolder. In 1964 the Johnson White House experienced its first hint of
trouble to come when Rochester, Harlem, and Bedford-Stuyvesant, New

York, erupted in violence, burning, and looting. The following summer, the black neighborhood of Watts in Los Angeles erupted. Ramsey Clark, like most Americans, watched in disbelief.[13]

A seasoned arbiter of civil rights crises and a trusted aide to President Johnson, Clark headed up the presidential task force on Watts.[14] On the president's orders he was to identify the causes of urban upheaval and co-ordinate federal aid and relief efforts with state and local officials. Always conscientious and curious, Clark went beyond the president's initial mandate. His experience in the South during desegregation and voting rights drives taught him to distrust local institutions and their vision of local problems. Hoping to identify the roots of the uprising from the residents themselves, Clark's team spent hours meeting with "every type of ghetto group and organization." Clark personally attended small gatherings of "completely unorganized" folks in churches, parks, at people's homes, in youth centers, wherever people were congregating, "to see what they were thinking, how they analyzed the riots and the cause of the riots."[15]

Clark inserted the perspective of Watts residents in a lengthy section of the task force report titled "Community Attitudes." Explaining to President Johnson his decision to include their perspective, Clark wrote that residents' voices "reflect attitudes . . . [that] do much to explain behavior in the community." With much emotion and some urgency, African Americans articulated to Clark the root cause of black frustration and alienation. They described how powerful structural forces limited economic opportunity and circumscribed individual access to the bounty of postwar cornucopia. Identifying the "burdens borne by those who live outside the circle of today's prosperity, outside looking in," African Americans bemoaned the institutional structures that denied them the same economic opportunities to prosper as their white counterparts.[16] High rates of unemployment and only marginal access to a "menial" job market undermined African American efforts to exit the vicious cycle of poverty.[17]

Federal welfare and poverty programs could not and would not solve the problems of the ghetto, residents insisted, "if the people in the depressed areas [did not] participate in the planning and execution" of those programs. Underscoring the need for community participation in the rebuilding of their communities by rejecting federal and state paternalism, these residents envisioned organic, grassroots efforts to address community problems. Residents demanded that local government do more to "help the people help themselves." Yet they distrusted the "white power structure" and its "false promises" that denied them the ability to "participate in planning or in action" in their own communities and "rammed" welfare relief "down [their] throats." The riots, for some blacks, were a way to express their frustrations to officials in Los Angeles. "A lot of us are beginning to feel that riots are . . . the only way to talk to [officials] downtown," commented one resident. The sense of alienation from white society reverberated throughout the black community. Clark identified "the preservation of law and order" as both a national and local priority. But he remained personally committed to improving the socio-economic conditions of black urban ghettos to decrease the likelihood of future urban disorders. With recommendations echoed in later presidential commissions, the task force identified "the problems which exploded into violence in Los Angeles" as fundamentally issues "of how human beings treat one another, not only through the institutions of their society, but individually."[18]

Clark thought that the report offered the president the opportunity to reaffirm the liberal commitment (embodied in the social welfare programs of the War on Poverty) to attack institutional forces that structured inequality. Clark personally believed that only powerful federal institutions had the capacity to address these deep, systemic problems. President Johnson, however, was under fire for failing to reaffirm "law and order." The political challenge for the administration was to balance liberal calls for social justice with conservative demands for social order.[19] The president considered the report "unpleasant" and believed that it emphasized that inner city blacks were "very angry people." Consistent with his stance that urban disorder was best handled at the local level, Johnson thought it best to allow the judgments of California governor Pat Brown's appointed commission, headed by Los Angeles resident and former CIA Director John McCone, to stand as the final assessment of the riot. As Clark remembered, the McCone investigation and report had the advantage of coming from "homefolks," without the "coloration of a bunch of feds." McCone could potentially tell the harsh truth of race relations and systemic institutional inequality in the United States free from the taint of federal imposition into a local problem. And yet, the McCone commission, as a local investigatory body, had political considerations of its own, namely, not to be too critical of existing local and state institutions in California. As a consequence, the commission report largely reaffirmed the need for greater law and order, excluded voices from the Watts community, and relied on top-down solutions to local problems. President Johnson put the "Report of the President's Task Force on the Los Angeles Riots" in a drawer, never to take it out again.[20]

Johnson's decision to ignore the report proved a point of "continuing frustration" to a number of people in the Justice Department, Clark later recalled. Not dissuaded, Clark pushed forward, determined to use the limited resources of the Justice Department to aid the inner-city poor. Meetings with Watts residents left Clark with a lasting impression: the urban poor needed "jobs first." He reasoned that Justice should tackle employment discrimination, a program that moved slowly but with measurable results. Clark's recollection of the Justice Department's efforts to tackle discrimination in employment—both as a result of the Watts report and as a relative success—underscored his faith in liberalism, in the power of the federal government to solve social problems.[21]

Clark's trust in federal institutions informed his views on urban crime and disorder; both were legitimate responses to institutional failures. Crime, Clark believed, was a natural response to rapid social changes that had beset urban centers. These changes produced opportunities for some, but not all of the nation's citizens. In a speech to the Washington, D.C., Bar Association, Clark identified the urban ghettos as pockets of the disadvantaged cut off from an "affluent and technologically advanced society." Respect for the law had to reside "within the hearts of the people" and "short of a police state, crime in the streets can be significantly and permanently reduced only by attacking its occurrence, not its causes." Government, according to Clark, had a central role to play in crime reduction, "provid[ing] a moral example and leadership" by eliminating "poverty . . . ignorance [and] unequal opportunity." Reducing crime and urban disorder, Clark believed, was only possible if the federal government made a "continuous conscious effort toward equal opportunity for all, toward decent conditions of living and toward just laws."[22]

In the late 1960s increasing numbers of white Americans found the liberal approach to national problems of poverty and equality, so paradigmatically articulated by Clark, to be unpersuasive. Public opinion polls suggested that far more Americans saw the nation's major domestic problems to be increased criminality, not inequality, and violence in the streets, not poverty. A September 1968 Harris poll reported that 81 percent of Americans polled agreed with the statement "law and order has broken down in this country." Eighty-four percent agreed with the statement that "a strong President can make a big difference in directly preserving law and order." Fifty-nine percent of those polled found the causes of breakdown in law and order attributable to "Negroes who start riots"; fifty-six percent identified "Communists" as a cause. Mass protests, the increasingly unpopular war in Vietnam, the frequency of urban riots, and rising crime rates made the American public more skeptical about liberal politicians' focus on injustice as the underlying cause of public disorder and liberals' big government antipoverty programs as the means to solve the nation's problems. When President Johnson appointed Clark acting attorney general in 1966, many on Capitol Hill considered him an able bureaucrat but not tough enough to attack the lawlessness that so infuriated the voting public. Critics called Clark a "cream puff," questioning his masculinity and underscoring criticism that the Johnson administration was "soft on crime." His tall, thin frame, youthful appearance, Hollywood looks (a face "something like Gary Cooper"), and "casual and unflappable demeanor" made him an easy target. Careful observers found Clark at once "folksy, informal, and naïve."[23]

Ramsey Clark was not the type of man many Americans would have chosen to tackle civil disorder, but President Johnson believed that Clark could do the job. In 1966, the trouble just kept coming. While mass protests against the Vietnam War had yet to emerge, 1966 was the year of Black Power. Stokely Carmichael, the new head of the Student Nonviolent Coordinating Committee (SNCC), publicly embodied the shift from a peaceful civil rights movement led by Reverend Martin Luther King, Jr., to a more militant, violent movement among African Americans, particularly those in the urban ghettos.[24] Frustrated by slow progress, Carmichael called for black-run institutions to solve black problems. Blacks, Carmichael reasoned, needed to wrest power from white institutions and elected officials. That struggle, he and many other Black Power advocates believed, would not come without violence, without blood running in the streets.[25] In 1966, for the third summer in a row, black Americans revolted in cities across the nation with thousands arrested, hundreds injured, and seven dead.

As urban unrest and mass protest increased in frequency and intensity, Attorney General Clark did not need to look further than the Federal Bureau of Investigation (FBI) to know more about what was going on in the urban ghettos of America. Nevertheless, Clark was well aware that under the direction of J. Edgar Hoover, the FBI was far from an objective source of information on racial issues in the United States. The Bureau had been fighting its own private war against African Americans' struggle for justice and equality in the United States since the early twentieth century, often at the behest of officials in the White House and Justice Department. J. Edgar Hoover, FBI director from 1919 to 1974, personally believed in racial segregation and racial inequality. The FBI, however, was not merely an institution operating under the direction of one racist. As historian David Garrow has convincingly argued, "The Bureau functioned not simply as a weapon of one disturbed man, not as an institution protecting its own organizational interests, but as the representative, at times rather irrational representative, of American cultural values that found much about [the civil rights movements] to be frightening and repugnant."[26]

From the beginning the FBI (and especially Director Hoover) opposed the civil rights movement and viewed African American calls for greater social and economic equality as evidence of Communist influence and subversion. In particular, the Reverend King's relationship with a former Communist Party member, Stanley Levinson, confirmed Hoover's suspicions. William Sullivan, fourth in command at the Bureau and head of the Domestic Intelligence Division, authored an analysis in 1963 linking communism to the movement. During the Kennedy administration the Bureau and its director enjoyed the tacit, if not explicit, approval of their efforts to link communism to the civil rights movement from prominent elected and appointed officials, including Attorney General Robert Kennedy. This same pattern continued under President Lyndon Johnson. In 1964 the Bureau established a special desk within the Intelligence Division to look into potential Communist influence in "racial matters." It continued wiretapping home telephones and planting bugs in the hotel rooms of prominent movement leaders, most notably Martin Luther King, Jr. Hoover personally loathed King, calling him a "burrhead" and "a tom cat with obsessive degenerate sexual urges."[27] Hoover distributed reports throughout the executive branch agencies, linking communism with the civil rights movement. Hoover frequently regaled anyone who would listen with lurid details about the Reverend King's sex life, details gathered from bugs planted in King's hotel rooms.[28] Ramsey Clark often heard these accounts from Hoover himself. He loathed Hoover's penchant for such tasteless voyeurism.

By all accounts the Department of Justice generally, and the attorney general specifically, offered "little guidance for FBI intelligence investigations" on matters related to race and civil rights. Robert Kennedy approved the King wiretaps, for example. In 1965 Kennedy's successor as attorney general, Nicholas Katzenbach, attempted to curb the Bureau's autonomy by ordering Hoover to obtain approval prior to planting wiretaps and bugs. Katzenbach never enforced his directive, and the Bureau continued to surveil Dr. King without prior approval. Even when the Bureau found no evidence of communist influence on civil rights groups, Katzenbach continued to approve wiretaps on organizations like the Southern Christian Leadership Conference (SCLC).[29]

Clark was determined to run his Justice Department differently. As deputy attorney general, Clark observed how the FBI and Hoover used anti-Communist rhetoric to support the continued surveillance of King and the movement. He grew to believe that attorneys general had not always been "sufficiently critical" in approving wiretaps and authorizing electronic surveillance, in the name of national security. Clark publicly claimed that some FBI bugs and wiretaps had been "a waste of time." He believed that the Bureau and Hoover overused the rubric of "national security" in order to justify secret and extralegal behavior. Surreptitiousness was contagious, Clark argued, and "police tactics" like bugs and wiretaps used "against political enemies or unpopular persons" were "intolerable."[30]

Clark's resistance to the "traditional" methods employed by FBI officers to obtain intelligence inevitably produced a strained relationship with his powerful and famous subordinate. Hoover made it clear to his underlings that he did not like or trust Clark, calling him a "bull butterfly." Clark's restrictions on Hoover's wiretapping infuriated the director. During the height of urban unrest and mass protest, Hoover drafted a three-page memo listing all the wiretaps that Clark had denied, which included those to spy on Stokely Carmichael, SNCC, SCLC, Students for a Democratic Society, and the National Mobilization Committee to End the War in Vietnam. On one occasion, President Johnson requested Director Hoover to place a wiretap on the South Vietnamese embassy. Hoover demurred and told the president to request authorization directly from Attorney General Ramsey Clark, implying that Clark would not approve the tap unless the request came directly from Johnson. Clark did his best to restrict Hoover's agency from continuing its secretive practices. In 1967 he rejected Hoover's request to continue wiretaps of the SCLC office in Atlanta, arguing that the director failed to present adequate evidence that the organization was a "direct threat to the national security."[31]

For all of these reasons Clark did not want to rely directly on the FBI for intelligence on militant black activists or urban conditions. He chose to circumvent Hoover's agency in the summer of 1966, creating an ad-hoc intelligence clearinghouse within the Justice Department. The so-called "Summer Project" consisted of law school interns who gathered intelligence from the FBI and other sources—including newspapers and U.S. attorneys general—to help the White House better anticipate urban flashpoints.[32] The Summer Project was Clark's immediate answer to the problem of urban disorder.

Historically, the executive branch had employed military capacities since the nation's founding to put down civil disorder. In the 1790s the Whiskey Rebellion, led by farmers in Western Pennsylvania, drove President George Washington to mobilize the new national army to put down the domestic disturbance. In the nineteenth century the federal government deployed the army to combat civil disorder on several occasions, to help quell domestic unrest during the Indian Wars, to maintain security at the border with Mexico, and during domestic insurrections including Bleeding Kansas and the Mormon War. During the First Red Scare following World War I, the Department of Justice targeted immigrants and socialists as potential enemies of the state. Infamously, President Herbert Hoover ordered General Douglas MacArthur to use army troops to disperse the Bonus Army encampments from Washington, D.C., in 1932.[33] These domestic security capacities were very much a part of the state's response to unrest by the mid-1960s.

Clark further enhanced the Department of Justice's capacities to respond to disorder by utilizing computer technologies, which enabled the bureaucracy to maintain vast quantities of domestic intelligence. During the Johnson administration expansive federal initiatives such as the War on Poverty and new social welfare programs such as Medicaid and Medicare required the government to collect and maintain data on millions of Americans. As institutional demand for data management solutions grew exponentially, the nation's preeminent computer manufacturer, International Business Machines (IBM), saw its profits soar—from $1.8 billion in sales in 1960 to $7.2 billion by the end of the decade. Computer solutions made Clark's programs both possible and practicable.[34] As useful as these new technologies were, however, computers could not save Clark's Summer Project from being swamped by the multiple crises that rocked the nation during the summer of 1967 when more than 100 cities experienced riots. The violence and destruction in Detroit was so acute that Michigan Governor George Romney requested federal assistance from President Johnson, who reluctantly deployed the army—the first time federal troops had been used to stop riots since the Detroit race riots of 1943. The civil disorders seemed to rage out of control.

Clark quickly realized that the Justice Department's small intelligence clearinghouse was inadequate to meet the administration's needs. Attorneys were "trained to think in terms of due process and deliberation" and were ill equipped to respond to White House demands for information in times of crisis. Clark reasoned that Justice needed to expand its institutional capacity in order to prepare the president for another Detroit. Clark demanded the development of a "systematic means . . . of compiling and analyzing . . . information" related to the perpetrators of, and participants in, urban unrest. He emphasized the need to make better use of intelligence from agencies outside the FBI and to review more thoroughly FBI data.[35]

On the recommendation of Assistant Attorney General John Doar, Clark established the IDIU in December 1967. The IDIU would act as a "single intelligence unit to analyze . . . information . . . about certain persons and groups who make the urban ghetto their base of operation." The FBI alone, Doar urged, could not meet the department's needs. This was partly a problem of capacity, since the agency employed only forty African American officers out of six thousand, making counterintelligence work in these communities difficult, if not impossible. But one large data source remained wholly untapped: the databases maintained by Great Society social welfare programs. Doar urged that social welfare agencies could prove invaluable sources of information about ghetto residents and their activities. For example, the "intelligence unit of the Internal Revenue Service . . . [a] unit under the direction of John Olszewski, had by far the best knowledge of the Negro areas in Detroit." Doar conceded that obtaining intelligence from social welfare agencies was a "sensitive," if not potentially explosive, matter. Young lawyers working for the agency should be encouraged, Doar suggested, "to move about" so that "they become familiar with urban areas." Persons in this position must exercise "discretion" and "must like and respect Negroes as individuals, be in tune with them and have a feeling of sympathy and understanding for their situation."[36] But the "factual information" that federal agencies like Neighborhood Legal Services could provide far outweighed any concerns for individual rights and privacy that Justice may have had. War on Poverty databases, Doar believed, would offer invaluable information about black inner-city residents.[37]

His respect for individual rights aside, Clark agreed. In the wake of the Newark and Detroit riots Clark stated that the federal government needed to establish an "intelligence system" in the black ghetto. The Justice Department, Clark explained to majors and chiefs of police at a conference on the prevention of civil disorder, was a bit overwhelmed by the riots. He called the urban riot, "vaster, much more obscure, fluid, uncoordinated, loose, difficult to identify—and it's black." The problem of coordinating and obtaining intelligence about the black community was, Clark stated plainly, "the toughest we've had. Ordinary police intelligence won't do it. This is not like [identifying] hustlers or cons."[38]

Probably Clark also appreciated that the IDIU would allow the Justice

Department to rely less on Hoover's FBI for intelligence. Clark placed the IDIU under the command of the assistant attorney general of the Internal Security Division, a unit charged with the investigation and prosecution of all cases affecting national security including espionage and sabotage, institutionally linking the problems of domestic unrest and civil disorder with national security issues. Aware that Hoover would undoubtedly object to encroachment on his bureaucratic territory, Clark carved out a role for the FBI, even when the IDIU itself undercut some of the agency's traditional analytical responsibilities. The Department of Justice and the FBI, Clark wrote Hoover, "have not heretofore had to deal with the possibility of an organized pattern of violence, constituting a violation of federal law, by a group of persons who make the urban ghetto their base of operation and whose activities may not have been regularly monitored by existing intelligence sources." The Bureau, Clark urged, should locate black informants within black nationalist organizations, SNCC, and other "less publicized groups" to identify those who might be involved in instigating riots. The FBI, unbeknownst to Clark, was already engaged in these activities, and had been for years.[39] Clark's letter suggests how ignorant the attorney general remained of the programs initiated under Hoover, specifically COINTELPRO, the agency's secret program to neutralize dissent in the United States.

The new IDIU provided Clark with an alternative intelligence source and analytic team to the FBI. The IDIU created bureaucratic competition with the FBI based on the opposing political viewpoints of two powerful administrators, Hoover and Clark. Unlike COINTELPRO, the IDIU has escaped public scrutiny. Its Communication Center—a "situation room" for coordinating response to civil disturbance and urban disorder—connected the Justice Department with the White House Situation Room, the army's Directorate for Civil Disturbances for Operations and Planning, the U.S. Attorney for Washington, D.C., and a number of police departments throughout the District of Columbia. The center also maintained telephone contact with the army's emergency Centrex system that was linked with several civil disturbance command posts throughout the United States.[40]

U.S. attorneys general proved to be another invaluable resource. Scattered about the country, federal officers worked closely with local and state government and law enforcement. Any disturbances within their district were immediately reported to the Communication Center. If a situation provoked concern, the U.S. attorney or assistant attorney took a position in the command post of the state or local police and relayed information at least on an hourly basis directly to the Communications Center at the IDIU in Washington. The center, at that point in constant contact with the army authorities, would advise the U.S. attorney via telephone of federal plans for intervention. The IDIU's analysis team processed and organized incoming data into easily retrievable paper and computerized dossiers. Subject files included brief biographies, known affiliations, and descriptions of personal political views. For example, the dossier on Mr. Andrew Benjamin Haynes, a Black Power advocate residing in Portland, Oregon, included his known former organizational affiliations and his support for "tactical violence" to achieve civil rights goals and racial equality; such reports were meant to meet the immediate goals of the IDIU and the Center—analyzing and organizing intelligence for the purpose of keeping the attorney general and other officials informed in the event action must be taken by a federal agency to put down a civil disturbance. [41]

Along with data management, the IDIU vastly improved communications among federal, state, and local law enforcement. Using the latest in computer technology and opening new lines of communication with state and local officials, Clark hoped to eliminate the need for federal intervention in times of civil unrest. Taking Cyrus Vance's recommendation, Clark arranged more formal relations with local police officials through the IDIU. Specifically, he encouraged local police departments to set up "intelligence units" of "undercover police personnel and informants" and "draw on 'community leaders, agencies, and organizations in the ghetto.'" These squads would then pass intelligence up the chain to the Communication Center at the IDIU. Without establishing a system of checks and balances or even parameters for intelligence gathering, Clark encouraged the development of a vast surveillance apparatus.[42]

Sponsoring a five-day training program for mayors and chiefs of police from across the nation in January 1968, Clark heralded a new federal effort to coordinate with local and state agencies, and he stressed the importance of the Communication Center as central to the administration's new civil disorder prevention efforts. The Communication Center, Clark assured the assembled chiefs, would ameliorate the problem of "overwhelming existing communication and emergency networks." To bolster communication efforts Clark offered new radio equipment. The IDIU's Communication Center, claimed Clark, was the best answer for local agencies that encountered civil disorders.[43] Indicating his own uncertainty about what he was creating, even as he developed capacities within the Department of Justice to gather intelligence from local, state, and federal agencies (with no legal framework for determining how such information was obtained), Clark adamantly opposed congressional efforts to legalize wiretapping and surveillance.

Clark was indeed uneasy about uncontrolled surveillance capacities, but given his antipathy to working with Hoover and his not trusting the intelligence coming out of the FBI, he thought it the best solution. As acting attorney general, Clark called for a sweeping review of all department cases. He declared that the Justice Department would not "proceed with any investigation or case which includes evidence illegally obtained." Any information obtained through illegal wiretaps or electronic wiretapping, Clark declared, must be "purged [until the Department of Justice is] in a position to assure [itself] and the court that there is no taint or unfairness." When the Senate approved the nomination of Ramsey Clark as attorney general in March 1967, he issued a sweeping ban on wiretapping that went far beyond the president's own 1965 directive. Clark thought wiretaps and electronic monitoring "inefficient" tools for law enforcement ("It takes twenty-seven men to install one of those things and monitor it") and "insidious." Congressional Republicans blasted Clark's wiretap ban and questioned "the authority of the Attorney General to meddle in this fashion in the purely investigative affairs of other departments."[44] Others criticized the apparent paradox of the attorney general's approval of wiretapping in national security cases as "tantamount to a concession that wire interception and eavesdropping are essential weapons of detection against elaborate, organized criminal conspiracies."[45] Yet even as Clark banned the use of such devices at the executive level, the IDIU encouraged state and local officials to provide intelligence, without regard for how that intelligence was obtained.

To counter political criticism and to at least appear to be addressing the concerns of average Americans that the country was coming apart at the seams while the administration stood idly by, the administration introduced sweeping legislation in 1968 aimed at curbing crime, the Safe Streets and Crime Control Act. Dissatisfied with the bill, Democrat John McClellan attached Title III, a statute to legalize wiretapping and electronic surveillance for law enforcement purposes. Many legislators and law enforcement officials believed that identifying criminals and gathering much-needed intelligence about their activities should be a continuous right granted to those on the front lines of the war on crime. In the House of Representatives, Republican Minority Leader Gerald Ford of Michigan cosponsored wiretap legislation. Taking up the recommendations approved by the Judicial Conference of the United States (which included chief justices from federal district courts and top judges from some district courts), Ford and his colleagues crafted legislation to legalize court-approved wiretapping for law enforcement purposes. The Association of Federal Investigators, the National Association of Attorneys General, and the National District Attorneys Association supported the legislation.[46]

Clark strenuously opposed Title III. When the Safe Streets and Crime Control Act passed the House and Senate, including Title III, he complained that Congress had passed a "bad bill" that "barely resembles [what] we sent the Congress with such high hopes and ardent pleas." The bill did not offer a thoughtful approach to law and order, Clark insisted, but instead reflected "the fears, frustration and politics of the times" and failed to address "the urgent need to professionalize police, coordinate criminal justice and effectively protect the public." Clark found "a profound and tragic moral in the fact that Congressional forces that favor wiretapping generally oppose professionalization of police, prisoner rehabilitation and research. They want to ignore any relationship between crime and slums, racism, poverty or mental health. To them, poverty is just an excuse; 'bad people' commit crime. The elements of racism in the insistent political demand for law and order also become manifest when the same leaders oppose enforcement of civil rights."[47] Outlining several components of the bill that he found most insidious, he reserved his vitriol for Title III—authorizing wiretapping and electronic surveillance. Clark warned the president that portions of the bill would grant federal and state law enforcement broad new authorities and "could set a trend that would destroy privacy and liberty in the difficult years ahead." Clark urged President Johnson to consider a "right and courageous" veto. He hoped such action would compel Congress to revisit the more egregious portions of the bill, with the added bonus that it would send a message to the American public and "increase confidence among youth, minorities and others in our government, [in] our laws and our national purpose." From a strictly legal perspective, Clark realized that Title III was not unconstitutional, but he worried that it opened the door for unconstitutional practices. Recognizing that a veto was politically impossible given the public's call for "law and order" measures, the attorney general urged Johnson to encourage the repeal of Title III in a signing statement.[48]

Clark was not alone in his principled opposition to the bill. White House counsel Harry McPherson also voiced reservations, calling Title III "extremely dangerous" and worrying that it had the potential to "turn any given town or state into a little soviet." McPherson warned the president that the Safe Streets and Crime Control Act would be "the worst bill you will have signed since you took office." Though he knew the president had little political room to maneuver, he urged Johnson to "blast" the "obnoxious" provisions of the bill, especially Title III. Taking McPherson's advice, President Johnson signed the bill and noted his objections to Title III in a signing statement. Congress had taken, the president stated, the "unwise and potentially dangerous" step of authorizing wiretapping and electronic eavesdropping by local, state, and federal officials in "an almost unlimited variety of situations."[49]

The passage of Title III haunted Clark right through his last days in office. In January 1969, days before Richard Nixon would be sworn in as the thirty-seventh president of the United States, Clark reflected on his legacy as attorney general in a conversation with journalist Fred Graham of the *New York Times*. Though the interview covered a range of topics, Clark made clear that nothing troubled him as much as the legacy of Title III. He voiced his concerns in Orwellian terms, predicting that by becoming "captive[s] of our technology" the nation was bent on a course that would ultimately "alter the meaning of the individual in a mass society." Clark was no Luddite. He recognized that technological advances helped drive modern society, but he warned: "If we create today traditions of spying on people when they do not know it, it may not be too far distant when a person can hardly think, much less speak his mind to any other person, without fear of police or someone else knowing his thoughts or words." That Orwellian nightmare, Clark supposed, could become a reality if American society did not face the challenges that such technologies posed to individual privacy and integrity. He remained resolute that "electronic surveillance is not necessary to law enforcement. It is a peril to freedom."[50]

Clark still held firm in his belief that technology could and should advance modern society. Presciently, he recognized that new technologies made surveillance not only more prolific but also more effective. Clark's concerns, however earnest, suggest an effort on his part to write the administration's response to urban disorder out of the historical record. Clark himself was an active proponent of intelligence gathering and used the latest in computer technologies to implement a nationwide catalogue of dossiers that, intentionally or not, included persons with no connection to urban riots. Even as Clark blasted surveillance as a threat to civil liberties, the use of these modern technologies was an almost inevitable, if unforeseen, consequence of a liberal state apparatus that strove to solve myriad problems through the technocratic management of volumes of data.

Clark's legacy as attorney general was mixed and paradoxical. A dedicated liberal, Clark battled over how best to approach the issue of urban disorder in the late 1960s. Committed to federal support for racial and economic justice, he believed the state must eliminate poverty before tackling other issues, including urban unrest. He firmly believed that only the federal government had the capacity and the will to deliver the American Dream to all its citizens, black and white. During his last days with the Johnson administration, Attorney General Ramsey Clark continued to emphasize federal social welfare programs as the best remedy against violence and civil disorder. Speaking at one of his last public engagements as the nation's top law enforcement officer, Clark recounted the "milestones of his tenure" with an "emphasis . . . on 'economic and legal justice'" and made no mention of law and order successes.[51] And yet, Clark's trust in the power of the state to solve the nation's greatest problems informed his decision to establish a new agency within the Department of Justice to gather intelligence on urban African American residents. The IDIU was a logical manifestation of liberal conviction that the state could ameliorate society's ills if managed by technocrats drawing on the latest technologies and gathering all the necessary information. Well-informed technocrats, Clark believed, could make well-informed decisions in the best interest of the nation and its citizens.

The unintended consequence of this unflagging faith in government and those who managed it lent legitimacy to "ends over means" practices of various agencies at the local, state, and federal level. Asked by the attorney general to provide intelligence on urban ghetto dwellers (without regard for how such data was obtained), agencies renewed their efforts to gather intelligence on American citizens. At the close of the Johnson administration in January 1969, the Department of Justice presided over a grand intelligence clearinghouse with extraordinary new capacities for data collection and retrieval. The administration of President Richard Nixon, less concerned with protecting individual rights, would use this apparatus to battle its political foes.

CHAPTER THREE

"A Communist behind Every Bush"
The Army Spies on Civilians

The whir of the helicopter blades overhead drowned out the loudspeaker, effectively silencing the young, long-haired man. The appearance of the four massive helicopters circling low over the protest evoked confusion among the activists. Confusion turned to panic as protestors recognized a long telephoto lens jutting from open doors and windows on either side of the low-flying choppers. Dozens of protesters began to run.

About forty of the protesters, however, did not panic; several even gazed up admiringly at the circling birds. These "activists" displayed no surprise or dismay at the sight of helicopters overhead. While young fresh faces, beards, unkempt and loose-fitting clothing suggested that they, too, were antiwar protestors, they were not. They were army counterintelligence officers. Like the men in the helicopters hovering overhead, they were gathering information for their government. They were spying on civilians exercising their constitutionally protected rights.[1]

In December 1966 *New York Times* associate editor and Washington insider James Reston predicted that disorder in American cities would be the most important issue of 1967. The "strongest man available" to wage the "war at home," declared Reston, was "undoubtedly [Secretary of Defense Robert] McNamara." Following three summers of increasingly volatile and unpredictable civil unrest, many Americans like Reston had become frustrated with the Johnson administration's inability to impose law and order on the streets. Reston reasoned that only the nation's most powerful institution—the Pentagon—could bring the United States back from the brink of civil war.[2]

While Attorney General Clark absorbed much criticism for the Justice Department's handling of lawlessness, in 1967 President Johnson ordered McNamara and the Department of Defense to assume more of the burden of managing and executing the administration's civil disturbance strategy. The president's decision to mobilize the U.S. Army to put down the Detroit uprising in July proved the catalyst for this shift. Heeding Deputy Defense Secretary Cyrus Vance's warning that Detroit was just the beginning of a summer of violent upheaval in the nation's cities, the Department of Defense spearheaded strategic planning to better anticipate disorder in American cities.[3]

Throughout the nation's history the U.S. government had called upon the army to control domestic disturbances and quell political dissent. Although the 1878 Posse Comitatus Act prohibited the use of the military in law enforcement capacities unless expressly authorized by Congress, the federal government had liberally interpreted the law throughout the twentieth century.[4] The army stood at the ready in the 1940s as labor strikes erupted across the country, prepared to move in and quell unrest. When southern opposition to desegregation threatened to become violent, President Eisenhower, in addition to nationalizing the Arkansas National Guard, sent in units of the army's 101st Airborne division to protect black students at Little Rock High School in Arkansas in 1957.

Given the extraordinary volatility of the 1960s, presidential administrations frequently ignored or overlooked the restrictions on the use of the military to enforce the rule of law. In the decade's early years this institutional response was confined mainly to racial violence in the South related to civil rights protests and struggles for racial equality. Army troops served as backup to federal marshals and National Guard units in Oxford, Mississippi, in 1962 and 1963, and Tuscaloosa and Huntsville, Alabama, in 1963. Similarly, army units watched over Martin Luther King, Jr.'s, civil rights march from Selma to Montgomery, Alabama, in 1965.[5]

When President Johnson tasked the Pentagon with developing a plan to combat riots, McNamara was confident the army could handle the job. As historian Michael Flamm explained, "Army units also had considerable minority representation and fire discipline, in sharp contrast to the virtually all-white National Guard whose indiscriminate discharge of weapons had inflated casualty rates so dramatically in Newark and Detroit."[6] If called upon by the president, McNamara felt confident that the Pentagon had the capacity to use military troops to maintain order though he worried that it did not have the intelligence it needed to assess the root causes of urban unrest and especially dissent. McNamara tasked his deputy, ardent cold warrior Paul Nitze, with developing the army's civil disturbance plan. Nitze, taking the recommendations of the Department of the Army Civil Disturbance Plan, proposed expanding the army's existing intelligence-gathering capacities to better anticipate urban upheaval.[7] Following the Detroit riots, the army implemented

Nitze's plan, developing a vast domestic surveillance program. "Repatriating" intelligence officers and military officers who had served abroad, the army tasked thousands of officers in the United States with gathering intelligence to better predict social upheaval. These officers practiced Cold War counterintelligence methods honed in Berlin, Saigon, and Seoul—use of spies, disinformation campaigns, and electronic and technological surveillance—on Americans who dissented from the foreign and domestic policies of the U. S. government.[8] These counterintelligence tools represented just a small portion of the American state's Cold War security capacities.

Like the FBI, in the 1960s the army's domestic organizational imperative—to establish law and order—led officers to blur the distinction between lawful dissent carried out by American citizens and unlawful, insurrectionary activities planned by foreign communist foes of the United States. In FBI Director J. Edgar Hoover's view, American youth were exposed to "more extremists and radicals than ever before" in the nation's history. Subversives who dealt in "bigotry, hate and falsehoods," Hoover warned, had the sole purpose of "turn[ing] young Americans against their country." Security officials like Hoover viewed dissent as an avowal "to overthrow the existing order." Even if radicals were not reds, he argued, they were dupes of the international communist conspiracy and were aiding and abetting communists by challenging authority and weakening the American state. This worldview led some domestic security experts to conflate the Soviet-led communist threat to the American way of life with the lawful, if disorderly, conduct of racial justice radicals and antiwar protestors.[9]

As a result, U.S. Cold War counterintelligence programs worked to root out all subversive forces and destroy their ability to foment disorder. On an institutional level the army's domestic surveillance program did not distinguish, as one scholar explained, among "opponents of the status quo."[10] Many commanding officers and counterintelligence officers perceived dissent in the United States as a subversive threat because they believed it weakened the nation during a time of war—both cold and hot—and so served the interests of the United States' enemies. As a result, officials in the Pentagon and other agencies enthusiastically developed the capacity to surveil, disrupt, harass, and persecute lawful, constitutionally protected political dissent on American soil. President Lyndon Johnson arrived reluctantly at the decision to commit army paratroopers to the urban revolt in Detroit in 1967, because he preferred that state and local officials have the "primary responsibility" for controlling civil disorder.

He based his decision to commit the army more on political calculation than personal commitment.[11] As a man with perhaps unparalleled political acumen, Johnson was eager to deflect the Republican Party's effort to paint the Democrats as soft on crime before the upcoming presidential election.

Republican critiques struck a chord with many Americans, who believed that the president should act more vigorously to halt urban violence. "Widespread rioting and violent civil disorder have grown to a national crisis since the present Administration took office," Republicans declared. "Today no one is safe on the streets, in his home or in his property." The country, they warned, was "rapidly approaching a state of anarchy." Republicans blamed the president who, they argued, opposed legislation aimed at restoring "law and order." Johnson's "pleasant platitudes and statements of good intentions," the GOP charged, were wholly insufficient to address "the critical state of the nation."[12]

President Johnson thought his defense secretary, Robert Strange McNamara, well prepared to respond to Republican demands for action. A holdover from the Kennedy administration, McNamara brought a keen eye for efficiency and management to the Pentagon. During World War II, working under the direction of Colonel Charles Thornton, McNamara and a small group of highly talented young men streamlined data flow to make American air power, then a nascent but blossoming force, a more effective weapon for the Allied forces. Based on this experience McNamara came to believe that intelligently applied data could solve the toughest bureaucratic problems. Following the war the Ford Corporation hired Thornton and his team of "whiz kids" to bring efficiency to the auto company's bottom line. McNamara's civil service, as well as his fifteen years improving Ford Motor's bottom line (serving part of that time as president of the company) earned him his place on the short list for the top job at the Department of Defense in the Kennedy administration. The team did not disappoint and rose rapidly through the executive ranks of the company. McNamara's experience in business administration made him well qualified to assume "the burden of directing and administering the gigantic department responsible for the defense of the United States," a job that that the *New York Times* believed was "as big and tough a job as can be found in the Government below the Presidency itself."[13]

McNamara had been a "phenomenon" in Detroit, but many top defense experts believed that he faced an "impossible job" in Washington—to "bring efficiency to a $40 billion military establishment beset by jealousies and political pressures while maintaining American military superiority." McNamara went right to work, promising to make "big decisions" and break with past practices after a careful "study and analysis" of Pentagon programs. Speaking before the annual Associated Press luncheon in one of his first public appearances as secretary, McNamara outlined his plans to "eliminate waste, duplication and unjustifiable expenditure" while still maintaining American defense superiority. This was a formidable task, considering that spending for the American defense establishment represented more than half of the federal budget.[14] McNamara believed the challenges of the Department of Defense could be solved by making the bureaucracy more efficient.

Tasked by President Johnson to coordinate the state's response to urban unrest, McNamara drew upon existing resources. Urban experts within the Department of Defense had, since the early years of the Cold War, worked closely with officials and organizations in American cities to combat unrest and eliminate subversive elements. Defense intellectuals relied on "command, control, computers, intelligence, surveillance, and reconnaissance," according to historian Jennifer Light, already "essential components in military planners' decision-making arsenals," to solve the nation's urban problems. In this historical context, national security managers, as well as President Johnson, cast the urban crises of the late 1960s as national security crises. Even the administration's efforts to attack social inequality—the Great Society and the wars on poverty and crime—were, according to Light, interpreted by defense intellectuals as efforts to construct an urban bulwark against subversion and communist infiltration. During the Kennedy and Johnson administrations national security planners moved easily from positions within the defense establishment to assume powerful roles as domestic policymakers. Adam Yarmolinsky, special assistant to the secretary of defense, assumed the position of deputy director of Johnson's Task Force on Poverty. Joseph Califano, who served as assistant to the secretary of defense, later became the president's special assistant for domestic policy. These defense intellectuals applied their security management skills to the problems of domestic policy and civil disorder.[15]

Secretary McNamara believed the administration could respond better to urban disorder by drawing on existing resources. To reduce waste and duplication, McNamara established an intelligence clearinghouse at Fort Holabird. Known as CONUS Intelligence Branch (Continental United States), this computerized hub linked eight military intelligence groups around the country, centralizing control for army intelligence under the Army Intelligence Command.[16] Fort Holabird directed its groups to collect urban intelligence in the event that the president deployed federal troops. Intelligence groups passed their information through the Counterintelligence Analysis Branch (CIAB) operating out of the office of the army's assistant chief of staff for intelligence, Lieutenant General William P. Yarborough.[17]

Affectionately known as "Big Y" for the way he signed memoranda, Yarborough came from a family of intelligence experts. His father had been an army colonel and intelligence officer. After World War II, Yarborough commanded counterintelligence and psychological warfare operations in Stuttgart, Germany, and in 1961 he took command of the Army Special Warfare Center and Special Warfare School at Fort Bragg, North Carolina. As director of army intelligence and the CONUS Intel program in the late 1960s, Yarborough's approach to civil disorder in the United States was deeply informed by his training in Cold War counterintelligence methods. In Germany he had personally directed and participated in counterinsurgency programs against foreign foes. He approached his task as head of CONUS Intel with the fervent belief that "outside influences were aiding and abetting" Americans who practiced their constitutionally protected right to protest. He could not believe that the spontaneous eruption of dissent, revolution, and mass protest in the United States could be possible without the funding and organizational capacities of the international communist movement. Yarborough's insistence upon the communist backing of rioters and protestors pointed CONUS Intel resources to the wrong targets. Consequently, the army failed to predict the explosion of violence and disorder in Newark, New Jersey, in July 1967. McNamara believed that multiple civil disturbances were likely to follow Newark and the president would need to mobilize the army to augment the National Guard. He directed the army to establish an early civil disturbance warning network, linking the army's 300 nationwide domestic intelligence officers with CONUS Intel at Fort Holabird.[18]

When Detroit erupted in violence, burning, and looting a few weeks after Newark, Yarborough told his staff to "get out your counterinsurgency manuals. We have an insurgency on our hands." Yarborough's Cold War counterintelligence training left the lieutenant colonel ill prepared to distinguish civil disorder in the United States from insurgency abroad. As one officer later recalled, "There we were, plotting power plants, radio stations, and armories on the situation maps when we should have been locating the liquor and color-television stores instead." Indeed, Detroit revealed the weaknesses of Yarborough's strategy, based as it was on the precepts of Cold War counterinsurgency methods. Institutionally, the army relied on a language and strategy for fighting international foes—real insurgents—rather than understanding the nature of domestic problems. Army counterintelligence officers lacked the skill set and experience to assess and respond to the domestic troubles of 1960s America. Besides being rather ridiculous in practice, the army's program of domestic surveillance made the violation of the constitutional rights of thousands of American targets unavoidable collateral damage. After the army's failure to predict the urban uprisings of 1967, McNamara and Nitze reevaluated the Pentagon's institutional capacities. Given the right information, McNamara and Nitze believed they could adequately respond to future disturbances. Nitze focused on expanding the army's existing intelligence capacities. National security planners remained unwavering in their conviction that international agitators backed civil disorder in the United States. In an effort to identify these elements, the army expanded CONUS Intel efforts to include dissidents in general and antiwar protestors in particular.[19]

Across the executive branch officials ordered domestic security agencies to find the link between the international communist movement and those who fomented disorder in the United States. As the radical Black Power movement became more vocal in its opposition to the Vietnam War, intelligence experts linked international and domestic movements. Black Panther Bobby Seale called on urban blacks to take up arms against their own country, predicting that as "the aggression of the racist American government escalates in Vietnam, the police agencies of America [will] escalate the repression of black people throughout the ghettos." Seale was right, in part. U.S. security agencies responded to domestic unrest by using the off-the-shelf institutional tools that had been developed for international efforts, like the war in Vietnam. Historian Michael Flamm has documented the Pentagon's close collaboration with state and local police. When McNamara took over the administration's response to civil disorder, the marines trained local and state police in counterinsurgency techniques and guerrilla warfare. The administration encouraged army personnel to go into police work after retirement. State and local police borrowed from the Pentagon's war toolkit, but more than that, they were literally the recipients of the Johnson administration's guns and butter programs. Flamm writes that the Department of Defense distributed weapons to state and local police through the Law Enforcement Assistance Administration, including "electronic movement sensors, armored troop carriers, and sophisticated scout helicopters."[20]

Antiwar protestors declared an implicit connection between the U.S. government's policies in Vietnam and the urban revolt at home. At a press conference in August 1967 announcing plans to march on Washington, the National Mobilization Committee to End the War in Vietnam (Mobe) claimed that there was *"only one struggle—for self-determination—and we support it in Vietnam and in black America."* These public pronouncements, explicitly connecting U.S. foreign policy to the social unrest, seemed to some top-level national security planners evidence of the links between international movements and domestic unrest. Army intelligence officers infiltrated the March on the Pentagon in the fall of 1967. President Johnson and other top officials came down hard on senior army officers in the wake of the protest—catching what one called "undiluted hell"—for failing to accurately predict the number of protestors and their intended plans.[21]

These consecutive "failures" on the part of Army intelligence prompted a seemingly paradoxical response from national security planners. Even as CONUS Intel expanded its intelligence capacities, gathering intelligence from local and state police, the FBI, and Secret Service, the army outlined restrictions for intelligence operations. Recognizing the potential danger to civil liberties if the army began to broadly sweep up intelligence, the army authored guidelines to restrict some counterintelligence activity. Counterintelligence officers, according to the new regulations, would not "directly ... obtain civil disturbance information" unless authorized by army headquarters. Neither would army personnel participate in so-called "covert operations" unless authorized with the prior approval of the Assistant Chief of Staff of the Army for Intelligence William Yarborough.[22]

The new restrictions, however, were only as effective as Yarborough would require them to be. He was not personally inclined to restrict anything; in fact, he encouraged, and in some cases ordered, CIAB analysts to find evidence to support his theory that subversive elements in the United States conspired with international officers to coordinate urban violence and civil disorder. In spite of their best efforts, analysts located no such evidence. Nevertheless, Yarborough remained resolute in his conviction that fifth column elements existed in the ghetto, and he assured his analysts that they would eventually find proof that the rioters "were tied in with each other—they were trained in Havana or Peking or some damned place." This intelligence was gathered along with intelligence from the FBI and the Secret Service and sent back to Fort Holabird. Officers fed this raw data into the new computer system and created the "compendium." This desktop "encyclopedia" included the names of people and organizations of interest—including their political beliefs and affiliations—which the army distributed among federal agencies.[23]

According to one former officer who often prepared reports for the lieutenant colonel, Yarborough had "a deep and abiding interest in groups in [the United States] engaged in dissident activity." He demanded weekly intelligence briefings about a variety of organizations and expected the analysts to find material to support his suspicion that New Left and civil rights organizations were "engaged in unlawful activity, civil disturbance activity." Though his analysts were rarely able to corroborate his theories, they nonetheless felt obliged to produce charts and graphs, financial records, leadership information, and the history of the organization to satiate the general's predispositions. Yarborough was not alone in his obsession with ferreting out "subversive forces" in the United States. Some intelligence officers liked to play "James Angleton."[24] Many found infiltrating civil rights groups and trailing peace and antiwar activists much more engaging work than attending to the boring tasks of routine security clearances. Absent clearly defined intelligence protocol from the defense secretary, army intelligence officers used Cold War–era procedures for compiling information about so-called subversive forces. The army's own intelligence collection plan so broadly defined "subversive activities" that, as one counterintelligence officer later recalled, it "implied that the Army viewed litigation, sit-ins, voter registration drives, and mass rallies as subversive activities warranting surveillance by Army officers."[25]

Regional and local commanding officers rarely distinguished between those who exercised First Amendment rights and those who advocated violence or committed crimes. When the army charged intelligence officers with identifying "subversive activities" in preparation for civil disturbance outbreaks in the summer of 1968, institutional guidelines identified "dissident elements" as civil rights movements, anti-Vietnam and antidraft movements, and "subversive and conspiratorial" organizations such as the peace movement and the Progressive Labor Party, the Student Non-Violent Coordinating Committee, and the Revolutionary Action Movement. The only "friendly forces" identified were U.S. military agencies including USCONARC, CONUS, and the U.S. Army Intelligence Command![26]

In an age of data banks and computers, the army's broad application of the term "subversive" had potentially devastating consequences for targeted individuals. CIAB blacklists were officially meant "to keep track of people who might cause trouble for the Army," but neither civilian nor military officers established guidelines for analyzing the accuracy of collected data. Consequently, the very existence of a file within the army's compendium or computer data bank suggested subversive activity. The sharing of data—accurate or not—across executive agencies could leave an indelible black mark on individuals who neither knew of the existence of their record, nor had any recourse to challenge the validity of the information held therein. In previous decades the label of communist or sympathizer in the United States could have devastating consequences for one's economic stability, family, and professional life. The CIAB's computerized intelligence reports proved popular with many government agencies, including the FBI, the Justice Department, and state and local police departments. One insider claimed that CONUS Intel "created addicts for this stuff [intelligence] all over the Government." Several volumes included intelligence taken verbatim from the Alabama Department of Public Safety and included white supremacist condemnation of civil rights leaders and organizations as "criminals and degenerates."[27]

Top army brass acknowledged the gray area of domestic intelligence work. The army conceded that an "overwhelming majority" of antiwar and civil rights movement participants were "sincere Americans." Nevertheless, to identify the "small but virulent number" who aimed to "tear America apart," the army encouraged broad surveillance and intelligence collection. To mollify critics, army commanding officers surely underscored that the program was a provisional response to social upheaval. They undoubtedly envisioned a swift return to the army's more traditional domestic intelligence role when law and order had been reestablished. Perhaps this reassured some that their mission to identify "the well springs of violence and the heart and nerve causes of chaos" was a reasonable task given the social upheaval of the late 1960s. Army intelligence commanders believed they would be remiss if they allowed "the professional violence purveyors" to perpetuate "law breaking, social disintegration, chaos, violence, destruction, insurrection, [and] revolution" to take place on their watch on American soil.[28]

Some army counterintelligence officers shared Yarborough's views of civil disorder. This group, as one former analyst recalled, tended to see a "communist behind every bush." This Cold War mentality led some to collect what one counterintelligence officer called "social intelligence." One such report observed a protest by welfare mothers who were "sick and tired of not having enough money to feed their children." Such "intelligence" met none of the army's informational needs pertaining to civil disturbances. The army's needs were "simple," recalled one participant.

"They had to know about the physical geography of the city; they had to know what was happening on the ground at the moment [of briefing], and what they could expect to encounter in the way of resources when they arrived on the scene."[29]

Most army counterintelligence officers expressed little appreciation for the complicated social and cultural tensions in the United States during the 1960s. "The professional soldier," observed one CIAB officer, "is trained for war. He is steeped in a tradition which emphasizes force as the final arbiter and instills a moral code which, however well suited to the exigencies of warfare and military service it might be, has little relevance to the process of understanding and solving our complex social and urban problems." Men like William Yarborough were lost in the domestic realm. Intelligence officers were trained for missions abroad and cycled into domestic service after their overseas missions. One officer commanded a tank unit in Vietnam and had little or no experience in intelligence work. Yet his domestic intelligence assignment required him to be "conversant with radical activities." One graduate of the U.S. Military Academy, who had served in an infantry unit, worked the racial desk for the CIAB. Though he was capable and intelligent, the assignment left him with a "sense of being at sea, of not really being able to reconcile his background training with this kind of duty which, he felt, was inappropriate for the Army to be involved in [in] the first place."[30]

Most domestic counterintelligence officers were steeped in an institutional Cold War culture that encouraged them to see "conspiracy" as the "key to understanding events." Most had spent their adult lives overseas and were not familiar or even acquainted with domestic life in the United States. Like Yarborough, many "approached civil disturbance problems with the conspiratorial theory and the inclination to gather all the data they could amass" to prove their theory. Army officers frequently briefed CIA liaison officers on "subjects" of interest. At the request of the director of security for the CIA, one former army intelligence officer thoroughly investigated *Ramparts*, a New Left magazine. Much to the chagrin of his army superiors, the officer could not establish a link between the magazine and foreign financiers, or "Comintern backing," as one army official called it. The CIA and the officer's army superiors were furious and told the officer he had "essentially failed" in his assignment.[31]

In this cultural climate, no one was above suspicion. In Illinois, the 113th Military Intelligence Group put Adlai Stevenson III (member of the Illinois House of Representatives, 1965–1967, and Illinois state treasurer, 1967–1970), Congressman Abner Mikva, and federal circuit court judge

Otto Kerner on its watch list. Army counterintelligence made Stevenson a target when he was photographed with Jesse Jackson, then head of the Southern Christian Leadership Conference's "Operation Breadbasket." Like Mikva, Stevenson came under scrutiny too for his anti-Vietnam war views. The army created a file on Kerner after the National Advisory Commission on Civil Disorders, which he chaired, published its final report in 1968. The Kerner report found no evidence of conspiracy with foreign officers in its examination of the urban uprisings of 1967.[32]

Not all army counterintelligence officers were comfortable playing the James Angleton role. Some communicated their concerns about army counterintelligence methods to their civilian and military superiors. The army assigned Officer Oliver Peirce, trained in counterintelligence methods from December 1968 through April 1969 at the U.S. Army Intelligence School at Fort Holabird, to the 5th Military Intelligence Detachment at Fort Carson, Colorado. He was ordered to infiltrate the Young Adult Project (YAP), an umbrella organization for a loose affiliation of groups of the Pikes Peak Council of Churches. Peirce's commanding officer explained that one of YAP's founders was a former member of SDS and had been active in the antiwar movement. This "radical" might use YAP to "influence soldiers from Fort Carson against the Army, [and] against the war."[33]

Peirce's commanding officer instructed him to collect any information he could obtain about the "civilian young adult members of this project" as well as identify any military personnel who attended meetings or visited the project center. Peirce watched this group and attended meetings from June through November 1969. He witnessed nothing to indicate that YAP promoted violence or was "disloyal" to the U.S. government. Peirce believed his intelligence work was redundant; he was one of many counterintelligence officers who had infiltrated local and regional peace movement organizations. When he hinted to his superior that his "intelligence" was useless, Peirce was told to continue attending meetings. He was later dismayed to find that, despite all evidence to the contrary, his commanding officer included YAP on an army chart of "extremist" political groups in Colorado, a distinction it shared with the local branch of SDS.[34]

Peirce's experience was the norm. Department of Defense intelligence guidelines for domestic surveillance granted army intelligence sweeping authority in the name of establishing law and order. Local and regional intelligence officers interpreted this mandate broadly. The army assigned one intelligence officer to White, South Dakota, after a local college party got a little out of hand. The police quelled the disturbance quite handily, but army intelligence decided to investigate in order to be sure that another drunken brawl would not go "undiscovered." Because the army had such resources, and because it had been tasked with predicting domestic civil disturbance, its officers and commanders were more likely to go far beyond their duty of preparing the army for federal troop commitment. In effect, recalled one officer, army counterintelligence officers spent time "chaperoning college students . . . taking part in their discussions and monitoring their private lives"—a waste of army intelligence resources.[35]

In spite of the disconnect between the Department of Defense intelligence needs and the work of army officers on the ground, institutional imperatives continued to promote useless, and in some cases, extraconstitutional surveillance practices. Presidential commission findings bolstered the Cold War counterintelligence, counterinsurgency approach of national security elites to the twin problems of protest and urban revolt. In 1968 President Johnson's Kerner Commission issued its long-awaited report on civil disorder. The commission recommended the creation of an intelligence unit "to gather, evaluate, analyze, and disseminate information on potential as well as actual disorders." The commission recommended the use of "undercover police personnel and informants" to gather intelligence, but also "community leaders, agencies, and organization in the ghetto."[36] Intelligence, the commission affirmed, was at the heart of any institutional effort to combat undesirable political and social behavior—at home or abroad. In effect, the Kerner commission legitimated the use of institutional techniques expanded in the Cold War and applied at home. Civil servants cited the commission's recommendations to justify the development and expansion of domestic intelligence programs including the Interdivisional Information Unit (IDIU) within the Department of Justice and the army's CONUS Intel.[37]

It was in this context of expanding state power in the name of law and order that the presidential campaign of 1968 unfolded. Republican Richard Nixon took up the theme as his banner issue. According to historian Michael Flamm, Nixon's electoral victory reflected a "growing sense among whites that liberal programs could not prevent social disorder, which in turn reinforced the growing popularity of 'law and order.'"[38] The Nixon campaign capitalized on a fear haunting many Americans— unabated lawlessness in the streets of America. Nixon's triumph over liberal Hubert Humphrey in 1968 suggested an electoral mandate to use any means necessary to impose law and order.

A second component of Nixon's campaign (and one far less politicized) was a pledge to reform "big government." During a 1969 televised address on federalism, Nixon declared that as president he would curb the growth of the federal government and roll back some Great Society programs. When President Nixon took office, his administration did restrict the social welfare state (though much less than his campaign would have suggested). In the area of domestic unrest, however, Nixon and his advisors expanded state power and grew the government.[39] Nixon's attorney general, John Mitchell, restructured the IDIU to better coordinate with local police and law officials to predict violence and effectively quash it. In March 1969 the deputy attorney general established an Interdepartmental Intelligence Evaluation Committee to review the intelligence collected by the IDIU and prepare a report about areas with a potential for civil disorder. The new intelligence committee included representatives from the Department of Justice's Criminal Division, the FBI, the Internal Security Division, the Community Relations Service, and the Department of the Army. The committee's first assignment was to identify locations where civil disorder seemed likely to occur on the first anniversary of the assassination of Martin Luther King, Jr.[40]

While the Nixon administration may have found justification for its domestic security policy in the Kerner Commission report, a second commission headed by former Republican president Dwight Eisenhower's brother, Johns Hopkins University's emeritus president Dr. Milton Eisenhower, offered a more complicated assessment of disorder. Released in December 1969, the report of the National Advisory Commission on Civil Disorders took the long view of recent protest movements and violence as a new expression of an old American tradition. Violent civil disorder—including events like the Whiskey Rebellion, "bleeding Kansas," the violence the Ku Klux Klan perpetuated against freedmen during Reconstruction, and the growth of organized labor—concluded the report, "runs through the American experience." To prevent and control group violence, American political institutions should aim to make violence as a political means to an end "both unnecessary and unrewarding." To do so, American institutions should make every attempt to address perceived social and political injustices throughout society.[41]

The Eisenhower commission conceded that violence was inevitable. The state should counteract disorder "firmly, fairly, and within the law." The challenge lay in striking a balance between protecting lawful expressions of dissent and establishing an appropriate federal, state, and local response to violent upheaval. The best method for controlling group violence, urged the commission, was "prompt, prudent deployment of well-trained law enforcement personnel [who] can extinguish a civil disorder in its incipiency." Furthermore, the report urged "police departments throughout the nation to improve their methods of anticipating, preventing, and controlling" group violence.[42] The report offered something for everyone. On the one hand, it called for a better government effort to eliminate the causes of social disorder and political unrest. On the other hand, it called for the expansion and enhancement of local domestic intelligence operations to better predict unrest. Notably, the report did not call for a federal role in law enforcement.

Even as the commission implicitly approved of expanded state action in response to social upheaval, it noted "society's failure to afford full protection" to those who wished to express their freedom of speech as a probable explanation for recent unrest. Consequently, the commission recommended that the president propose legislation to allow courts to issue injunctions (requested by the attorney general or citizens) "against the threatened or actual interference by any person," with First Amendment rights including "freedom of speech, freedom of the press, peaceful assembly and petition for redress of grievances."[43]

The commission's recommendations underscored a historically contentious constitutional issue. How could the state at once enhance and expand the powers of federal, state, and local law enforcement while respecting the First and Fourth Amendment guarantees of freedom of speech and individual privacy? To address inequities in the United States, wrote the commission, democratic institutions must reflect the racial and cultural diversification of the society they represent. "For speech, petition and assembly to be effective, they must be heard and seen." Claiming that media groups offered fewer and fewer perspectives to represent the "growing size and diversity of the nation," the commission grappled with how to encourage the press to report more frequently about the societal problems of underrepresented minority groups: "Private and governmental institutions" should "encourage the development of competing news media and discourage increased concentration of control over existing media." Recalling Thomas Jefferson's observation that American institutions must be flexible and keep pace with the human mind, the report cautioned, "Today the pace of change has become far more rapid than when Jefferson wrote, and the need for adapting our institutions to the changing environment has become greater still." The commission thus offered a somewhat contradictory approach to the problem of urban disorder—simultaneously recognizing the democratic right to protest while advocating enhanced and better coordinated law enforcement.

Both the Johnson and Nixon administrations struggled over these contradictions.[44]

The proliferation of domestic surveillance and counterintelligence operations in the late 1960s raised fundamental questions about the vitality of constitutionally protected civil liberties in Cold War America. Appointed officials within the Justice Department, like Attorney General Ramsey Clark, worried about the long-term repercussions of legal surveillance on the health of American democracy. But First Amendment rights were fleetingly, if ever, a consideration of top officials in the Department of Defense. Rather, they applied institutional capacities developed to combat insurgents and subversives abroad to domestic civil rights battles, urban uprisings, and mass protest. The Department of Defense was ill equipped to differentiate legitimate political protest from "disorder," and was not inclined to make constitutional protections an institutional priority. In Cold War terms, threats, even if uncertain or unproven, must be identified. The possible social and political consequences of intelligence gathering—violating constitutionally guaranteed rights to freedom of speech and privacy, for example—were not top priorities for some civilian and military leaders. In the last half century historians of American foreign relations have developed a rich literature that explores how domestic imperatives (economic growth and the spread of democracy, for example) have driven American foreign policy.[45] During the 1960s, the state responded to social disorder and civil unrest in the United States with tools, strategies, and capacities developed to fight a global war against communism.

The army proved a powerful force in American political and social life throughout the 1960s. By the end of the decade, however, cracks had begun to appear in the previously impenetrable wall of the national security state. Some army officers believed that government surveillance programs to monitor dissent violated the Constitution and undermined the very freedoms that the state claimed to protect. Most worried quietly over these contradictions. But the waves of discontent that rolled through American society in the 1960s suggested that Americans found it increasingly difficult to reconcile the rhetoric of Cold War America with the practice of its most powerful institutions. A few army officers decided to challenge these contradictions openly. Their revelations created a public outcry and launched a congressional inquiry into the domestic applications of national security capacities.

Senator Sam, or How Liberals Learned to Stop Worrying and Love a Southern Segregationist

As a former army officer and instructor in counterintelligence, Christopher Pyle knew when he was being tailed. He also knew that a well-trained counterintelligence officer would likely try black-bag tactics in order to get as much information as possible on his target. For all these reasons, the retired army captain proceeded with his investigation very carefully. In order to protect his own research—taped interviews, personal papers, and handwritten notes—from prying eyes, he built a wooden box and secured it with a heavy-duty padlock. Determined not to let the "watchers" know about his sources or the extent to which his story revealed their tactics, he endeavored to carry the box with him wherever he went. This led to some comical results. Each and every time he left his one-bedroom walkup near Columbia University, he lugged the heavy box with him. He made the box to fit perfectly in the trunk of his Volkswagen Beetle. It was an exhaustive regime, however, even for a young man. As an extra precaution, he recruited a buddy and former counterintelligence officer to follow him with a telephoto lens camera, instructing him to snap a picture of any suspicious person on the street. All this effort, he reasoned, served the goal of making public the Army's secret program of domestic surveillance.[1]

The urban riots, antiwar protests, and civil unrest throughout the 1960s prompted an immediate, often violent, reaction from "the Establishment." Within the Manichean framework of an American Cold War political culture that posited a bipolar world divided between good and evil, those who dissented from the foreign and domestic policies of the United States frequently found themselves targets of local, state, and federal law enforcement and intelligence agencies.[2] Had they known of these secret surveillance programs, a majority of Americans likely would have supported them. Weary of civil unrest, urban revolts, and protests, an overwhelming majority of Americans polled in 1970—76 percent—said they did not support the First Amendment right to assemble and dissent from government policies. Blaming the press for sensationalizing protests and fomenting disorder, a majority did not even support the freedom of the press.[3]

Though such intolerance for dissent and disorder was widespread, it was not uncontested. In 1970 Army Captain Christopher Pyle blew the whistle on the U.S. Army's secret domestic surveillance program in a daring exposé published in *The Washington Monthly (The Monthly)*. His account ignited fierce debate among lawmakers on Capitol Hill. In particular, Pyle's story worried civil libertarian and southern Democrat Senator Sam Ervin, chairman of the Constitutional Rights Subcommittee of the Senate Committee on the Judiciary. Taking cues from a broad array of 1960s radicals who had been calling for greater transparency and accountability in national politics, a loose coalition of reformers—including Charles Peters, founder of *The Monthly*, Pyle, and Aryeh Neier, executive director of the American Civil Liberties Union (ACLU)—battled to check executive power. Working closely with reform-minded elected officials in Congress, like Ervin, their efforts to promote institutional reform culminated in a series of congressional hearings on government surveillance, privacy, executive privilege, and freedom of the press in 1971.

Congressional inquiries addressed a fundamental question about the state of American democracy: Did citizens in Cold War America have a "right to know" what their government was doing? The political culture of the 1960s created fertile soil for the movement to rein in the state. During the first major anti-Vietnam war rally in 1965, the president of Students for a Democratic Society (SDS), Paul Potter, denounced the Vietnam War as a "symptom of a deeper malaise" in American society. Potter declared that "faceless and terrible bureaucracies" were largely responsible for the immoral war in Vietnam. Identify "the system," Potter told his audience. "For it is only when that system is changed and brought under control that there can be any hope for stopping the forces" of injustice and reviving democratic practice in the United States.[4]

Like their radical predecessors, reformers like Pyle wanted to deliver greater power to the people.[5] To do so, they meant not to overthrow America's political institutions but to reform them. Onetime president of SDS Todd Gitlin explained that radicals intended to wrest control from American institutions and return power to the people. "Participatory democracy," he later wrote, "meant inserting yourself where the social rules said you didn't belong." The movement was a "revolt against all formal boundaries and qualifications, which it saw as rationalizations for illegitimate or tedious power."[6] Only through greater citizen participation in the politics of everyday life, radicals argued, could the polity rein in the state power.

As militancy and polarization increased during the late 1960s and early 1970s, and social and political problems seemed to many to be more intractable, Americans became increasingly cynical about their leaders and their ability to solve the nation's greatest problems. Some political activists and reformers responded to such feelings of hopelessness and cynicism by turning their backs on politics and looking to more personal remedies to societal crises. Others, like Pyle, Neier, and Peters, struggled to find new solutions to the political crises they witnessed. Scholars have, as yet, failed to explore how the citizenry's distrust of and anger with their government resulted in a large-scale and largely successful campaign to limit the power and reach of the national security state.

Charles Peters was at the forefront of the loosely affiliated network of people and organizations that refused to give in to alienation, dead-end radicalization, or political burnout. Peters had not spent the 1960s as a political radical, but he had been deeply enmeshed in the liberal reform movement of the era. As chief evaluator for the new Peace Corps program from 1963 to 1967 under Director Sergeant Shriver, Peters observed troubling trends in the culture of state institutions. Bureaucrats shielded their organizations from public scrutiny for fear that any criticism might expose them to unwanted budgetary reductions in the next fiscal cycle. Career civil servants jealously guarded their positions. Risk-averse, they avoided actions that might threaten their own advancement, especially criticizing institutional processes. Peters decided in 1968 that the best way to fight these governmental failures was from the outside. Like other presidential appointees, Peters's frustration with the political status quo suggested a splintering of consensus among political elites about the best ways to approach the multiple crises that gripped the nation in the late 1960s. He left the federal civil service determined to shed light on opaque, ineffective institutions and the officials he believed were responsible for their democratic and policy failures. *The Washington Monthly* (*The Monthly*) would be his torch.[7]

In 1969 Peters published the first issue of *The Monthly,* a political magazine, he said, that would examine "Washington [D.C.] the way that an anthropologist looks at a South Sea Island." The magazine would explore "the institutional imperatives that govern what organizations and the individuals who work for them do." Using New Left–like rhetoric, Peters and his young assistant editor, Taylor Branch, promised to be "serious critic[s] of those people and institutions" that wielded "tremendous power over every American."[8] The bureaucrats and government appointees who ran the federal government, Peters believed, would not willingly submit to greater transparency. The success of the magazine, he recognized, depended upon the investigative talents of the writers he could attract to the magazine and the connections those writers—and he—had or could develop within the federal establishment.

Peters made *The Monthly* an exciting place to work, and the magazine attracted a rising cadre of journalists, many of whom had cut their teeth reporting the political culture of mass movements.[9] As participants in, and observers of, 1960s street heat, these young men and women came to question in their articles and in their personal politics the legitimacy and authority of government officials. *The Monthly*'s focus on the establishment reflected a larger popular movement to examine the efficacy of the nation's institutions and its powerful managers. Though the magazine had a rather modest circulation in its first years of around 23,000 subscriptions, *The Monthly* attracted the attention of all the right people. Peters skillfully mediated between a contentious movement culture and established political and media elites. *Time* magazine, a stalwart of the mass media establishment, called *The Monthly* "must reading at the White House, on Capitol Hill and elsewhere in Government." I. F. Stone, a longtime critic of the establishment, called Peters's style "responsible" and claimed the magazine "doesn't go in for half-assed hysterics."[10]

As a former insider, Peters enlisted whistle-blowers—insiders who divulge wrongdoing within an organization in hopes of stopping it—to inform the magazine's reporting. Peters legitimated critiques of the establishment and ignited fierce public policy debates.[11] Investigative journalists who published in *The Monthly* further justified American cynicism about their elected officials. More important, they provided an outlet through which a network of reformers could legitimately challenge the failures of the political status quo and offer solutions.

The Monthly was one of many new nonradical, essentially mainstream media forms in the late 1960s and early 1970s to challenge the political status quo and ignite public debate about democratic practice and governance in the United States. Experimenting with more in-depth coverage

Taped

TAPED: A 1970 Herblock cartoon, copyright by *The Herb Block Foundation*

of the biggest national stories, CBS created its immediately popular news magazine *60 Minutes* in 1968. NBC followed in 1970 with *First Tuesday*. The newspaper of record, the *New York Times*, institutionalized its opinion-editorial page (Op-Ed) in 1970. The paper's editors wanted to devote more space to "stimulating new thought and provoking new discussion on public problems."[12] This rising cadre of journalists, driven by the political polarization and challenges to political legitimacy of the 1960s era, created vocal and far-reaching outlets through which reformers could challenge the political and governmental status quo. Politically savvy, these well-placed, reform-minded citizens believed that formal political change would only come by establishing networks to connect them with powerful elected officials.

In January of 1970 *The Monthly* featured a carefully researched account of the U.S. Army's secret program to monitor domestic politics, authored by former army captain Christopher Pyle. Offering shocking details of a three-year-old program to watch dissidents, Pyle charged the army with maintaining a coast-to-coast operation of 1,000 plainclothes officers who spied on individuals and organizations critical of the domestic and foreign policies of the U.S. government.[13]

Pyle's own background made his whistle-blower account difficult to dismiss; he was not a radical. A graduate of Bowdoin College, he taught at the Intelligence School in Fort Holabird, just outside Baltimore, Maryland. On a student's recommendation Pyle took a personal tour of the army's CONUS Intelligence Section, where he learned firsthand of the army's domestic surveillance program. The millions of computerized dossiers that the army maintained on political dissidents and organizations, Pyle argued, had all the trappings of a police state. When he left the army in 1969 to pursue a law degree and PhD in political science at Columbia University, he was determined to make the army's secret program public. His mentor, Professor Alan F. Westin, a prominent New York attorney, civil libertarian, and head of the ACLU Privacy Committee, encouraged him to write an article detailing the army's program. Pyle submitted it to the *New York Times*, which rejected it. Charles Peters did not.[14]

Pyle's article fit *The Monthly*'s mission perfectly. Determined that his magazine would challenge powerful institutions, Charles Peters believed the army was an irresistible target. The cloak of "national security" had kept the army's surveillance program secret from the American public and Congress for three years, until Pyle's exposé. His account electrified Capitol Hill. Members of Congress fired off angry letters to the Pentagon demanding to know more about the army's political surveillance program. Maryland Republican senator Charles Mathias called for "clear and consistent rules to protect individuals by controlling the types of information to be stored, the uses to be made of it, and the extent to which it should be disseminated."[15]

Adept at taking the pulse of the American electorate, Congress did not need polls to know that by the late 1960s Americans had grown deeply distrustful of political institutions, and especially their elected representatives.[16] Driven by a sense of self-preservation, bolstered by a national political culture that favored reform, and encouraged by a new cadre of public advocacy groups such as Common Cause, prominent Republicans and Democrats favored institutional reform. To avoid direct confrontation with President Lyndon Johnson, Senate Majority Leader Mike Mansfield (D-MT) encouraged committee chairs to flex their oversight muscles. Congress moved simultaneously to check the slow aggrandizement of institutional power by the executive and judicial branches. In 1966 Senate leaders Mansfield and Everett Dirksen (R-IL) cosponsored a resolution establishing the Separation of Powers subcommittee within the Committee on the Judiciary, chaired by conservative Democrat Senator Sam Ervin, Jr., of North Carolina. The subcommittee investigated how, over time, the executive and judicial branches of government slowly assumed powers traditionally reserved to the legislative branch.[17]

Sam Ervin, the Senate's expert on the Constitution and a longtime defender of First Amendment rights, was deeply troubled by Pyle's account of the army's domestic spy program. He believed that surveillance programs chilled dissent. Determined to know the extent of domestic spying, and rebuffed by the army and Pentagon in his attempts to obtain further information about the problem on "national security" grounds, Ervin pursued his only remaining option. He would use his Constitutional Rights Subcommittee (CRSC) as a bully pulpit to investigate the legality of the executive branch's domestic surveillance programs. Ervin faced one of the greatest political challenges of his long career in public service: to penetrate the dark recesses of the national security state.

From Ervin's vantage point in the early 1970s, the civil disorder and public protest generated by the crises of the 1960s offered a testing ground for American democracy. He personally despised the Black Panthers, the Weatherman faction of SDS, and all those who advocated violence as a means of political change. However, Ervin vocally supported their First Amendment rights, claiming that "those people have the same right to freedom of speech . . . that I have."[18] Pyle's account troubled Ervin. It charged that some agencies within the U.S. government embraced the rhetoric of national security as justification for political surveillance of dissenters.

Senator Sam (as his staff liked to call him) is best remembered for his role as chair of the Senate Select Committee on Presidential Campaign Activities (also known as the Watergate Committee) in 1974. Through their television sets, millions of Americans came to respect and trust the southerner with the heavy jowls, thick black eyebrows, and grandfatherly demeanor. Even as he pressed former White House staff and appointed officials on their less-than-respectable activities, his thick southern drawl and his frequent interjections of homespun yarns of southern wisdom ("the constitution should be taken like mountain whisky—undiluted and untaxed") reassured Americans, as one later wrote, "that there were still people in Washington with moral bearings solidly fixed."[19] Before his Watergate fame, however, many Americans viewed Ervin with more ambivalence.

Sam Ervin grew up in a world of white supremacy. Born in 1896, the year the Supreme Court's *Plessy v. Ferguson* ruling upheld the constitutionality of racial segregation under the guise of "separate but equal," he lived in the small town of Morganton, North Carolina. At his father's knee, young Sam learned two irrefutable truths: government was the antithesis of individual liberty and freedom, and the U.S. Constitution was, like the Bible, immutable. Determined to become an attorney like his father, Ervin entered the University of North Carolina in 1913, where he excelled in history, literature, and law. A popular student (voted senior class vice president, most popular, and "best egg") he also excelled in his studies, attending law school while finishing his bachelor's degree.[20]

Before he had the opportunity to take the bar exam, the country went to war. An army infantryman, Ervin served during World War I on the French front where he was twice wounded and well decorated, earning a Purple Heart, a Silver Star, and a Distinguished Service Cross. When he returned to North Carolina in 1919, he easily passed the state bar exam. Then, for reasons he never fully explained, he enrolled at Harvard Law School.[21]

Ervin took courses from many keen legal minds during his tenure at Harvard, though none proved quite so influential to his career in public office as Zechariah Chafee. As the Red Scare gripped the country in the wake of the Bolshevik Revolution, Professor Chafee refused to succumb to "red fever." He deplored President Woodrow Wilson's assault on freedom of speech and Attorney General A. Mitchell Palmer's anti-Communist witch hunts. As a legal scholar, Chafee sought a rational approach to free speech that would balance the nation's need for security with the Bill of Rights. In 1919, the year that Sam Ervin enrolled at Harvard, Chafee published an article expounding the virtues of free speech in times of war. One of the greatest outlets for free speech, according to Chafee, was a free press. Chafee's teachings left deep impressions on Ervin's young mind; as a U.S. senator he remained a vocal proponent of First Amendment rights.[22]

After Harvard young Ervin easily ascended the political hierarchy in North Carolina. He served three terms in the state legislature and was appointed to the Burke County Criminal Court and the North Carolina Superior Court. In 1946 Ervin went to Washington to fill a seat in the

House of Representatives left vacant by his brother's suicide. In 1954 the governor appointed Ervin to serve in the U.S. Senate following the unexpected death of Senator Clyde Hoey. Ervin held that seat until his retirement from public life twenty years later.

Before Watergate whitewashed his record, Ervin was best known in his home state and nationally for his virulent opposition to the civil rights movement. As one journalist astutely observed, however, Ervin was "no Cotton Ed Smith." Another close observer recalled that Ervin "took pains to disassociate himself from the anti-Negro racism apparent in many of those who share his distaste for civil rights laws." In fact, he bristled at the suggestion that his resistance to civil rights stemmed from anything other than a true understanding of the Constitution. When pressed on his strident opposition to the civil rights movement, Ervin argued that his advocacy of equal civil liberties for *all* Americans and his opposition to "special civil rights for Americans of minority races" were totally compatible with the equal protection clause of the Fourteenth Amendment. Ervin proffered that civil rights bills effectively stole rights from some (whites and presumably white southerners) to deliver unto others.[23] Despite such arguments, Ervin did nothing to oppose Jim Crow laws and black disenfranchisement. This behavior is hard to square with his principled claim that he supported limited government because he believed in maximum individual freedom for every American. These apparent contradictions situated Ervin directly within the mainstream of southern politics and culture of the era.

When Ervin entered the Senate in the 1950s, southern Democrats held the most powerful committee and subcommittee chairs, an arrangement that would continue until institutional reforms forced change in 1970.[24] Ervin's work on the North Carolina State Supreme Court made him a considerable expert on the Constitution in the Senate.[25] As a former justice of the Superior Court in his home state, his fluency in constitutional jurisprudence made him a natural for assignment to the Senate Judiciary Committee. By 1961 he had secured the chair of the CRSC. Another southern senator now controlled a powerful subcommittee. Ervin quickly became the bane of the civil rights movement, infamous for his one-man filibusters that stymied the civil rights legislation of Presidents John F. Kennedy and Lyndon B. Johnson.[26]

Throughout the 1960s, even as he opposed civil rights legislation, Ervin advanced a legislative agenda to expand and protect the rights of federal employees and a wide range of disadvantaged Americans—the mentally ill, the physically and mentally handicapped, criminal defendants, and

Samuel James Ervin, Jr., member of the U.S. Senate, 1954–1974 (U.S. Senate Historical Office)

Native Americans. Because of his position on a number of issues related to individual rights and the First Amendment, Ervin enjoyed an amicable relationship with the ACLU, strained as it was at times by his opposition to civil rights legislation.

As the nation focused on the battle over racial inequality, Senator Ervin turned his subcommittee resources to exploring issues dear to his own heart, specifically violations of First Amendment rights. In an era of burgeoning social welfare programs, Ervin worried about the executive branch's unchecked accumulation of personal data and worked to become a relative expert in the field of computer technology and data banks. Could the computer, as some suggested, make a person's life story available to Washington bureaucrats "at the push of a button"?[27]

Congressional efforts to reform government were bolstered by a plethora of public interest groups in the late 1960s and early 1970s. Ralph Nader and his "Raiders," and Common Cause, working alone or in concert with older reform-minded groups such as the League of Women Voters and Americans for Democratic Action, proved effective at generating public support for institutional reform with vigorous public relations campaigns. Common Cause founder and Washington insider John Gardner claimed his organization represented "the interest of the individual" in the face of "vast and complex institutions that dominate our national life today." Gardner envisioned Common Cause as the embodiment of "a true 'citizens' lobby" that would bring "pressure to bear" on important issues before Congress.[28]

One of these powerful public advocacy groups was the ACLU. Founded in 1920 during the first Red Scare, the ACLU promoted itself as a civil liberties bulwark, willing to protect the rights of all Americans, "regardless of the views they espouse." By the late 1960s the organization had become a forceful voice for institutional change and in particular a vocal critic of the ever-expanding power of the executive branch. The protest movements of the 1960s proved to be a public relations boon for the organization as it represented in litigation the free speech rights of radicals, college kids, and dissenters. But trials were costly, and the ACLU's tradition of relying on pro bono legal representation soon proved inadequate. The organization needed full-time attorneys dedicated to advancing rights jurisprudence to be effective. Taking advantage of new tax codes, the ACLU established a foundation in 1967. The foundation, in addition to attracting philanthropic support and leading to burgeoning membership rolls—from 50,000 in 1960 to more than 150,000 in 1970—helped the organization to develop research and legal capacities in the late 1960s to advance a rights agenda.[29]

Aryeh Neier was one of the young lions who charted a legislative strategy and litigation rights agenda for the organization during this transitional decade of the 1960s. A German-born Jew whose family escaped the Nazi regime, Neier was in his early thirties when he joined the ACLU as field director in 1963. He was a lifelong leftist and a member and future president of the Student League for Industrial Democracy (SLID) at Cornell University. At the young age of twenty-one, Neier had become the director of LID, SLID's parent organization. He focused his efforts on reviving the flagging student organization, giving it a new, catchy name: Students for a Democratic Society. But Neier quickly became disillusioned with SDS. A self-described "anti-Soviet" anti-Communist, Neier was appalled by the group's ideological "Port Huron Statement" for its claims that "Soviet repression and the invasion of Hungary were defensive actions in response to Cold War aggression for which the United States bore prime responsibility." He also found the concept of "participatory democracy" hard to swallow—calling it "justification for demagogy."[30]

Neier's own politics in this period defy easy classification. He opposed all forms of oppression and maintained a healthy skepticism of all ideology. He invited socialists like Norman Thomas to speak at the inaugural SDS meeting and served on the LID board with socialist Michael Harrington. While he found the SDS form of anti-anticommunism abhorrent, he also came to oppose LID's drift to the right. Under the influence of Trotskyite Max Shachtman, the organization adopted a decidedly hawkish stance on the war in Vietnam. Neier found himself ideologically adrift. Though he lacked a law degree, the ACLU liked his politics and community organizing experience and hired him. Neier rose quickly to become executive director in 1970, and under his leadership the ACLU became the preeminent voice for individuals' rights throughout the decade. Presiding over a great expansion of the organization's mission, Neier's aggressive program made some older civil libertarians uneasy. He charged ahead, determined to keep the ACLU relevant to the needs of a changing time.[31]

When Neier joined the organization in 1963, the New York State chapter, NYCLU, was struggling to develop a program to combat alleged police brutality against protestors and dissidents. Such violence against protestors was not new to the 1960s. Since the organization's founding in the 1920s, ACLU lawyers had defended victims of government repression. But the police abuse of the 1960s reached unprecedented levels of violence. Metropolitan police responded to the violent civil disorder that rent the decade—first urban unrest, and later mass protests—with undue force and brutality. The NYCLU pursued police brutality as its flagship civil liberties issue, but Neier quickly realized that the affiliate lacked the necessary resources to litigate against such abuses.[32] Neier turned to the ACLU Foundation for funds. Under the newly created Police Practices Project, attorneys worked full-time to amass data for litigation.[33] Neier himself was arrested during one peaceful protest as he attempted to observe police treatment of protestors. The national office became a data bank of sorts on issues of police surveillance, brutality, and abuse. Compelled to act in the name of protecting the First Amendment right to protest, the foundation intensified its efforts to gather data in the latter part of the decade. Seeking new funding from the Stern Family Fund, the ACLU expanded the project to include political surveillance. Neier turned the project over to two extraordinarily capable men: Yale Law Professor

Aryeh Neier (Mudd
Manuscript Library,
Department of Rare
Books and Special
Collections, Princeton
University Library)

Frank Donner and ACLU Legal Director Mel Wulf. Calling "political surveillance by government officers" a "spreading cancer," the ACLU embarked on a project with a two-pronged approach to documenting political surveillance: "a litigation program and a series of publications." The
project's immediate problem was obtaining "accurate and reliable data"
that offered concrete evidence of surveillance of "dissident groups and
activities by undercover officers, photography, planted informers and
infiltrators, compilation of political files and dossiers, electronic eavesdropping."[34] Neier encouraged state affiliates to pass along any information they obtained on police practices and surveillance. These reports included vital information about municipal and state police, infiltration of
protest meetings, and organizations associated with political dissent.[35]

Neier envisioned a litigation program to challenge First Amendment
violations based on techniques successfully developed and employed by
civil rights groups in the 1950s and 1960s. This "public interest litigation"
would be more effective, Neier believed, than all the civil rights dem-

onstrations or government programs combined. By bringing cases before courts, Neier hoped to force public policy development on issues of surveillance and individual privacy. The ACLU would join other public interest groups like the NAACP that were forming a "public interest" bar to advance the interests of various groups throughout civil society.[36]

Neier thought Donner perfectly suited to organizing the research that would be required to support the litigation strategy. The Yale professor had made the pursuit of justice for dissenters his professional focus. A civil rights attorney, Donner had collected materials "dealing with official attacks on nonconformity" since the late 1940s. Donner, who as one colleague fondly remembered, "looked like a disheveled Tom Edison but wrote like Tom Paine," worked as a trial consultant and later wrote appellate briefs for a number of lawsuits filed as sedition cases under the Smith Act, or Alien Registration Act of 1940, which made it a crime to advocate violent overthrow of the government. It was here that Donner became curious about government surveillance practices, as he recalled that "the government's case in all of these trials was uniformly based on an assortment of secret political intelligence practices." His legal support for alleged communists made him a target, and Donner was brought before a congressional committee in the 1950s. Since then he had been an "unrelenting critic of the hunters."[37]

Since the onset of the Cold War, national security bureaucracies and the White House resisted public scrutiny, usually with success. But Donner had an idea. During the 1968 Democratic National Convention, Chicago mayor Richard Daley had his police geared up to shut down and even beat down the radicals who descended upon the city. One of Donner's friends represented some of the protestors in Chicago. In connection with a lawsuit to obtain parade permits for the demonstrations, he subpoenaed documents of the Chicago Red Squad, a secret municipal intelligence unit within the Chicago Police Department. These documents showed that the squad indiscriminately gathered dossiers on anyone who applied for permits. This technique inspired Donner. He explained to the ACLU board that "when information uncovering such clearly unconstitutional dossier-gathering can be gotten only through lawsuits, litigation should be seen as indispensable to the research-gathering arm of the project."[38]

Donner's good fortune with the Chicago Red Squad was a breakthrough, but it was not easily replicated. Though student protesters and political radicals often claimed to be the targets of government surveillance, the ACLU had a hard time uncovering proof of it. Particularly at the federal level, evidence that the executive branch authorized widespread surveillance of political dissidents had proven to be nearly impossible to gather. Then, dramatically, in 1970 the ACLU found its proof.

As computer technology and capacity developed along with a growing suspicion of Big Brother during the 1960s, Americans worried that a large government could create a real-life Orwellian nightmare for its citizens by harnessing the power of computers and data banks. This concern played out in political debates over the creation of a National Data Center. The controversy erupted in 1965 when the Bureau of the Budget recommended to President Johnson that all statistical information be gathered in one central location. Measuring the success of the War on Poverty, many social scientists argued, required analyzing mountains of data about the lives of millions of recipients of federal aid programs. The White House appointed a commission, and the final report recommended the creation of a national data clearinghouse. The goal was innocent enough, to give "both governmental and academic analysts a much sharper view of the nation's problems and possibilities." The data center, officials agreed, would not maintain dossiers on individuals, but would apply the latest computer technologies to the purpose of national social and cultural advancement.[39]

But the public and the media were not so easily convinced. The computerization of everyday life threatened individuality, many thought. The rise of multiuniversities epitomized this social change. Students were "computerized," identified for all intents and purposes with their IBM cards. One college newspaper reported that a new student had a lot to learn at college, most especially "not to fold, spindle or mutilate his IBM card." The prevalence of these new technologies aroused strong public sentiment against the depersonalizing effects of modern society, the loss of individual freedom, and the threat to personal privacy that a computerized, data-driven world posed.[40] Popular journalist and social commentator (and author of *Naked Society* and *Hidden Persuaders*) Vance Packard neatly summarized this sentiment with a warning: "bureaucratic efficiency could put us in chains of plastic tape—don't tell it to the computer." The ACLU and a score of newspaper editors and privacy experts adamantly opposed such a powerful data bank. In the wrong hands, they cautioned, the accumulation and storage of personal data on millions of Americans posed a threat to individual privacy rights.[41]

It was in the context of this swirling public debate over computer technology and privacy that Ervin prepared to chair hearings of the CRSC to investigate Pyle's account of army surveillance of civilian politics published in *The Monthly*. Ervin was not interested in the short-term scandal the army hearings might engender. Instead, he leveraged the public's interests in the sensational army story to explore broader public policy issues related to computers, government data banks, and personal privacy. Echoing the rhetoric of New Leftists, Ervin called for a democratic revival, stating that Americans must have the ability to "express their views on the wisdom and course of governmental policies." A healthy democracy, he insisted, depended upon active civic participation, and "policies themselves must be the product of the people's views." Ervin would offer his subcommittee dais as a forum to "help elected officials determine how to use constitutional tools to meet the demands of the modern age."[42] In so doing, he offered a direct challenge to the constitutionality of secret government security programs and promised to deliver a public forum for citizens to debate national security policies.

Like most elected officials in Washington D.C., Ervin gauged public opinion on critical national policy issues through the steady stream of constituent mail that came through his office. From the nation's founding Congress recognized the importance of public opinion and debate generated by communication between legislators and their constituents. In 1789 the legislative branch promoted this relationship with the franking privilege, allowing elected officials to use only their signature as "postage" through the U.S. mail. The privilege ensured a steady exchange of ideas and opinions through the post, and constituent mail became, over the centuries, a normative and vital aspect of American democratic practice. Ervin, again like many elected officials, demanded that his staff respond promptly to all letters, usually within twenty-four hours. Ervin was energized by the overwhelming public support he received for his investigations of domestic intelligence operations from citizens around the country. In their letters to the senator, Americans explained that they had lost their faith in national leaders and that they feared the government's unchecked power and habitual secrecy. Many firmly believed in the immutability of the rights articulated in the Constitution and compared their government's surveillance techniques to those of the despised Soviet Union. Some argued that government agencies that thwarted the right to dissent brought the nation dangerously close to a "police state." Surveillance of dissenters, they believed, violated the basic constitutional rights of all Americans.[43]

Letter writers overwhelmingly supported Ervin's call for greater transparency and broader civic participation in issues of national import. A few called for more thorough investigations of the nation's domestic security apparatus. One noted, presciently, that the army's domestic surveillance program was likely just the tip of the iceberg, a point that would prove accurate in subsequent investigations over the next two years. Many letter writers believed that further investigation would reveal "Big Brother is watching over many more of us than we would have guessed." Some Americans expressed certainty that FBI activities violated civil liberties and called for public investigation of the nation's top law enforcement agency. Many recognized the need for institutions to take appropriate measures to halt the bombings and "terrorist activities" that tore at the fabric of American society. But one stressed the irony of army tactics: "How can we, except in the name of law and decency, reason with them [bomb throwers], when the government is also engaged in activities which are questionably lawful and hardly decent?"[44]

Many Americans questioned the Cold War framework that pitted American democracy and freedom against communism and slavery. Their rhetoric echoed the New Left's critique of the Cold War dichotomy of "us" versus "them," suggesting that protest movement culture informed the political rhetoric of the 1970s. Some warned that the tactics of the national security state would prove America's downfall in the battle to win the hearts and minds of nonaligned people in the newly liberated Third World. The United States, one wrote, "will most definitely lose the ideological victory both at home and abroad if by our own actions we prove to the world that a democratic and free society is unworkable. . . . The politics of manipulation, fear and distrust are extremely dangerous and pose a distinct threat to a free society." Hundreds of Americans pleaded with Ervin to force the state to make intelligence dossiers public. Many underscored the Orwellian themes of the army's program. As one concerned Texan wrote: "On the national level—this [Army surveillance program] sounds more like 1984 than the USA . . . on the personal level: how do I know I'm not in someone's file?"[45] For Senator Ervin, these letters confirmed that the American public yearned for public debate and greater transparency in government, especially regarding the nation's security apparatus.

The public outcry reassured Senator Ervin and his subcommittee staff that Americans would support their agenda. Committee staff worked closely with Chris Pyle, who gathered information on government data banks and surveillance programs. They found in Pyle an able and diligent researcher. Young, ambitious, and meticulous in his research techniques, Pyle wanted to see Congress pass legislation to prevent the government from intruding into the lives of its citizens in violation of the First Amendment.[46] Driven by a conviction that nothing short of congressional legislation could save the reputation of his beloved army, Pyle encouraged congressional leaders to exercise their "power of inquiry" because few Americans or elected officials knew the extent to which the domestic intelligence community had grown.

The Nixon administration declined to cooperate with Ervin. On national security grounds the army (and later the Pentagon) refused to supply the subcommittee with any information regarding the army's program. The army assured Senator Ervin that intelligence gathering was a necessary response to urban disorder and civil unrest, and since 1967 "ha[d] been a subject of constant attention and refinement in order to narrow the Army's actions to only those which are absolutely necessary." The army repudiated Pyle's accusation that it "watch[ed] civilian politics." Army legal counsel justified the establishment of the CONUS program without prior congressional approval or oversight by referring to President Dwight Eisenhower's Executive Order 10450. Under Secretary of the Army Thaddeus Beal assured Ervin that the "operation or establishment of any computer data banks concerning civilians or civilian activity [was prohibited] unless the specific data bank is approved by the Chief of Staff and the Secretary of the Army." Congress had virtually no authority over such matters, argued Beal, and the "Subcommittee and other interested Committees of the Congress will be informed" of domestic intelligence activities at the discretion of army officials.[47] But lofty legal justifications failed to temper the public outcry, and the army's programs became a political problem for the Nixon administration. Secretary of Defense Melvin Laird closed the army's database at Ft. Holabird in February 1970 because, in the words of one official, "the information in the computer was not useful in view of the Army's limited civil disturbance mission."[48] Nixon officials hoped the public would soon lose interest in the story, and Ervin's hearings would prove nothing more than a sideshow event.[49]

The administration's stalling techniques forced Ervin's hand; he postponed the hearings until February 1971. Staff worried that a delay would prove disastrous if the public lost interest. Through Alan Westin, Pyle met the ACLU's Mel Wulf. Wulf was ecstatic: this was the case that the legal director of the ACLU Foundation's Privacy Project had been waiting for—irrefutable evidence that an institution secretly monitored civilian political behavior. When *The Monthly* syndicated Pyle's article, and edited versions came out in the nation's largest regional papers, Pyle's phone rang off the hook.[50] Some former army intelligence officers, like Pyle, were disquieted by their activities in the army. These former insiders offered crucial evidence of surveillance techniques and protocols that army officials had refused to supply to Ervin's subcommittee. This was the evidence that Pyle (and Ervin's committee) needed to proceed with a congressional investigation. For the next nine months, in preparation for the hearings, Pyle and a former counterintelligence officer, Ralph Stein, traveled across the country collecting testimony to inform Ervin's committee (all travel was paid for by the subcommittee). Pyle diligently investigated the army's program for both professional and personal reasons. He thought the program dangerous to the credibility of the institution. Second, he had decided to write his doctoral thesis for Columbia on the army's program and its implications for democracy.

The ACLU solicited Pyle's assistance, and his research ultimately helped to advance the legislative and litigation strategies of Donner and Wulf. Pyle's work effectively advanced the discovery phase for the organization's legal team. Donner carefully catalogued the testimony of former army officers, collected by Pyle. Wulf's legal team used this evidence as the basis for a number of lawsuits pursued on behalf of victims of army surveillance.[51] The basis of the ACLU's litigation strategy, securing evidence, also advanced the organization's legislative strategy. Pyle, acting as liaison, passed crucial information to Ervin's subcommittee. Rather than remaining stonewalled by the Pentagon's refusal to discuss the details of its programs, Ervin's staff arranged a witness list that drew heavily upon the information obtained during ACLU discovery. As one staffer recalled, a subcommittee's "regular diet of legislative responsibilities" sapped the attention of congressmen and their staff. The ACLU, flush with talent and the resources to pursue an investigative and litigation strategy, proved a crucial ally to Ervin's congressional investigation in the nascent effort to reform the national security state.[52]

Ervin's witness list reflected the ACLU's influence on the proceedings. Privacy experts and former intelligence officers, civil libertarians, and attorneys all were in some way affiliated with the organization, either as members, plaintiffs, or expert witnesses in ACLU lawsuits against the government. In exchange for delivering their professional network of connections, the hearings ensured that the political debate would bolster public support for a broad legislative agenda to curb surveillance cases and protect First Amendment rights.

Senator Ervin recognized the political risks of challenging the constitutionality of the nation's most secret (and in some cases most revered) institutions. Though Ervin himself was politically invulnerable in his home state of North Carolina, many of his congressional colleagues whose support would prove crucial to a real investigation (and the resulting legislation) did not have the same political cover. As one senator later recalled, FBI Director J. Edgar Hoover protected his agency from congressional inquiry by blackmailing prominent elected officials with "secret" files about their personal life, which he kept in his office. For these reasons Ervin instructed his subcommittee staff to investigate only those agencies for which they had irrefutable evidence of constitutionally questionable activities. One false accusation, Ervin reasoned, would discredit the investigation and derail the reform effort.[53] They had to get it right the first time; they were not likely to have a second opportunity.

Delaying the hearings offered congressional staffers, including Pyle, time to gather more evidence of army surveillance, but the delay also threatened to test the public's interest in the story and the media's feeling that the story had "played out." Staff members carefully managed the flow of information they received from government agencies and Chris Pyle to the public. Historically, congressional investigations could be, in the crudest sense, "a form of entertainment" that allowed legislators to compete in the crowded arena of politics and political events "for the voters' attention." Well-managed investigative hearings in the age of television allowed Congress the opportunity to combat the reality that, as one scholar has written, "a president cutting a cake has more news value for the media of communication than almost anything a congressman does in his non-investigative capacities."[54] The media, eager to charge ahead with a sensational story, maintained close contact with the committee. In exchange for insider scoops reporters like the *New York Times'* Richard Halloran offered committee staff information obtained from anonymous agency insiders. This cooperation helped maintain and assure public interest in government surveillance.

The ACLU proved indispensable to piquing the media's interest in Ervin's hearings. For months Mel Wulf orchestrated a media campaign in New York, pushing the *Times* and the *Times Sunday Magazine* to investigate the government's use of surveillance and computers and the privacy implications. Like Progressive-era reformers, Wulf recognized the centrality of the press to his efforts to usher the issue into the public sphere. The more public debate on the issue, Wulf reasoned, the greater the pressure on democratic institutions to respond. His efforts demonstrated how neo-progressives sought to strengthen ties with a burgeoning group of neo-muckrakers. In his letters to the editor of the *Times*, Wulf called for an immediate cessation of government surveillance, or he expounded on the role of the courts in defining a legal right to privacy in the age of the super computer.[55]

The ACLU and Ervin's subcommittee rightly worried that Americans would turn their attention elsewhere. Two events, however, both beyond the control of subcommittee staff, kept the issues of surveillance and privacy alive. In December 1970 NBC aired a program that breathed new life into the story of government surveillance of civilian politics. The news journal *First Tuesday* broadcast a dramatic exposé of the army's program. It featured interviews with former army intelligence officers as well as privacy experts and elected officials like Senator Ervin, who eloquently articulated their concerns about unchecked executive power and privacy. Television proved to be a more powerful medium than newspapers. One Ervin staff member remembered, the program "conveyed to the public the story on Army surveillance in a way that made it immediate and hard-hitting."[56]

Former army intelligence officer John O'Brien watched the *First Tuesday* report. Encouraged that Washington was ready to listen to his story, he wrote to NBC and to elected officials who figured prominently in the NBC documentary, including Senator Ervin. Recounting his years with the 113th Military Intelligence Group in Evanston, Illinois, O'Brien claimed that he personally observed army spy operations that went beyond watching radicals and dissidents. O'Brien asserted that his intelligence group had maintained "subversive files" on prominent elected officials. In addition, his unit kept hundreds of files on any organization or individual that spoke out against the Vietnam War or that opposed any domestic policies of the Nixon administration.

When the news media got wind of O'Brien's accusations, Ervin's staff worried that O'Brien's story would turn the otherwise carefully scripted hearings into a media circus. As Pyle remembered, the intelligence operations of the 113th differed dramatically from the operational missions of any other regional army CONUS program. Ervin and Pyle had misgivings about the accuracy of O'Brien's account and his personal motivations. Did he aim to discredit the proceedings with an inaccurate story? Did he want to be a star? If his story could not be corroborated, the whole investigation could be discredited before the hearings even commenced. Pyle immediately flew to Chicago and spent four long hours interrogating O'Brien, whose account withstood Pyle's considerable interrogatory abilities.[57] It likewise withstood the intense scrutiny of the press and government agencies. Breathing a collective sigh of relief, and pleased over the revived public interest in the subcommittee's hearings, staff moved forward with hearing arrangements.

The subcommittee staff tackled hearing preparations like the stage crew for a Broadway show. They aimed to impress the audience—the American people. The performers—subcommittee members as well as witnesses—must immediately command the respect of their audience. A poor performance might mean bad press and waning public interest. All of these things could adversely affect the subcommittee's bottom line: informing the public and elected officials in order to garner support for a particular legislative agenda. Preparations began by distributing a press release to the Senate press gallery. Subcommittee staff handled the media cautiously, both needing their attention and dreading it at the same time. Ervin stressed the importance of obtaining the whole picture of government surveillance and data management. The media's tendency to focus on sensational stories—such as O'Brien's account—could on the one hand derail long-term legislative aims. On the other hand, if the hearings failed to capture and sustain media interest, Ervin's legislative aims would never gain the much-needed support of the public and his congressional colleagues.[58]

Ervin's staff set the ideal stage, opening the hearings in February 1971 in the Senate's grand Caucus Room in the old Senate Office Building, the site of a number of notable Senate investigations, including the hearings on the Teapot Dome scandal and the Army-McCarthy hearings. To head off a media frenzy that focused exclusively on the army's surveillance program, subcommittee staff packed the first day of testimony with ACLU privacy experts and legal counsel and professors who would focus on privacy concerns in the age of technology. Ervin himself proved an adept dramatist. In the opening act he expounded the virtues of privacy as a constitutional right. Leaning over the grand wooden dais, peering down over his thick-rimmed reading glasses, Ervin hefted, in one hand, a thick, hardbound, eleven-pound Bible. In his other hand Ervin held aloft between extended thumb and forefinger a perfect two-inch square of microfilm, which he explained, contained the same 1,200 pages of text! Computer technology, Ervin thundered, now makes the storage of information infinite. "Someone remarked," Ervin recalled, "that this meant the Constitution could be reduced to the size of a pinhead." Senator Sam chortled. "Maybe that was what they had done in the executive branch because some of those officials could not see it with their naked eyes." This dramatic opening act reminded the public of Ervin's primary concern: the unfettered growth of government data banks and the threat new technologies posed, if unchecked, to individual privacy. The *New York Times* ran a front-page story on the hearings.[59]

The ACLU's handpicked privacy experts led off the hearings with dramatic testimony. They contended that most Americans "were only vaguely aware of the extent to which they are watched" by government agencies. Government intelligence gathering was virtually unchecked. The nation was traveling headlong, cautioned one witness, "toward a 'dossier dictatorship.'" University of Michigan law professor Arthur Miller, author of *Assault on Privacy*, stole the show, detailing how "intruders in society, aided by modern science" through the use of microphones, electronic eavesdropping, and "cameras equipped with esoteric optical devices," have "destroyed many of our traditional bastions of privacy." Miller described the dossier of the average American, complete with information about credit history, past employment, and tax returns. These files, warned Miller, "can tell a great deal about his activities, movements, habits, and association when collated and analyzed." Typically, agencies maintained personal information to "achieve socially-desirable objectives." But, Miller continued, without "effective restraints" on the federal government, there are no safeguards to "insure that individuals are protected against the misuse of the burgeoning databanks." Ervin steered Miller's testimony to the real crux of the information-gathering issue. Collection was only one part of the problem. Without effective restraints on information sharing among government agencies, argued Miller, personal data may be "bandied about in some subterranean information exchange network."[60]

Ervin pushed further. What kind of effect, he wanted to know, could unchecked government surveillance and dossier-gathering have on a citizen's constitutionally protected political behavior? Dr. Jerry Rosenberg, a psychologist and the author of *Death of Privacy*, testified that computer technologies and dossier data banks maintained by the federal government would likely cause Americans to "clam up" and "hide." Already aware of this "Orwellian nightmare," Rosenberg claimed that student unrest was largely the result of a perceived loss of individual privacy.[61] Chris Pyle considered the constitutional problems that unchecked government surveillance posed to a democratic society. He cautioned that unchecked surveillance may have a psychological, "chilling" effect on the American polity—if people believe they are being watched, they are less likely to enter the public domain and voice their opinion. In a clever twist on President Nixon's "silent majority," Senator Ervin warned that dossier building and surveillance created a "silent American." This man "refrains from any public controversy and from any political activity. . . . He has been frightened out of his great birthright—the right to speak his mind."[62]

Throughout nine days of testimony Ervin presided over a lively media event. The Senate Caucus Room offered an outstanding forum for the senator and the ACLU to present their case to the public (through the filter of the media) and to legislators on issues of First Amendment rights and privacy.[63] Counterintelligence officers revealed that they had spied on congressmen, as well as state and local elected officials; they had posed as dissenters at antiwar meetings; and they had in some cases fomented violence. They admitted that they had monitored the legal political activity of millions of law-abiding American citizens.[64] When asked why they decided to speak publicly about their previous work with the army, many echoed the sentiments of former special officer Richard Allen Kasson. Troubled by the army's extralegal activities, Kasson believed the army's missions and programs ought to be brought fully in line with the Bill of Rights.[65] The hearings underscored two major problems: the executive's unwillingness to share information with Congress, and the White House's lack of concern for broader First Amendment rights.

Not all Americans were satisfied with the scope of Ervin's subcommittee investigation. Activists, many of whom had faced years of government surveillance and attacks on their civil liberties, believed that Ervin had only scratched the surface of the problem. By focusing so narrowly on the army program, they thought, Congress failed to demonstrate the magnitude of the problem. These critics had a point, though they failed to take into consideration the political risks associated with challenging America's most revered institutions like the FBI. Though Ervin and his staff privately suspected the FBI of engaging in illegal activities, publicly they handled FBI Director J. Edgar Hoover and his agency with kid gloves. Indeed, Senator Ervin enjoyed amiable relations with Hoover, regularly exchanging pleasantries. In the early 1970s the FBI was still off-limits to congressional inquiry or oversight. The bold (and illegal) actions of one organization in 1971, however, deeply undermined the public trust that the FBI had so long enjoyed.[66]

On March 8, 1971, the Citizens' Commission to Investigate the FBI burgled the Bureau's regional office in Media, Pennsylvania. Stealing more than 1,000 topsecret dossiers, the group mailed copies to the *New York Times* and the *Washington Post* and to three congressmen, including Democratic senator George McGovern of South Dakota. The stolen files revealed what many radicals had long suspected—that the FBI also engaged in massive domestic surveillance of nonviolent, lawful political dissent. One memorandum from FBI Director J. Edgar Hoover encouraged FBI officers to harass dissenters to "enhance the paranoia endemic in these circles and . . . get the point across there is an FBI officer behind every mailbox." The files offered proof that one of the nation's most revered domestic security and law enforcement agencies ran roughshod over the First Amendment rights of many Americans.

Little is formally known about the members of the Citizens' Commission. The FBI never uncovered the identity of the burglars. The office location of Media, Pennsylvania, was no coincidence. Media, ten miles southwest of Philadelphia and bordering on Swarthmore College, was a small hotbed of antiwar activity in the 1960s and early seventies. Following the secret U.S. bombing of Cambodia, the Street Messenger Community Project was formed, joining an already large contingent of Quaker peace activists in the area. Demonstrators were well aware of the FBI field office in their midst. And the office was neither well guarded nor difficult to access.[67] The organization's stated goals, however, suggested a growing restlessness in the United States with politics as usual. The group hoped, not only to "correct the more gross violations of constitutional rights by the FBI," but also to "contribute to the movement for fundamental constructive change" in society.[68] Like the writers and editors at *The Monthly* and attorneys at the ACLU, this organization was determined to challenge the political status quo, albeit using more radical and direct tactics.

Attorney General John N. Mitchell issued a plea to the media not to publicize the story when the Justice Department got word of the burglary. "Disclosure of national defense information," Mitchell claimed, "could endanger the United States and give aid to foreign governments whose interests might be inimical to those of the United States." *Washington Post* editors, ignoring pleas for self-censorship, ran the story on the front page, above the fold, on March 24, 1971. The *Times* followed with a page-one story the next day.[69] The *Post*'s decision, motivated in part by professional determination to "out-scoop" the *Times*, was both politically courageous and financially risky; the newspaper was on the eve of a $35 million public stock offering.[70] Explaining their decision to publicize the files in an editorial, *Post* editors condemned the government's domestic security methods as appropriate tools "for the secret police of the Soviet Union but wholly inconsonant" with American democracy. Calling the FBI's program to monitor political dissent dangerous to democracy, the *Post* editors believed it was their professional duty to inform the American public about the state's activities, especially when those activities violated the basic constitutional rights of many Americans. *Times* editors similarly condemned the administration's "policies of paranoia" and wondered of the FBI's activities, "who watches the watchmen?" Without condoning the tactics of the Citizens' Commission to Investigate the FBI, the *Times* condemned the FBI for "incursions into political surveillance which far exceed legitimate efforts to protect the national interest." Ervin and his staff denounced the tactics of the radical organization to avoid the appearance of collaborating with radicals. But the dossiers, as part of the public domain, proved useful in later congressional inquiries.[71]

Washington Post executive editor Ben Bradlee's editorial decision, risky though it was, underscored the ferocious competition among powerful news organizations for the next big scoop, the next exposé. Structural forces opened wide opportunities for courageous media outlets, like the *Post*, to challenge the federal government in unprecedented ways. CBS News was the next mainstream media organization to offer a direct challenge to powerful national institutions. While the country buzzed over Ervin's hearings, CBS aired a special documentary titled "The Selling of the Pentagon." Splicing a hard-hitting exposé with what historian Beth Bailey has called "the credibility of network news (no irony intended) and all the most persuasive techniques of documentary filmmaking," the program carefully examined how the Pentagon used its public relations budget. Trusted CBS journalist Roger Mudd reported that the Pentagon used a portion of its public relations monies (perhaps $190 million) to fund a domestic propaganda program, including speaking tours and films, to bolster public support for the war in Vietnam.[72] "The Selling of the Pentagon" followed on the heels of a series of public relations disasters for one of the nation's most powerful institutions, saddled as it was with the debacle in Vietnam and forced to explain its domestic surveillance program to an incredulous Congress and the American public.

The Nixon administration responded rabidly to the documentary. Vice President Spiro Agnew, the administration's media watchdog, embarked on a personal campaign to soil the image of the American news establishment in general, and CBS in particular, with the American public. He called the documentary "clever propaganda," proffered by CBS "to discredit" the U.S. defense establishment. In an ironic twist Agnew argued that the "Selling of the Pentagon" belied "the widening credibility gap that exists between the national newsmedia and the American public." CBS President Frank Stanton fought back, arguing that the establishment's disagreement with the media was a "vivid example of the traditional conflict between Government and the free press." Stanton stood by the accuracy of the "Selling of the Pentagon" documentary.[73] A subcommittee of the House Commerce Committee subpoenaed materials relating to the making of the documentary, questioning whether the documentary "accurately" depicted the Pentagon's public relations program. The Nixon administration without apology attacked the very notion of freedom of the press, of government transparency, and of a people's "right to know," claiming that national security always trumped such democratic concerns. The executive branch under both Democratic and Republican presidents had been waging this battle with ferocity since the onset of the Cold War, and beginning in the 1950s, journalists had organized to fight back. The 1960s protest movements revived a movement for greater government transparency. These activists had secured a major victory when President Lyndon Johnson signed the Freedom of Information Act into law in 1966.[74]

The media's claim to information and a public's right to know was already at a head when a spectacular event put the issue at the nation's center stage. Daniel Ellsberg was another establishment insider-turned-critic. During his time as a staffer at the Pentagon in the 1960s, he had gone from hawkish supporter for the Vietnam War to resolute opponent. In early 1971 he approached another establishment critic, a journalist at the *New York Times*, with a story that he promised would be big. He had a copy of what came to be popularly called the Pentagon Papers. These were documents compiled under the direction of then secretary of defense Robert S. McNamara detailing the history of the U.S. policy-making process in Vietnam, from President Dwight Eisenhower through President Johnson. Ellsberg wanted the *Times'* assurance it would use the information and not bow to White House pressure to keep it under wraps. Though the report made some editors and the *Times* legal counsel nervous, the newspaper decided to publish excerpts. The report included evidence that the Pentagon had expanded the war into Cambodia and Laos but kept this information hidden from the American public. Overall the report underscored the duplicity of presidential administrations and widened the credibility gap between government officials and the American polity.

The Nixon administration enjoined the paper to halt publication. The ACLU joined the *Times* legal team in *New York Times v. United States*, entering an amicus curiae brief. Attorneys for the *Times* agreed to halt publication of the documents if the White House could offer evidence that publication endangered the nation's security. But as the ACLU concluded, such a standard "ignores the public's right to know information which will help shape its views on public policy questions." The Supreme Court decided in favor of the *Times*. The ruling undercut executive claims to absolute authority in national security matters, and, according to one journalist, offered "dramatic evidence that Government officials . . . do not possess some mysterious high wisdom . . . one could make the case that the outside public exhibits more good sense." But the ACLU did not see a resounding legal victory; the justices remained deeply divided on how much "freedom" to grant the press under the First Amendment. In other words, the ACLU failed to convince the court to consider the larger First Amendment issues at stake. Instead, the court offered a narrow interpretation: the government had failed, in this instance, to provide evidence that such publication would leave the nation vulnerable either at home or abroad.[75]

From 1970 to 1971 an unlikely coalition created a public framework for institutional reform. Senator Ervin's committee, the ACLU, the Citizens' Commission to Investigate the FBI, *The Monthly*, NBC, and CBS worked to make government surveillance and the suppression of civil liberties headline news. In spite of tremendous gains, however, ACLU Executive Director Aryeh Neier predicted a long, hard battle ahead when he reflected on his organization's progress at the close of 1971. The Ervin Senate hearings on surveillance, privacy, and data banks ignited much-needed public debate on critical constitutional issues. Ultimately, the army buckled under political pressure and discontinued its program—a temporary victory. The challenge remained, Neier believed, to create a legal framework to strictly limit government surveillance. And while some issues, like privacy, seemed poised for legislative resolution, others such as executive privilege, government transparency, and rampant disregard for the Bill of Rights, remained untouched. The public's "right to know," argued Neier, was stymied by the administration's "widespread use of classifications and 'executive privilege' to keep material in the possession of the federal executive department." The Pentagon Papers case highlighted, according to Neier, the need for an expanded ACLU "program of legislative and litigative action to challenge secrecy in government."[76] From 1972 to 1973 the organization would continue to recruit allies and develop networks to challenge the national security regime.

CHAPTER FIVE

It's "Poppycock"

Congress Challenges Executive Privilege

*When Republican William Roth ran for the U.S. Senate in
Delaware in 1966 his constituents told him they wanted more
information about federal programs—who qualifies and what
kind of assistance is available. Just put me in the Senate, he'd say,
and I'll get all the information you need. When the newly elected
senator arrived in Washington in early 1967, he and his staff got
right to work. Roth wanted to catalogue all the federal domestic
assistance programs and send the list back home to his constituents.
He thought it would take a month or so. He was already thinking
how this might help his reelection campaign in five years. Nothing
went as Roth planned. Among the many rejections he received from
federal agencies to his request for information, the one from the
Office of Economic Opportunity was the strangest. The OEO denied
his request for a copy of its telephone directory. This information,
the agency wrote the senator, was "confidential." Roth faced similar
rejections from other agencies. His requests for information were
met with "resistance and subterfuge, and frequently with outright
opposition or refusal." Welcome to Washington, Senator.*[1]

When the army announced plans to dismantle its domestic surveillance program in a letter to congressional critics in 1970, many heralded
the move as a major victory for First Amendment rights in the United
States. But a loosely affiliated network of reformers remained dissatisfied.
Even if the dossiers were destroyed (which they were not), the larger issue
of unrestrained executive power remained unresolved. The Nixon administration refused to cooperate with congressional inquiries into domestic surveillance programs or produce documents in legal proceedings
about the program, claiming "executive privilege."[2]
Frustrated by the opacity of the Nixon administration, Congress fought

back. Believing that they were witnessing a historic perversion of democratic practice in the United States, Senator Sam Ervin and Congressman William Moorhead (D-PA) used the investigative tools available to them. Working closely with the news media and powerful public interest groups, Ervin and Moorhead led a small cohort to publicly debate the role and power of the executive over the state, including the limits of "executive privilege," "freedom of the press," and the public's "right to know."

Ervin and Moorhead received support from a small coterie of public interest groups like the ACLU and Common Cause and the news media. The public's "right to know," these organizations believed, was a basic tenet of American democracy, and the lack of transparency in the modern American state severely restricted democratic practice. Presidential administrations had always tended toward secrecy, but critics claimed that the Nixon administration particularly abused the "national security" claim in order to restrict the flow of information to the American public. Critics argued that the Freedom of Information Act of 1966, a law intended to throw back the curtains on the executive branch, had failed to open the state to public scrutiny. News organizations that dared to peek under the state's dark cloak and reveal what they saw were targeted—"enemies"—for public condemnation and intimidation by the administration. Some critics viewed the administration's attack on the press as yet another effort to subvert the First Amendment. Reformers sought to protect freedom of the press as a vital component of American democracy. Civil libertarians and national security and congressional reformers united to debate freedom of the press, government transparency, and executive power.

While some moved to check executive power through legislative inquiry, others worked through the court system. The ACLU sought to carve out a role for the judicial branch in defining the limits of executive power in the realm of national security in the Cold War period. In *Tatum v. Laird* the ACLU contested the constitutional legality of the army's surveillance program, arguing that it "chilled" First Amendment rights of free speech. *United States v. United States District Court* disputed the executive's claim of "inherent power" to wiretap citizens without court approval. At stake was the very definition of "executive privilege" itself. How far outside the bounds of the Constitution could the president legally act to ensure "national security?" Who or what constituted a threat to the nation? Answers to these questions struck at the heart of the American Cold War culture that had defined the relationship between citizen and state for decades.

When investigative journalists Carl Bernstein and Bob Woodward doggedly pursued the story of the break-in at the Watergate hotel and office complex in June 1972, they were caught up in a tide of swirling public debate about executive power. In the traditional grand narrative of recent American history, the Watergate scandal has taken on gigantic proportions. Historians have called it a "watershed" event that resulted in a congressional reassertion of checks and balances. They exaggerate. Though important, Watergate was but one event among many that underscored the exigencies of executive power. Watergate did weaken the state. It fractured agreement among the nation's powerful elected and appointed officials and created political opportunities for a grassroots movement to unite on issues such as the right to privacy, freedom of speech, and government transparency.[3]

In 1971 CBS White House correspondent Daniel Schorr was not a muckraker. He wasn't even an investigative journalist. That's why the Nixon administration's decision to single him out as an "enemy" made little sense. Schorr came to television late in his career and always considered himself a "journalist *in* television [rather] than a journalist *of* television." This distinction stemmed from his background as a foreign correspondent where he felt compelled to give "shape" to the news to make it more palatable for the American domestic audience. Homely, with a thick voice, Schorr was uncomfortable with "the stagecraft, image-making and slogan-selling to which television seemed so susceptible." Reporting from behind the Soviet Union's Iron Curtain in the 1940s and early 1950s, he developed a penchant (as much out of a sense of professional survival as personal curiosity) for information that was difficult to access, for news that the establishment wanted to withhold from the public.[4] When Schorr joined CBS television news in the late 1950s he found that presidential administrations didn't much like the "shape" that he gave to his stories. Schorr was a nonpartisan offender. He turned the same critical eye on Democrats and Republicans. Administrations of both parties viewed him as a gadfly, with every administration expressing its disapproval in its own way. President Johnson made his dislike for Schorr's reporting on Great Society programs known in no uncertain terms, calling the reporter at his home late one night and deriding him as "a prize son-of-a-bitch." But at least on the surface Schorr and the administrations he covered maintained a civil, if strained, relationship. Unbeknownst to Schorr, however, his relationship with the Nixon administration became anything but cordial. Sometime in 1971, after Schorr broadcast a few reports critical of White House programs, the reporter became the brunt of some ugly jokes inside the Nixon White House. Nixon and his staff, it seemed, took a "siege mentality" with those who criticized their programs rather than attempt to sway journalists to their way of thinking. Their displeasure with certain journalists manifested in what Schorr would later call "secretive in-group humor," such as adding the middle initial "P" to the names of some reporters. The "p" stood for "prick."[5]

One morning, after a typical dispute with the White House over his reporting, an FBI officer greeted Schorr at his CBS office. The officer claimed the White House was vetting Schorr for a position. Which position, Schorr wanted to know. The officer couldn't say. For a brief moment Schorr fancied that his excellence in reporting had finally brought him not only the admiration, but the approval of White House officials. He imagined how his skills could be put to use by the executive branch. But Schorr had to be honest with himself. He had been no friend to this, or any, presidential administration. And the mystery job seemed suspicious (especially coming as it did after another row with the White House). For the remainder of the day Schorr answered bewildered phone calls from friends, family, and associates who had also been contacted by the FBI. The investigation was embarrassing and potentially damaging to his career. The formal inquiry made his colleagues, his sources, and, most importantly, his supervisors, nervous. He finally asked the FBI to suspend the inquiry—he didn't want a government job. The White House clumsily admitted that it had never considered him for a position. Nixon had ordered the name check to intimidate the reporter.[6]

Presidential administrations had battled an adversarial press since the nation's founding. The Adams administration had gone so far in 1798 as to enact the Sedition Act to forbid unfavorable and malicious reporting about the government and members of Congress.[7] But Nixon's decision to use the national security apparatus to intimidate a critic into silence was a particularly heavy-handed technique. The Schorr episode was but one of the Nixon administration's efforts to intimidate the news media: the administration sued the *New York Times* to halt the publication of the Pentagon Papers; turned Vice President Spiro Agnew loose on CBS news for airing an investigative report critical of the Defense Department's public relations work ("The Selling of the Pentagon"); and sought subpoenas for journalists who refused to reveal their sources.[8] Some viewed the administration's attacks on the press as evidence that the president and his staff preferred secrecy to open government. ACLU Executive Director Aryeh Neier suspected that the White House aimed to punish the media for doing its job—informing the public about affairs of government. Neier believed that the administration's preference for secrecy made the role of the media more important than ever.[9] The ACLU called upon its ally in Congress, Senator Sam Ervin and his subcommittee on Constitutional Rights, to investigate.

Ervin himself was no friend of the administration. The conservative southern Democrat and Richard Nixon were both "law and order" men. In fact, Ervin voted with Nixon 60 percent of the time during the president's first term. But Ervin was opposed to the methods the president proposed to fight crime. He publicly called Nixon's omnibus crime bill "a garbage pail of some of the most repressive, nearsighted, intolerant, unfair, and vindictive legislation that the Senate has ever been presented." Ervin's steadfast support for First Amendment rights made him a vocal critic of the administration's tactics. The senator appreciated the historically contentious relationship between the executive branch and the press, but the Schorr case seemed to Ervin an unconscionable abuse of power. Little did he know the extent to which Nixon and his aides were willing to use intelligence agencies against the president's so-called "enemies." Fearing the erosion of the concept of a free press and determined to "reexamine and reemphasize First Amendment principles," Ervin gaveled to order hearings on freedom of the press in late September 1971. Schorr testified as a star witness.[10]

Ervin's staff worked assiduously to maximize press coverage by packing the hearings with media darlings. The nation's most trusted television journalist, CBS news anchor Walter Cronkite, told his audience that Congress should write legislation to protect the free press. Cronkite described a media troubled by government secrecy and harassed by elected officials. He acknowledged the "immense power" of the news media (for which he certainly felt pride) but dismissed administration claims of bias. Offering his "personal assurance" as proof, Cronkite denied that "political or ideological consideration" ever determined the making of the news.[11]

One of the men responsible for the publication of the Pentagon Papers, *New York Times* Executive Vice President Harding Bancroft, also minced no words. He claimed that the Nixon administration's efforts to silence the media amounted to intimidation. The enjoinment of the *Times* set an ugly precedent and cast a "chilling effect" over the news industry. "A reporter who, in the past, routinely checked his facts with Government officials might well think twice before doing so, always fearful that by revealing his knowledge he will put into motion the Government censorship machine." The greatest challenge faced by the media was the overclassification of information, and Bancroft urged Congress to reexamine the Freedom of Information Act's efficacy. Hailed in 1966 as a law that would ensure the "people's right to know," the Freedom of Information Act, according to Bancroft, had not "deterred Government bureaucrats from routinely denying proper informational requests." Since journalists did not have the luxury of "enter[ing] into prolonged negotiations, or litigation with the agency in question," these delaying tactics killed stories.[12]

Ervin's hearings proved a great success in publicizing the challenges of modern journalism, and his efforts earned him the respect and gratitude of the press. In December 1972 the Radio and Television News Directors Association awarded the senator the Paul W. White Memorial Award for outstanding contribution to broadcast journalism. Past recipients included Edward R. Murrow, John F. Kennedy, William Stanton, and Walter Cronkite. Jim McCulla noted in his remarks at the association's meeting that "Sam Ervin is very much the right man in the right place at the right time."[13]

Representative William Moorhead, a Democrat from Pittsburgh, followed Ervin's freedom of the press hearings closely. As chairman of the House Subcommittee on Foreign Operations and Government Information, he had a professional and personal interest in challenging the opacity of the executive branch. Like many of his colleagues, Moorhead had grown increasingly frustrated with the executive branch's failure to comply with the basic principles of FOIA. He wondered why the law failed to work as its architects had originally envisioned. Moorhead was not alone, and by the early 1970s the euphoria following the passage of FOIA had dissipated. The Nixon administration's attacks on the press, so eloquently described by respected members of the media at the Ervin hearings, prompted Moorhead to investigate. If transparency remained the exception, not the rule, Moorhead was determined to revise FOIA to make it effective.

Architects of FOIA had envisioned it as an institutional and organizational revolution—a democratic tool for institutionalizing a new process of information transfer from the dark recesses of the executive branch to the public squares of American society. But as FOIA practitioners revealed in Moorhead's hearings, the law had failed to make government more transparent or more accountable to the American polity. With few exceptions, current and former government officials, representatives of print and broadcast media, public interest groups, and attorneys echoed the assessment of FOIA as "fine in principle and purpose but poor in practical terms."[14]

The hearings exposed the degree to which executive agencies reluctantly responded to FOIA requests, claiming civil servants had to "balance the Government's rights against the people's rights [to know]."[15] Requestors described cases of bureaucratic "foot-dragging," suggesting "widespread reluctance of the bureaucracy to honor the public's legal right to know." A study of the first four years of FOIA conducted by the Congressional Research Service revealed the time for response varied widely from agency to agency: the Small Business Administration took an average of eight days to respond to requests, while the Federal Trade Commission took an average of sixty-nine days. It took a staggering fifty days, on average, for requestors to receive a response to an appeal. For these reasons, the report noted, journalists had "made little use" of FOIA. Agencies employed techniques to dissuade requests, including charging excessive copy fees. Critics complained that government agencies overused the nine exempt categories to avoid complying with FOIA requests.[16]

Moorhead's subcommittee hearings offered a forum for an emerging knowledge network of organizations and individuals—such as the ACLU, Common Cause, and the American Bar Association—to collaborate on issues related to government transparency and executive power. Common Cause proposed reinforcing the statutory provisions of the law by requiring each federal agency to publish an annual report of FOIA requests, rejections, and approvals. Because attorney fees often dissuaded requestors from mounting legal challenges to top-secret classifications, the American Bar Association urged Congress to require agencies to pay legal fees for successful plaintiffs. These organizations vociferously supported a citizen's "right to know" and challenged broad claims to executive privilege employed by both Democratic and Republican presidential administrations. More importantly, this network worked closely with congressional allies to author legislative amendments to the 1967 FOIA Act.[17] During the course of an otherwise thorough congressional inquiry, Moorhead did not challenge the law's exemptions relating to national security. Even if he personally believed such exemptions to be illegitimate and undemocratic, Moorhead probably recognized that these agencies were beyond his committee's oversight jurisdiction. At least for the time being, the congressman was content to leave issues related to national security outside the scope of his inquiry.

Senator Ervin had demonstrated a similar reluctance to challenge the extrademocratic security agencies when he investigated the army's domestic surveillance program in 1971. The administration's stonewalling tactics—either explicitly denying requests or delaying so that information was no longer relevant—had effectively halted Ervin's inquiry. Ervin wondered about the administration's repeated claims of executive privilege: "How can a government be responsive to the people if it will not answer the people's questions, explain its actions, and describe its policies to the only national body directly responsible to the people?"[18] Ervin warned, "when the people do not know what their government is doing, those who govern are not accountable for their actions—and accountability is basic to the democratic system."[19]

President John F. Kennedy had promised Congress that only he, and not his advisors, would invoke the claim of executive privilege. President Lyndon B. Johnson followed Kennedy's lead, and the claim of executive privilege was used infrequently during both the Kennedy and Johnson administrations. While President Johnson claimed to "cooperate completely with the Congress in making available to it all information possible," many congressmen were frustrated by the opacity of federal agencies, especially regarding information about the war in Vietnam. President Nixon had promised that executive privilege would be narrowly construed and not "asserted without specific Presidential approval." Nixon also claimed that his administration would be "dedicated to insuring a free flow of information to the Congress and news media—and thus, to the citizens."[20]

Ervin was determined that Nixon would be the last president to broadly apply executive privilege. Using his power as chairman of the Separation of Powers Subcommittee (created in 1967 as a congressional response to perceived infringements on legislative prerogatives by the executive and judicial branches), he declared he would investigate "conflicting principles: the alleged power of the President to withhold information, the disclosure of which he feels would impede the performance of his constitutional responsibilities; the power of the legislative branch to obtain information in order to legislate wisely and effectively; and the basic right of the taxpaying public to know what its Government is doing."[21]

Ervin was particularly troubled by the administration's policies regarding disclosure of its wiretapping and surveillance practices. A colleague on his Constitutional Rights Subcommittee and chair of the Administrative Practices Subcommittee, Edward Kennedy (D-MA), had been battling the Department of Justice for months on the issue. Kennedy was curious about the consequences of the provisions of the Safe Streets and

Crime Control Act of 1968. The bill allowed the executive branch to use court-approved wiretaps to combat crime. It also legalized the use of warrantless wiretaps if the reason for doing so fell in one of five national security–related categories: (1) protecting the nation against actual or potential attack or other hostile acts of a foreign power; (2) obtaining foreign intelligence information; (3) protecting national security information against foreign intelligence activities; (4) protecting against the overthrow of the government by force or other unlawful means; and (5) protecting against other clear and present danger to the structure or existence of government. Though the administration publicly stated that "it fully complies with the 1968 Congressional standards before installing any tap or bug without a court order," Kennedy had his doubts. (He also harbored presidential ambitions and undoubtedly believed that challenging President Nixon was a politically savvy move.)[22] He asked the Justice Department for details about warrantless wiretaps currently on the books—under which of the five categories did each wiretap fall? Assistant Attorney General Robert Mardian told the senator that he could not categorize the wiretaps "exclusively under a single criterion." However, he assured Kennedy that each wiretap met "one or more of the criteria itemized" by law.[23] When pressed for a categorical breakdown of wiretaps from 1968 to 1970, Mardian replied, *no such categorization exists.* Mardian explained that the procedure for obtaining a wiretap was simple: the FBI director asks the attorney general and the attorney general approves or denies the request "acting for the President of the United States."[24] Kennedy was appalled, not only for the casual manner in which the department handled wiretap approval procedures, but also by the lack of transparency on the part of the administration related to a very sensitive issue.

In truth, the legislative branch was partly to blame for the abuse of executive power. Ervin admitted to colleagues that "the shifting of power to the Executive has resulted from [a congressional] failure to assert [its] constitutional powers." Nixon's reorganization plan of 1970—approved by Congress—allowed the president to consolidate his domestic and foreign policy planning staff within the corridors of the West Wing. (John Erhlichman ran the domestic council and Henry Kissinger headed up the National Security Council.) In the words of Ervin's biographer, Congress allowed the White House to "transfer the power of cabinet officers to unaccountable White House assistants."[25] This issue became acute early in the Nixon administration when the president decided to put congressional relations regarding foreign policy under the direction of National Security Advisor Henry Kissinger. This reshuffling almost guaranteed

"It's For Security --- It Makes <u>Us</u> Feel More Secure"

"IT'S FOR SECURITY—IT MAKES US FEEL MORE SECURE": A 1971 Herblock cartoon, copyright by *The Herb Block Foundation*

that Congress would have trouble gaining access to information related to Vietnam policymaking because, since World War II, the president had claimed that his personal staff was not subject under the Constitution to questioning by members of Congress. In spite of his campaign pledge to shrink the size of the federal government, Nixon's plan doubled the number of White House aides, all of whom were protected from testifying before Congress by the cloak of "executive privilege."[26] This consolidation of power and expansion of staff led some senators to complain that the White House had "access to information which the Congress cannot possibly match." It was no wonder, noted one senator, that when added to the "hydraheaded monster" of "executive privilege," the legislative branch had a difficult time gaining access to information necessary to perform both its legislative and investigatory duties. Ervin worried that "the steady increase of Executive power has come close to creating a 'government of men, not of laws.'"[27]

Ervin had a powerful ally in Senator William Fulbright (D-AR). As the respected chairman of the Senate Committee on Foreign Relations, Fulbright was indignant at Nixon's lack of cooperation with Congress on even the most mundane of foreign policy issues. The Pentagon Papers revealed to Fulbright how inconsequential the legislative branch seemed to be from the perspective of the White House. He concluded that the report revealed in stark detail the "almost total exclusion of Congress from the policymaking process." How could Congress be relevant and fulfill its constitutional duties, if secrecy was the rule, rather than the exception, Fulbright wondered.[28]

For all of Ervin's lofty talk about constitutional imperatives, protecting civil liberties and the fundamental tenets of democracy, and doing the work of the "people," political considerations surely underscored the legislative movement to challenge executive power. Ervin himself had faced his first formidable political challenge in 1968 when a young "modernizer" considered challenging him in the primary. Polls had Ervin and Terry Sanford, former North Carolina governor, in a dead heat. Sanford decided not to run, only because the matchup promised to deeply divide the state party. Though Ervin played naïve, he was not obtuse. The once-powerful grip that his generation held on party politics in his home state was weakening. Surely Ervin was looking to regain the trust and confidence of his constituents back home.[29]

The strengthening of congressional resolve to challenge executive power and privilege in the early 1970s suggests that, given the right set of circumstances, some of the nation's most powerful elected officials were ready to lay an unprecedented challenge at the president's feet. But legislative politics moves slowly. Some outside of Congress were unwilling to wait for Ervin or other sympathetic congressmen. They took their challenges to the courts. The ACLU was the organization best prepared, financially and administratively, to legally challenge executive power. Under Aryeh Neier's direction, the ACLU had taken an aggressive stance in its approach to pursuing a more democratic government. Shortly after Christopher Pyle published his tell-all article about army domestic surveillance in the *Washington Monthly*, a mutual friend introduced him to ACLU Legal Director Mel Wulf. Neier and Wulf wanted to challenge the constitutionality of domestic surveillance programs but lacked the hard evidence to bring forth a successful lawsuit. Pyle volunteered to gather evidence against the army's surveillance program. All they needed was a plaintiff.

Wulf persuaded Arlo Tatum, executive director of the Central Committee for Conscientious Objectors in Philadelphia (one of the organizations identified in Pyle's article as a CONUS surveillance target), to sue Secretary of Defense Melvin Laird in Federal District Court. The ACLU charged that the army's program violated Tatum's First Amendment right to free speech. ACLU legal director since 1962, Melvin Wulf had seen the organization at its worst and was enjoying the direction it was taking in the early 1970s in defense of First Amendment rights. Under Aryeh Neier's direction the organization was moving beyond its traditional legal strategy of submitting amicus curiae. Eighty-five percent of the organization's cases were amicus briefs in 1962. By 1965, under Wulf's direction, the organization litigated about half its cases directly. By the early 1970s ACLU attorneys submitted an amicus brief only when they could not get their "hands on the cases," about 10 percent of the time.[30]

Wulf had reason to be optimistic that the federal court would decide in his client's favor. Since the late 1950s the courts had cautiously guarded a legal right to privacy and protected First Amendment activities like the right to free speech and association. In the case of *NAACP v. Alabama* (1958), for example, the liberal Warren court ruled against the state of Alabama when it sued the NAACP for access to its membership rosters. The First Amendment, wrote the court, guaranteed the constitutional right to privacy of one's association. Two years later the court overturned a California statute prohibiting the distribution of anonymous political leaflets. In *Talley v. California* (1960), the court recognized the historical significance of anonymous political activity; the First Amendment granted citizens political anonymity as protection from government scrutiny. In the cases of *Griswold v. Connecticut* (1965) and *Stanley v. Georgia* (1969), the Court recognized a zone of privacy around certain very personal activities. Even the more conservative Burger court, in *Wisconsin v. Constantineau* (1971), struck down a state law permitting law enforcement officials to publicize lists of local alcoholics. The court declared that a government could not affix "a badge of infamy" to a person without offering the individual an opportunity to challenge the accuracy of such information. These five cases evinced new jurisprudential protection of certain private, political activity from government scrutiny, protecting a right to privacy especially when related to political activities protected by the First Amendment.[31]

The ACLU filed suit in Federal District Court in Washington, D.C. Suspecting that the army would attempt a cover-up by destroying the dossiers, Wulf filed a preliminary injunction to have the files delivered to the court. The army called for the case to be dismissed, arguing no one's rights had been violated. Judge George Hart, Jr., a graduate of the Virginia Military Academy, presided over the case. Hart demonstrated little patience with the ACLU's claims and quickly dismissed the case.[32] When the ACLU appealed to the Supreme Court, the Nixon administration asked the court to dismiss the case, claiming that the legislative and executive branches acted as sufficient "checks" on military intelligence (ironic given the Nixon administration's repeated failure to cooperate with Senator Ervin's inquiry). Senator Ervin argued *Tatum v. Laird* before the Supreme Court. The ACLU hoped that Ervin's celebrity status might influence the court. Ervin was delighted to have the opportunity to speak before the court, the first time in his long career in law. The court dismissed the case, and Justice William Rehnquist cast the deciding vote in the 5–4 ruling. The very fact that plaintiff Tatum filed a lawsuit against the army's surveillance program, wrote Nixon-appointee Chief Justice Warren Burger for the majority, suggested that his First Amendment right to free speech had not been chilled—a catch-22. The court noted that the judicial branch did not wish to play the role of "continuing monitors of the wisdom and soundness of executive action."[33]

As director of the Justice Department's Office of Legal Counsel, Rehnquist had testified before Ervin's hearings on *Federal Data Banks, Computers and the Bill of Rights* in 1971. During his testimony he had asserted that the president alone had the "inherent power" to conduct surveillance and that neither legislative nor judicial review of executive surveillance programs was necessary because "'self restraint' by the president sufficed." According to Rehnquist, dissenters had no constitutionally protected rights against the executive branch's collection of data on their political beliefs.[34] Infuriated by Rehnquist's participation in the case, the ACLU filed a motion to have the justice retroactively recused (a tie vote would have upheld the decision of the lower court). Neier and Ervin argued that Rehnquist "had been so closely related to the subject matter of *Laird* as to render impartiality highly unlikely."[35] Rehnquist conceded that questioning his objectivity in the case was reasonable, but refused to consider his own recusal.[36]

Though the *Tatum* decision initially struck a devastating blow to the ACLU's legal challenge to executive power, another landmark case was winding its way through the court system. In 1971 the Nixon administration sued radical members of the White Panther Party for bombing the CIA office in Ann Arbor, Michigan. During the course of the trial, government officers conceded that they had wiretapped the phone line of a defendant without a court warrant. When challenged by the plaintiffs to justify the wiretap, Attorney General John Mitchell articulated what came to be known as the Mitchell Doctrine. He claimed "the government had the right to conduct wiretaps and electronic surveillance" without court warrant in any case "that [the government] deems a 'national security' case." Mitchell believed the president drew such power from his constitutionally protected right to wage war and his duty to protect the country. He also relied upon a broad interpretation of the Safe Streets and Crime Control Act of 1968 that granted the executive the power of unrestricted wiretapping authority in "national security" cases. At stake was the Nixon administration's claim that the White Panthers constituted a threat to "national security.[37]

Federal District Court Justice Damon Keith presided over the case. A Johnson appointee and a graduate of Howard University Law School, Keith considered himself an ardent defender of the Constitution. As a student at Howard Keith observed Thurgood Marshall, then an attorney for the National Association for the Advancement of Colored People, practice his landmark civil rights cases before a "mock" Supreme Court. He later claimed these sessions instilled in him an abiding interest in seeing the Constitution protected.[38] Keith ruled for the plaintiffs, ordering the government to disclose the information it obtained by the wiretap or drop the case against the White Panthers. The judge rejected Attorney General Mitchell's implicit claim "that a dissident domestic organization is akin to an unfriendly foreign power and must be dealt with in the same fashion." Such claims undercut the "very constitutional privileges and immunities that are inherent in United States citizenship," that is, the right to receive equal justice before the law. Keith insisted, "The executive branch of our government cannot be given the power or the opportunity to investigate and prosecute criminal violations because certain accused persons espouse views which are inconsistent with our present form of government." Especially in times of great social unrest, "it is often difficult for the established and contented members of our society to tolerate, much less try to understand, the contemporary challenges to our existing form of government." In the most politically contentious times democracy must be defended. If, as the government would have it, "attempts of domestic organizations to attack and subvert the existing structure of the Government" are seen as criminal behavior, Keith argued, then dissent is effectively silenced.[39] The Nixon administration immediately appealed the decision to the Supreme Court, certain that the conservative Burger court would uphold the administration's broad definition of "national security."

The Keith decision (as it came to be known) severely undercut the prerogatives the executive branch had enjoyed for decades in the realm of national security. Civil libertarians, ecstatic over the ruling, worried that the "Nixon court" would overturn it. Wulf solicited like-minded organizations to submit amicus briefs, urging that they, too, had a vested interest in the outcome of the case because "electronic surveillance unchecked by judicial scrutiny can be directed against any organization whose activities at any time displease the government." The attorney general's broad claim to the right to electronic surveillance if "certain individuals or groups pose such a danger to the internal security of the United States" meant that any person or organization could become a target of surveillance and wiretapping. In such cases, the administration asserted, "the Fourth Amendment does not require the additional safeguard of a prior warrant." Wulf raised the specter of the McCarthy-era witch hunts, arguing that the administration sought to "discredit dissent against its policies by branding legitimate dissent as an attack upon the internal security of the nation." The administration's approach to domestic security, argued Wulf, circumvented all the protections afforded by the Fourth Amendment. Such unconstitutional activity, conducted under the broad banner of executive privilege in the interest of national security, would have significant and long-term repercussions for civil liberties in the United States if upheld by the Supreme Court. The ACLU closed its appeal with the ominous words of Pastor Martin Niemöller, a German pastor imprisoned by the Nazis during World War II, intimating that those who kept quiet about injustice were destined to become victims themselves.[40]

The success of the ACLU's amicus strategy is difficult to quantify. However, it was successful enough in the 1960s to prompt law professor Fred Inbau to create a counterweight. Called the Americans for Effective Law Enforcement, Inbau's organization authored amicus briefs in defense of law and order and on behalf of law enforcement agencies. In 1971 Attorney General John Mitchell formally endorsed the organization.[41]

In the amicus brief submitted to the court, the ACLU rejected out of hand the administration's broad claims to power in the name of national security: "Ignoring our traditions of limited delegated power, checks and balances, and clear Fourth and First Amendment restraints, the Government demands the right to apply the most penetrating and unlimited electronic spying devices on all individuals and groups who, in the Attorney General's eyes, appear 'dangerous.'" This concept, argued the organization, threatened the very fabric of American democracy: "No nation can survive such [absolute] power and remain free; no democracy can function where its prerequisites, dissent and free association, are so jeopardized; no society dedicated to the rule of law can tolerate so huge an official exemption from 'those wise restraints that make men free' without teaching its people that the rule of law is merely official rhetoric to keep dissenters in line." These words were enough to give even the most ardent proponent of law and order pause, as they raised the specter of totalitarianism at a time when the United States remained locked in a geopolitical struggle to contain the spread of communism.[42] Surveillance, the ACLU argued, "is inevitably surreptitious." As the government's case against the White Panthers demonstrated, such practices would rarely, if ever, be made public. Checks and balances could hardly be maintained with such practices conducted in secret. "Since the Attorney General does not include reports of such eavesdropping in his annual reports to Congress under 18 U.S.C. 2519, no one outside the Executive branch will know what electronic eavesdropping is taking place under this power." From the organization's point of view, the administration behaved as though there was "no limit to who can be eavesdropped upon." When pressed, the Nixon administration fell back on claims of "inherent presidential power." This claim was without legal grounding, argued the organization, and "sounds much like 'Big Brother knows best.'"[43]

The president defined his legal position as derived from the constitutional authority based on the president's responsibility as commander-in-chief and chief executive, asserting that "such power is necessary because judicial scrutiny would seriously compromise national security."[44] But with Congress reticent to check presidential power on these issues, the ACLU was determined that the judicial branch should exercise some prerogative. Precedent was decidedly in the ACLU's favor. In 1952, facing a strike at the nation's steel mills, President Harry Truman issued an executive order commanding his secretary of commerce to seize and operate most of the nation's mills to prevent a work stoppage. The president claimed the power in the interest of national security; Americans were fighting the Korean War. The Supreme Court denied such broad executive powers in its *Youngstown Sheet & Tube Co. v. Sawyer* decision.[45] In spite of legal precedent, the ACLU was acutely aware that times had changed. The organization harbored scant hope that the conservative Burger court would restrict the power of the president on issues of national security.

The court shocked civil libertarians when it unanimously upheld the Keith decision in 1972. (Justice Rehnquist abstained from judgment on the case.) Writing for the majority, Justice Lewis Powell, Jr. (a Nixon appointee), argued that the "Fourth Amendment [against 'unreasonable searches and seizures'] cannot properly be guaranteed if domestic surveillances may be conducted solely within the discretion of the executive branch." Constitutionally guaranteed rights were constants, not to be cast aside at the whim of the White House. The court rejected the executive's claim that it was constitutionally entitled to engage in electronic surveillance of American citizens without complying with the requirements of the Fourth Amendment "to protect the nation from attempts . . . to attack and subvert the existing structure of the Government." Even in national security investigations, the president had no constitutional authority to conduct electronic surveillance of American citizens on American soil without a judicially issued search warrant based on a finding of probable cause.[46] The court conceded that special times called for a special federal response. "At a time of worldwide ferment and when civil disorders in this country are more prevalent," the court recognized the government's desire to maintain law and order. However, the administration's claim that issues related to domestic security were "too subtle and complex" for judicial review seemed self-serving. Judicial review of wiretap requests was a "justified" inconvenience to the executive branch. In free societies, the court urged, the public must be reassured that "indiscriminate wiretapping and bugging of law-abiding citizens cannot occur." Without careful checks on the system, wrote Powell, "targets of official surveillance may be those suspected of unorthodoxy in their political beliefs." Upholding the Keith decision, the court delivered a stunning rejection of unfettered executive power in the name of national security.[47]

Powerful members of the media, still angry over the executive's attack on the press, lauded the court ruling. *New York Times* editors called the decision a "rebuke to those ideologues of the executive branch" that fall back on the "inherent powers" of the executive branch as justification for unconstitutional behavior. The ruling, editors declared, "completely demolished" the attorney general's claim that any effort to restrict those inherent powers in terms of wiretapping left the nation vulnerable and in danger: "The Court was not persuaded by a system of constitutional safeguards dependent on the Attorney General's, or even the President's, infallibility or, as Mr. Mitchell put it, on the 'self-discipline of the executive branch.'" The *Times* congratulated the court for recognizing that a "blank check of official powers is the prelude to their abuse."[48]

Still, as the *Washington Post* noted on its editorial page, the ruling was not a total victory for civil libertarians. Though it offered a "sharp slap" at unchecked executive power, the court opinion did not repudiate the "constitutional basis of the President's domestic security role." Rather, the court encouraged the administration to protect domestic security "in a manner compatible with the Fourth Amendment."[49]

The Nixon administration feigned indifference to the ruling. At a press conference on domestic policy Nixon stated defiantly that the decision did not "rule out wiretapping" if the administration made a "connection between the activity that is under surveillance and a foreign government."[50] Privately, however, the White House worried over the long-term repercussions of the decision, and how it restricted presidential power on issues related to national security. Arthur Kinoy, the crusading civil liberties attorney who successfully argued the Keith decision before the Supreme Court, later claimed that the break-in at the Democratic National Committee headquarters at the Watergate office complex was a mission to remove the wiretap devices from DNC headquarters. Someone privy to the court's decision with ties to the administration had alerted the White House staff of the likely outcome. The Plumbers then scrambled to remove the wiretaps before the court issued its ruling banning the president's broad claims to wiretap without warrant.[51]

Watergate, as a scandal, was precipitated by the decision, taken early in the Nixon administration, to use modern tools of surveillance against its political enemies. In the Cold War climate that fostered suspicion and barely tolerated dissent, Nixon and his aides—products as well as producers of this political culture—used the most expeditious route for achieving their aims. Their determination to blacken the records of their critics, as the case of Daniel Schorr suggests, and their belief that they could use the tools of the presidency for such deeds, exemplified the problems of executive privilege, the ambiguity of the term "national security," and the degree to which secrecy had undermined the democratic experience in the United States by the 1970s.

The Watergate debacle is well known. In short it goes like this: following the publication of the Pentagon Papers in 1971, top White House aides, including the president's domestic policy advisor, John Ehrlichman, created a "plumbers unit." The Plumbers were authorized by the president's Committee to Re-elect the President (CREEP, for short) to "plug leaks." To discredit Daniel Ellsberg, an author of the Pentagon Papers and the man who leaked the report to the *Times*, the Plumbers broke into his psychiatrist's office looking for information that they could use.

These same men performed the Watergate break-in—a mission that had nothing to do with national security and everything to do with politics. The Plumbers broke into the Democratic national headquarters in the Watergate hotel and office complex in Washington, D.C., to plant bugs on office phones. The break-in was another instance of "dirty tricks" and "black bag jobs" that CREEP had authorized to discredit Nixon's Democratic opponents in the 1972 presidential race.[52]

Washington metro police arrested the Plumbers after they bumbled the break-in. They did not fit the profile of ordinary burglars: one carried an address book with a telephone number for "W.H." Five men were Cuban émigrés and two were former CIA employees. As if that wasn't bizarre enough, this odd lot carried more than $2,000 in cash and high-end surveillance equipment. Two days after the Watergate break-in the Supreme Court announced the *U.S. v. U.S. District Court* (Keith decision) ruling.

DNC Chairman Larry O'Brien accused the administration of backing the break-in. Eager to clear the president's name, FBI Acting Director L. Patrick Gray (who owed his position to Nixon) pressed his officers to get to the bottom of the case. They did—the money found with the Plumbers traced back to CREEP. Nixon instructed his chief of staff, H. R. Haldeman, to coordinate a cover-up, with the CIA taking the fall. Haldeman called in favors with CIA Director Richard Helms, asking him to put pressure on the FBI to limit its investigations. Helms and his staff warned Gray that his investigation might have national security implications. Meanwhile, Nixon instructed Gray to continue to aggressively investigate the break-in. Determined to demonstrate his loyalty, Gray kept the White House apprised of his investigation. White House counsel John Dean sat in with FBI officers while they conducted interviews of White House staff. Gray had FBI reports of the investigation delivered to Dean at the White House. CREEP officials and those involved in the burglary destroyed files before FBI investigators could lay hands on them. White House aides lied to investigators, or gave them information that proved inconsequential or irrelevant. All this evasion was encouraged and in some cases orchestrated by officials at the highest levels of government. The cover-up reached all the way up to the president himself.[53]

Over the next few months, as more evidence linked the Plumbers to the president's reelection committee via a money trail, the White House became obsessed with keeping the seven men, now awaiting trial in Washington, D.C., quiet. The men wanted their "commitments" to be honored. Nixon and his staff managed to keep the whole affair out of the presidential campaign and pull off a landslide victory (CREEP worked full-time implementing a strategy to divide the Democratic Party, which certainly helped to keep the press focused on anything but the Watergate story). But the Watergate mess—thanks to the reporting of Woodward and Bernstein—continued to bite at the administration's heels. The two tenacious journalists uncovered more evidence in the months following the election that Watergate was just the tip of a large iceberg of presidential impropriety. At their trial, the Plumbers claimed their act had been done out of a sense of patriotism, for fear that a win by Democratic presidential candidate George McGovern would make the country vulnerable to communism. Judge John Sirica, an Eisenhower appointee, publicly expressed doubt about the "facts" that the burglars offered and hoped that the new Senate select committee would quickly uncover the real story.[54]

Majority Leader Mike Mansfield (MT) nominated Senator Ervin to head the new Select Committee on Presidential Campaign Activities (hereafter, Watergate committee). Republicans remained divided on the committee, some calling for an investigation into previous elections and denouncing the inquiry as deeply partisan. Though Republicans were reluctant to investigate one of their own, Ervin's reputation as a fair man, a constitutional "expert," and a conservative in his own party helped pull through a unanimous vote on the Senate resolution to establish the special committee (77-0). As historian Stanley Kutler argues, "What the Republicans finally voted for was more an expression of faith in Senator Ervin than of any real desire for a Select Committee."[55]

Many historians have written about the Watergate committee and its findings. Some have suggested rightly that Ervin leant legitimacy to an investigation that might otherwise have been dismissed as partisan. Ervin did bridge the partisan divide. But more than that, Ervin was deeply invested in issues surrounding the executive's domestic security overreach. For years he and a small army of committee staffers (from the Constitutional Rights and Separation of Powers subcommittees) had coordinated investigations delving into executive power, domestic surveillance, and personal privacy. Ervin was the nucleus of a burgeoning network of experts on these issues. He exploited these connections when he staffed the Watergate committee. It was because of his own reputation that he was able to persuade Sam Dash, a professor of law at Georgetown University and a former district attorney for the city of Philadelphia, to serve as chief counsel. Ervin had been impressed by Dash's work, particularly his "profound study of surreptitious activities," published as *The Eavesdroppers* in 1959. *The Eavesdroppers* explored the policies in ten states regarding law enforcement and the use of wiretaps in order to "be better able to formulate policies and opinions on the delicate question of individual privacy."[56]

Ervin staffed the newly formed committee with his own subcommittee staff. They possessed finely tuned skills in the art of publicity and media relations, and they had developed expert knowledge about the issues under consideration. By 1973 when the committee began its inquiry, this one-time ardent southern segregationist and leading foe of the ERA (whose views on many issues so offended some Americans) had the media and, therefore, the public eating out of his hand. His staff had cultivated media contacts at some of the nation's most powerful print and television news organizations. They knew how to leak information and how to use this information to pique public interest in topics that otherwise might generate little attention. When they earned the attention of the national media, they knew how to exploit it. Ervin's staff was practiced at the art of staging hearings to maximize press coverage and maintain public interest. It's perhaps no coincidence that Ervin again selected the Senate Caucus Room to stage the Watergate hearings—a room that he had so successfully used in the past to garner public attention to the army surveillance program. Ervin and his staff brought these skills in media manipulation to bear on the Watergate hearings.[57]

Three days before Judge Sirica's planned sentencing of the Watergate burglars the case blew wide open. James McCord, one of the defendants, delivered a note to the judge's chambers. He claimed that the defendants were being pressured to remain silent, that the CIA was not involved in the break-in, and that the Plumbers had perjured themselves in court. McCord wanted to speak to the judge, a request with which Sirica eagerly complied. In spite of White House knowledge of the letter, the payments to silence the Plumbers continued. Determined to get to the bottom of the story, Sirica urged the defendants to cooperate with the grand jury and the newly appointed Watergate committee. He suggested that he might take such cooperation into consideration when making the final sentencing.[58]

No doubt President Nixon realized that his administration teetered on the brink of political catastrophe. This is the only plausible explanation for his decision to declare the protection of individual privacy rights a top legislative priority in his January 1974 State of the Union address. The following month, Nixon devoted a public radio address entirely to the privacy issue. "At no time in the past has our Government known so much about so many of its individual citizens," Nixon declared. "This new knowledge brings with it an awesome potential for harm as well as good—and an equally awesome responsibility on those who have that knowledge." Nixon fretted (insincerely) that government records often held inaccurate, and damaging, information about American citizens. These individual files could potentially result "in the withholding of credit or jobs" for no good reason. Most Americans did not know what kind of information the government retained and had no means to find out. Nixon's concerns over privacy echoed those of many elected officials—including civil libertarian Sam Ervin. These earnest reformers had been clamoring for greater privacy protections, especially from state surveillance programs. Nixon explained the issue as though he had just discovered it. In all, it seemed a lame attempt to champion the issue to protect himself from forthcoming criticism. The *Post* was not afraid to call a spade a spade. Editors declared the president's concerns for privacy disingenuous: "To date Mr. Nixon has shown little concern for anybody's privacy except his own."[59]

To demonstrate his resolve Nixon appointed a Domestic Council Committee on the Right of Privacy (DCCRP). The presidential committee, he promised, would not be just "another research group" but something poised for "high-level action." He pledged to investigate how the government collects data and protects it and to explore how citizens can gain access to records and how to safeguard personal information. After careful research, his committee would offer policy solutions and propose regulations, executive actions, and legislation where necessary.[60] On October 11, 1973, Vice President Spiro Agnew resigned from office in the face of criminal charges of extortion, tax evasion, and bribery. Nixon nominated House Minority Leader Gerald R. Ford of Michigan as vice president, the first person to be nominated under the Twenty-Fifth Amendment to the Constitution. Ford took the oath of office on December 6, 1973. Nixon put Ford in charge of the DCCRP. Nixon's Domestic Council functioned, as one former staff member recalled, as a "key institutional innovation" of the administration. Part of the executive reorganization of 1970, the council offered the administration a way to prioritize domestic issues, including legislation, budget, personnel, and policy. The council took the pressure off presidential advisors and streamlined the process of evaluation and management of policy issues that could otherwise overwhelm the White House on any given day.[61] In early 1974, privacy rose to the top of the council's short list of issues of great political importance.

Critics found the president's embrace of the privacy issue laughable given that the administration had been charged with spying, illegal surveillance, and political dirty tricks. Senator Ervin might have explained to the president that his DCCRP was unnecessary. Ervin had explored privacy issues for more than four years. In fact, the growing public unease about government computers and personal dossiers could be at least partly attributed to Ervin and the ACLU's excellent publicity work. Nixon's radio address inspired the ACLU to work up a "blueprint" for executive and legislative branch action on the issue of privacy. Sensing a political opportunity in the making, ACLU privacy staff got to work drafting legislation that would protect privacy in two primary areas. First, the organization promoted laws to safeguard a citizen's right to political privacy from the state: surveillance, wiretapping, and political dissent. Second, the ACLU drafted legislation to regulate how data could be collected, held, and distributed by government data banks and computers. Nixon staffers had learned about the debate from the ACLU's widely read publication, *The Privacy Report*. The magazine circulated among academics, White House staff, elected officials, those in the computer industry, journalists and editors, and civil libertarians in the public at large. It had done much to awaken powerful politicians and nonstate actors to the issue.[62]

Democrats refused to allow this president to co-opt the issue of privacy. Speaking for the majority, Michigan senator Philip Hart ridiculed Nixon's sudden concern for individual privacy. If the president really wanted to protect citizens, Hart argued, he should order "everyone in his Administration to refrain from political spying of any kind." The DCCRP would be just window dressing, Hart argued, "rather than a broad program of action."[63]

Watergate hung like a rotting albatross around the neck of the Republican Party, and no elected officials could escape the stench. Some Republicans hoped privacy could help strengthen the image of the party among the electorate before the upcoming midterm elections. In the House, conservative Barry Goldwater, Jr., of California, son of Arizona senator and former Republican presidential candidate, Barry Goldwater, urged the development of privacy legislation. Goldwater had been a privacy advocate for years, and in 1974 he stumped for his party to embrace the issue as public policy. Goldwater sought to link the privacy issue with conservative values in an article he penned for the ACLU's monthly journal, *The Civil Liberties Review*. He wrote, "Privacy is an essential element of every individual's right to life, liberty, and the pursuit of happiness." In this sense, the issue of privacy was essentially "conservative." As a self-proclaimed "citizen legislator," Goldwater called for Congress to pass privacy legislation before the fall elections.[64]

Amid a bipartisan debate about surveillance and privacy, the White House desperately tried to cover up its ties to the Watergate break-in. McCord's decision to trade his secrets for leniency and the Senate's new special committee caused the White House to panic. Nixon settled on a strategy to limit the scope of congressional inquiry: his current and former staff would claim executive privilege and refuse to testify publicly before Congress. Watergate historian Stanley Kutler noted: "The control of information and access to it were at the heart of the Administration's strategy."[65]

Nixon's decision to claim executive privilege in response to Watergate investigators' queries forced a constitutional crisis of unprecedented proportions. This was not the first time that Nixon had claimed the privilege to avoid cooperating with an investigation headed by Senator Ervin. With public opinion turning in his favor, however, Ervin determined it would be the president's last such attempt. Laying all his political capital on the line, Ervin appealed directly to the American public, denouncing the president's claim of executive privilege as "poppycock." Such a privilege could never be extended to cover criminal behavior, the senator proclaimed. He threatened to authorize the arrest of White House aides who failed to cooperate with his committee.[66]

Nixon's polling numbers were sinking precipitously and he was the first to blink in the confrontation over executive privilege and allowed his aides to testify. The testimony of his former staff shocked the American people as they learned that the campaign of "dirty tricks" had been approved, if not planned, by the president's top advisors. White House counsel John Dean testified that the president himself approved of the Watergate cover-up and even participated in some planning. But proof of the president's direct involvement was hard to come by.

Then someone slipped up. Alexander Butterfield, an assistant to the president, told committee staff in a private interview that President Nixon had installed, in the words of Senator Ervin, "voice-activated eavesdropping devices" in the Oval Office, the Executive Office Building, and the Cabinet Room. Ervin and the special prosecutor requested access to White House tapes, especially conversations between John Dean and the president. When Nixon refused, the Watergate committee issued subpoenas to compel the president to release the tapes. Again Nixon refused, citing executive privilege and separation of powers.

The Watergate committee took the unprecedented step of suing the president in the Federal District Court of Washington, D.C., to gain access to the tapes. Ervin denounced the president's position as "incompatible with the doctrine of the separation of powers of Government. . . . the select committee is exercising the constitutional power of the Senate to conduct the investigation, and the doctrine of the separation of powers of Government requires the President to recognize this and to refrain from obstructing the committee." Even if Nixon possessed "autocratic power" as he claimed, the Constitution certainly did not "obligate him to hinder the search for truth or forbid him voluntarily to make the tapes and memorandums available to the committee."[67]

In another unprecedented move Judge Sirica ordered Nixon to produce the tapes for the court. The judge would review them *in camera* (in judge's chambers) to respect the president's claims to executive privilege. To this generous offer Nixon proposed supplying transcripts and tapes (prepared by the president himself) to Senator John Stennis of Mississippi. Stennis would listen to the tapes to verify that the president's summaries were accurate. The special prosecutor rejected this plan. A furious Nixon ordered him fired. When his attorney general refused, Nixon fired the attorney general. By the end of the "Saturday Night Massacre" of October 20, 1973, the president had fired one special prosecutor and the two top officials in the Justice Department. The president closed the Office of Special Prosecutor, returned the investigation to the Department of Justice, and sealed all files to prevent their removal.

Surprised by the public backlash against his actions, Nixon ordered his new attorney general to appoint a new special prosecutor. The battle for access to the tapes continued, with the new prosecutor, Leon Jaworski, appealing to the Supreme Court. In July 1974 the Supreme Court ruled in *United States v. Nixon* that the president must turn over the tapes and that executive privilege would not protect from prosecution presidential aides who may have committed a crime. In its decision, the court said: "Neither the doctrine of separation of powers, nor the need for confidentiality of high-level communications" could sustain "absolute, unqualified Presidential privilege of immunity from judicial process." The court found the president's argument that "even the very important interest in confidentiality of Presidential communications is significantly diminished by production of such material for in camera inspections" difficult to accept.[68] Instead, Nixon stubbornly offered transcripts of the tapes to Jaworski. The Judiciary Committee of the House of Representatives approved three articles of impeachment against the president. Before the full House voted on those articles, and at the urging of members of his own party, Nixon resigned on August 9, 1974.[69]

Watergate had dragged on for nearly two years. The scandal devastated the White House, stripping away the dignity of the executive branch. Watergate left in its wake abundant opportunity for political reformers. The ACLU hoped to use Watergate as a prism through which Americans could come to see the issues of political surveillance, government secrecy, and executive power as related and inherently damaging to the democratic process. In a 1973 mailing to members, the ACLU identified two interrelated political problems that the Watergate scandal exposed. First, the "creation of a governmental surveillance apparatus to monitor lawful political activities" undermined First Amendment rights of free speech and association. Second, the episode revealed the administration's battle to "prevent the dissemination of information to the general public," beginning with the Pentagon Papers, in the name of "national security." The extent to which the executive branch was willing to go, admonished the ACLU, to bury "the origins of the most controversial and divisive enterprise" of the century—the war in Vietnam—undermined the democratic process. Democracy thrives, asserted the ACLU, when citizens have access to the information they need to make informed decisions. The abuse of "national security" as a pretext for government secrecy hindered the "informed exercise of political judgment" and undermined "the basic commitment to this nation of free trade of ideas."[70]

As the ACLU's efforts to capitalize on the Watergate scandal suggest, the scandal proved a boon for reformers. It helped to garner public support for substantive policy reform on issues of government transparency, privacy, and domestic security policy. It severely weakened the power of the executive branch at a time when reformers were aggressively pursuing broad-based reform of the nation's most powerful and least transparent agencies and institutions. To some reformers Watergate was not evidence of aberrant behavior. As ACLU attorneys saw it, the scandal seemed a predictable outcome of a powerful, unchecked "governmental surveillance apparatus" to monitor "lawful political activity."[71]

Watergate was in some ways an aberration attributable to Nixon's own psychological insecurities, but to blame the man is to overlook what the episode of Watergate revealed. There was a breakdown and failure of American institutions to protect key civil liberties and democratic practices in the Cold War era. Watergate exemplified those issues that had begun to unify investigative journalists, Republicans and Democrats in Congress, whistle-blowers and former bureaucratic insiders like Charles Peters, and organizations like the ACLU. Focusing narrowly on the Watergate incident obfuscates the larger citizens' movement already under way in the period before the scandal exploded onto the national scene. Watergate catalyzed a loose coalition of unlikely allies who aggressively pursued legislation aimed at restricting state power. In 1974 reformers passed the Freedom of Information Act revisions and the Privacy Act. Ensuing debates about abusive and unchecked power further strengthened the broad coalition fighting to restrain the national security state.

CHAPTER SIX

An "Effective Servant of the Public's Right to Know"

Representative Moorhead Revises FOIA

The former president entered the room late and sat down, flanked on either side by attorneys from the Department of Justice. Deposing a former president was risky business, even if that president had resigned from office in disgrace, Shattuck thought. A lot was at stake today. Nixon's own admissions could determine whether or not the former president could be held liable in a civil suit filed by his client, Morton Halperin. Did the president authorize illegal wiretaps of Halperin's home telephone in order to stop so-called "leaks"?

Shattuck smiled, thinking how remarkable this journey had been. Only five years before he had been hired by the ACLU to lead civil cases against local, state, and federal surveillance practices. Now he was deposing the former president. It seemed remarkable to the young ACLU attorney to be sitting so near the man once considered the most powerful person in the world. Now all that separated him from Nixon was a small folding card table. How the mighty had fallen, he mused.[1]

In the wake of Watergate revelations Senator Sam Ervin and Representative William Moorhead led a broad coalition of Republicans and Democrats to enforce government transparency and to protect individual privacy. Following Richard Nixon's resignation, Congress passed two historic pieces of legislation creating a new statutory framework governing the flow of information between the executive branch and civil society. These laws formed the foundation of a new domestic information policy regime.

The first piece of landmark legislation was the Freedom of Information Act (FOIA) revisions, passed in 1974. This revised law required agencies—including the FBI and CIA—to respond to requests promptly and placed the onus on institutions to justify withholding of classified materials in federal court. The *Washington Post* called the new rules "reasonable" and noted that they would likely result in "more prompt and extensive disclosure of information." Another journalist predicted that the new law would offer the media and the American public a "genuine tool of discovery."[2]

The second bill, the Privacy Act, signed into law in 1974, was the darling of both conservatives and liberals. Since revelations in 1970 that the government maintained millions of dossiers on its citizens, legislators and their constituents had worried over government invasions of privacy. The new law aimed to balance the government's need for information with an individual's "right to privacy," creating mechanisms that restricted the sharing and distribution of personal information among executive-level agencies. The Privacy Act allowed individuals to access personal files maintained by federal agencies and correct inaccurate information contained therein.[3]

Public interest groups seized upon these new tools to probe the deepest recesses of the national security state—for so long a labyrinth of secrecy operating outside democratic processes. The ACLU launched a campaign to encourage journalists, scholars, and individuals to file requests for information related to national security programs. The material they successfully obtained through FOIA requests confirmed what many Americans already suspected: some agencies within the U.S. government operated outside democratic oversight and checks and balances.

The ACLU's organizational success was due, in part, to the strategy it established in the early 1970s to pursue reform through both litigation and legislation. Increasingly the organization relied on the expertise of a carefully cultivated network of current and former Washington insiders, elected officials, and powerful media interests to see its policy goals realized. The ACLU created new organizations with resources devoted exclusively to pursuing domestic security policy reform. The success of these organizations depended upon the input of professional critics— individuals who had once worked for these agencies, and therefore, were uniquely positioned to critique what one journalist called the "shadowland" of the security state.[4] Professional critics lent legitimacy to the reform effort and brought much-needed expertise to complicated jurisprudential and legislative strategies to reform national security institutions.

In addition to the information obtained through FOIA requests, the Senate Watergate investigation prompted yearlong House and Senate investigations into the nation's intelligence agencies. Scholars have credited these congressional committees, chaired respectively by Senator Frank Church (D-ID) and Representative Otis Pike (D-NY), with exposing the abuses of national intelligence agencies.[5] Though their work has accurately placed institutional reforms within a broader context of congressional-executive tussles for power, historians have rarely examined civil society's role in this reform effort, more specifically the contributions of public advocacy groups in promoting institutional reform. Public advocacy groups played a significant role in building a case for and bringing public attention to national security policy reform. Congress tapped the human resources of organizations like the ACLU and newly formed groups such as the Committee for Public Justice and the Center for National Security Studies. Drawing on the expertise of professional critics like Morton Halperin, these organizations promoted public debate about the abuses of the national security apparatus before congressional committees made such abuses popular.

Morton Halperin had never considered himself a radical. With a doctorate in government from Yale, which he parlayed into a promising career in civil service with the Department of Defense, he belonged to the establishment. He was stunned in 1971 to learn that he had been the target of an FBI wiretap ordered by his former boss, National Security Advisor (and later Secretary of State) Henry Kissinger.[6] It happened like this: while serving as deputy assistant secretary of defense for the Johnson administration, Halperin worked closely with Leslie Gelb to compile the Vietnam assessment known as the Pentagon Papers. In 1969 Halperin joined the National Security Council staff. It wasn't long before his boss, Henry Kissinger, began to suspect NSC staff of leaking information about the secret bombing of Cambodia to the press.[7] Through FBI Director J. Edgar Hoover, Kissinger arranged a wiretap on Halperin's home telephone. Making no secret of his disillusionment with the administration's expansion of the war into Laos and Cambodia, Halperin left the administration and joined the Brookings Institute.[8] Halperin became a vocal critic of the Nixon administration in 1971 when it attempted to halt the publication of the Pentagon Papers, which, Halperin claimed, "contained nothing which would cause serious injury to national security." When the Supreme Court ruled in favor of the *New York Times*, the administration sued the man responsible for leaking the report, former NSC staffer and Halperin's friend Daniel Ellsberg. At Ellsberg's trial the prosecution submitted evidence against Ellsberg that had been acquired through a wiretap on Halperin's home telephone. The Organized Crime Act of 1970 required the attorney general to disclose surveillance to a defendant in any proceeding. The Department of Justice violated this law with the Halperin wiretap by not informing Ellsberg at his trial that he had been overheard on the wiretap. Because the evidence was obtained illegally, the judge dismissed the criminal trial. Apparently, Director Hoover had been so uncomfortable with the Kissinger wiretaps that he kept the records separate from other domestic intelligence gathered by the agency, first in his own office, and later in his deputy's. Upon Hoover's death on May 2, 1972, the White House retrieved the records. Acting FBI Director William Ruckelshaus found the wiretap transcripts in John Erlichman's safe at the White House and publicly admitted that the White House had wiretapped a former NSC staffer's home telephone for twenty-one months.[9] Incensed over the invasion of his privacy, Halperin arranged a meeting with the local ACLU to discuss his legal options. John Shattuck, the legal director of the organization's Washington, D.C., office, encouraged him to sue the officials who had tapped him.[10]

Halperin turned to the ACLU for legal advice because the organization had earned a reputation for successfully challenging expansive executive power, particularly in the areas of wiretapping, surveillance, and personal privacy. Part of the ACLU's success lay in its decision in 1971 to broaden its power base by partnering with new interest groups. These organizations helped the ACLU expand its knowledge base, as well as reach broader audiences. One affiliation, the Committee for Public Justice (founded in 1971), brought big Hollywood names (Marlon Brando, Candice Bergen, and Warren Beatty, to name a few) together with Washington insiders who advocated institutional reform (former attorney general Ramsey Clark, former aide to Secretary of Defense Robert McNamara, Adam Yarmolinsky, and Roger Wilkins, former assistant attorney general and committee chairman) to speak out on select issues. ACLU executives hoped celebrities might garner public interest on a whole range of policy issues and "unite individuals from different segments of society who are concerned about the current situation in the country and who have not, in many instances, hitherto spoken out."[11]

Spurred on by the battle over the publication of the Pentagon Papers, the committee organized a conference on government secrecy. Invitees included historians, journalists, attorneys, public officials, and scientists. As planning unfolded, *Washington Post* reporters broke the Watergate story and Committee Director Stephen Gillers expanded the original program to include discussion of the country's secret national security government. As Gillers saw it, Watergate revealed that secrecy was not an "appendage to the constitutional system; it is a whole separate system, and it involves actions as well as information." The challenge for reformers, Gillers believed, lay in integrating these two "systems."[12]

Morton Halperin proved a persuasive advocate for reform. Since his initial contact with the ACLU, Halperin had become increasingly strident in his opposition to expansive executive power in the name of national security. As a former NSC staff member he offered expertise that few, if any, elected officials could claim on issues related to the inner workings of the national security apparatus. National security intellectuals like Halperin, Ellsberg, and other conference attendees bridged the divide between congressional efforts to reassert checks and balances over the executive branch and the movement among civil libertarians and other interest groups to develop broad policy reform in the areas of secrecy, classification, surveillance, and privacy. These professionals had a unique perspective of the tensions inherent in the relationship between an open democratic society and extrademocratic security agencies tasked with maintaining the nation's security.

Personally, Halperin had come to believe that the secret national security government was corrupting the constitutional system. Without transparency there could be no effective oversight. Without oversight the founding fathers' vision of carefully balanced power between the three branches of government could not exist. As he explained to conference attendees, neither the judicial nor legislative branches imposed adequate checks and balances over the national security apparatus. The legislative branch had been reluctant to challenge executive power in the realm of national security. The secrecy that blanketed national security agencies and their activities discouraged congressional oversight because elected officials had nothing to gain politically by exerting traditional oversight functions. As one story went, Senator John Stennis of Mississippi, chairman of the Armed Services Committee, had once told the director of the CIA, "You just go do your work, and you don't have to come back to me with all this information." The problem was one of access: executive secrecy made congressional investigations virtually impossible. The subcommittee of the House Appropriations Committee in charge of CIA oversight, Halperin noted, had a secret membership—many congressmen did not want their participation known! Denied the ability to keep their constituents apprised of their activities, politicians could not rally public support for institutional reform.[13]

Attendees did not expect to solve the problems of secret government over the course of the Committee for Public Justice's two-day conference. Few agreed on the appropriate level of oversight or transparency that was needed. Most, however, believed that compromise could, and should, be found to make government more transparent. Many advocated for legislation to define formally the limits of the national security government's power. Such reform could only come from within the halls of Congress, and attendees left the conference less than optimistic that lawmakers would move swiftly on the issues of government transparency.[14]

Watergate proved a powerful motivator to many on Capitol Hill. For years the public had been growing increasingly distrustful of their elected officials and institutions. The political scandal of the century exacerbated this trend.[15] Democrats hoped that the public would punish the Republicans, the party of Watergate, in the 1974 midterm elections, by delivering to the Democrats an overwhelming majority in both houses of Congress. In a post-Watergate age even popular incumbents like seven-term congressman William Moorhead worried that cynical voters would associate them with the Washington status quo. In 1974 Moorhead lamented, gone were the days when the average American voter "was occasionally willing to give a governmental official the benefit of the doubt in the performance of his duties." Given the recent problems of Vietnam, a lackluster economy, social upheaval, and the failure of institutions to solve these problems, "government officials no longer enjoy the good will of their fellow citizens . . . we often have two strikes against us before we ever get into the batter's box."[16] Watergate created, Moorhead believed, a public "crisis in confidence in government"—a problem of epic proportions, even greater than the energy crisis.[17]

Nevertheless, in times of crisis industrious politicians like Moorhead saw political opportunity. After years of futilely sponsoring laws about privacy and transparency, Moorhead believed that 1974 might be the right year to achieve reform. As *Times* editors noted, the year was marked by "an impressive array of legislators, administrators and citizen experts" who "have reached general accords on several basic principles to govern" the operation and maintenance of federal data banks.[18] These principles included the acknowledgment that all federal information should be accessible to the public, and that citizens should have access to files to review them for accuracy.

With bipartisan support, Moorhead moved to enhance government transparency and protect individual privacy. Moorhead's single-minded resolve on these issues belied his otherwise quiet demeanor in the Capitol and reputation as a "nice guy" who "did not "make waves." In the seven years since Congress first enacted freedom of information legislation, it had not, in Moorhead's opinion, created a "fully informed public in a democratic society." As chairman of the Subcommittee on Foreign Operations and Government Information, Moorhead had heard stories from journalists and organizations to prove his point; bureaucrats had failed overwhelmingly to comply with the principles of FOIA. Bolstered by this testimony, the congressman worked up revisions to the original statute. The "widespread use of government secrecy" to hide information from "the press, the American public, and their elected representatives in Congress," Moorhead believed, threatened the health of democracy. The overuse of the "nation's security classification system" allowed the executive to "withhold vast amounts of information needed by Congress to carry out [its] Constitutional responsibilities."[19]

Moorhead's FOIA revisions addressed two complaints commonly expressed by FOIA requestors. First, agency response time had been historically sluggish—taking months, and occasionally years. The new bill would require an agency to respond within ten working days, twenty for an appeal, with a possible ten-day extension. Moorhead also addressed the executive branch's penchant for overclassifying documents. The Watergate scandal exposed the executive branch's willingness to use the "national security" label in order to operate outside the law. Moorhead's revisions allowed exemptions for classified documents, but empowered federal district court judges to examine documents *in camera* to determine whether the documents were legitimately exempt from disclosure under one of nine categories. This marked a departure from past policies that had granted the executive branch the power to make the final decision. It set an important precedent, giving courts a role to play in ascertaining what information could and could not be made public in the name of national security, and it challenged long-held beliefs about executive branch prerogatives and presidential authority. Files related to law enforcement (including the FBI and CIA) could be withheld only if the agency offered proof that their release would interfere with criminal proceedings. To improve congressional oversight of FOIA compliance, Moorhead's legislation required government agencies to publish annual reports on FOIA requests, including the number of refusals and the reasons for them, judicial appeals, and the individual responsible for each denial. If an agency employee was found by a court to have acted capriciously in withholding information, the law empowered the Civil Service Commission to impose disciplinary action. The bill also required the attorney general to publish an annual report of all the freedom of information cases resulting from the act and the fees and penalties associated with them.[20]

The Nixon administration had virulently opposed FOIA revisions. White House counsel, staff, and the NSC had urged a presidential veto.

They reasoned that the White House would then load a revised bill with "objectionable features" to sustain a veto in the Senate.[21] If passed, FOIA revision legislation promised to solve one of the most urgent issues of reformers—lack of government transparency. But ACLU leaders had long warned that secrecy was only one part of a larger problem—the power of the executive branch to impinge upon the privacy of individuals. To deflect criticism and salvage his party, President Richard Nixon announced he would make privacy legislation a priority in early 1974. Republicans had seized upon the privacy issue as a rallying point to refocus legislative priorities and redeem their party in the minds of the American people. The House Republican Research Committee named the privacy issue a top legislative issue for the year, and the House Republican Task Force on Privacy denounced government surveillance as "repugnant," recommended legislation to prohibit "unauthorized surveillance," and called for further clarification on existing legislation. The committee welcomed the courts' recent move to "circumscribe unauthorized wiretaps," and it supported wiretaps and surveillance in national security cases if agencies could convince a court of "probable cause." To fend off criticism that privacy protections hindered law enforcement and weakened national security, Republicans assured the public that privacy protections need not "lessen the capability of the government to protect and defend the American people." Republicans shared concerns with civil libertarians about the federal government's collection and use of personal information. Government data banks held vast quantities of personal information, and "individual[s] possess inadequate remedies for the correction" of data abuses. Data inaccuracies were likely to go unreported "simply because the individual involved did not know of the data being collected about him." The misuse of a wide range of personal information including the social security number, personal financial information, consumer credit reports, school, juvenile and arrest records, and personal medical records worried Republicans that "George Orwell's *1984* may become a reality in 1976."[22]

The Republican Task Force recommended legislation to address these issues. An early ally in their effort was predictably conservative Democrat Senator Sam Ervin. No one had been a more ardent proponent of privacy legislation than Ervin. Since his first investigations into government data banks in the 1960s, the senator had tried unsuccessfully to pass privacy legislation. Ervin first attempted to pass privacy legislation for federal employees in 1967. In each successive Congress, a version of his privacy bill passed the Senate, but never made it out of committee in the House. Watergate changed that.[23]

In 1974, after years of meticulous research and probing into the federal government's data bank systems, Ervin's Subcommittee on Constitutional Rights published a comprehensive report examining the federal government's data bank system. The report offered robust evidence of the government's reliance on computer data banks to maintain personal information on millions of its citizens. Ervin's staff identified some 858 data banks maintained by 54 federal agencies with records totaling some 1.25 billion. Most disturbing to lawmakers was the committee's finding that a majority of executive-level data banks existed without congressional authorization. As a consequence, most elected officials (and therefore their constituents) knew little, if anything, about the information contained in those files and had no legal means to access them. The report concluded that, though many agencies promised the confidentiality of their records, executive data banks frequently exchanged data.[24]

Ervin and the ACLU had long been allies on the issue of privacy, and, like Ervin, the organization had made privacy legislation a top priority since the early 1970s. The ACLU had long opposed the "computerization of manual record systems of personal information by government and commercial bodies unless proper standards and safeguards for privacy and due process are first provided." ACLU attorneys recommended that all Americans be granted access to their government records, be allowed to contest the accuracy of those records, and be authorized to place explanatory information in their file. They likewise proposed that criminal charges be expunged if trials did not result in convictions. The First Amendment, urged the Board of Directors, was "so fundamental as to preclude completely the collection of information" about constitutionally protected activities, like the right to dissent, "however compelling the interest which the government may seek to assert."[25]

In the wake of Watergate this pro-privacy triumvirate—conservatives, liberals, and civil libertarians—joined together to support Ervin and Moorhead's bill, the Privacy Act of 1974. In the House, Moorhead and thirteen cosponsors including Democrats John Moss, Ed Koch (NY), and Bella Abzug (NY), joined by Republicans Barry Goldwater, Jr., John Erlenborn (IL), Gilbert Gude (MD), and Charles Thone (NE), offered a bill to protect individual privacy and force government transparency on individual records. In the Senate, Ervin had the support of members from across the political spectrum including Republicans Barry Goldwater, James Buckley (a Conservative who caucused with the Republicans), and Charles Percy, as well as Democrats Warren Magnuson, Phil Hart, and Hubert Humphrey. Congress ultimately passed Ervin's more moderate privacy bill, which placed the onus to ensure the accuracy of data on the individual, not the federal government.

The Privacy Act of 1974 required most federal agencies to register their data banks. Citizens would be allowed to petition to review their files and conect any erroneous infomation. To secure broad bipartisan support for the bill, liberals compromised with conservatives who demanded exemptions for law enforcement and national security agencies—such as the FBI and CIA—from its disclosure provisions.[26] Conservatives worried that disclosures would weaken the nation's defense. On this issue they straddled two seemingly incompatible ideological principles. While they often supported the growth of a vast national defense structure, they consistently sought to limit the gowth of govemment. As Senator Barry Goldwater succinctly explained in *The Conscience of a Conservative*, the United States needed an expansive national security apparatus to fight the "Soviet menace," even as Big Govemment threatened to be the "chief instrument for thwafting man's liberty." Privacy advocates, such as the ACLU, supported the landmark legislation though they protested efforts to exempt nalional security agencies from its requirements.[27]

Moorhead delayed the House vote on FOIA revisions until after the Supreme Court ruled in *U.S. v. Nixon*. The court's decision, issued on July 24, 1974, did recognize the constitutional basis for executive privilege—finding that the executive branch did have the need for some confidentiality in its decision making—but it also recognized the need for a balance of powers. As one scholar wrote, the justices found that executive privilege would not be "'significantly diminished' if the President produced the tapes for an *in camera* scrutiny by the judiciary." The case established the ground rules for use of executive privilege that were not inconsistent with Moorhead's bill.[28] Though Congress was eager to vote on the groundbreaking legislation, elected officials waited to see what a disgraced and besieged President Nixon would do. When Nixon resigned on August 9, 1974, he left his successor Gerald Ford (himself the House Minority Leader only nine months before) to battle over the finer points of transparency and privacy legislation.

Like his predecessor, President Ford adamantly opposed the FOIA bill, but a close examination of Ford's public record made many dismiss his objections as disingenuous and politically driven. During the Johnson administration, Congressman Ford and many of his Republican colleagues had clamored for greater transparency in the executive branch, particularly regarding the war in Vietnam.[29] National media outlets, overwhelmingly supportive of proposed FOIA revisions, challenged the new president to stay true to his past support for transparency. The *New York Times* reminded Ford that he had once called the executive branch's efforts to deny information to the legislative branch and the American public an espousal of "some power akin to the divine right of kings." The *Post* called the legislation a harbinger for the "future of openness in government" and predicted it would be an "effective servant of the public's right to know." It reminded the president that the bill was "in tune with [President Ford's] recent appeals for openness" and promised FOIA revisions would help to "reduce public mistrust of government."[30] Ford's staff (many of whom were holdovers from the Nixon administration) recognized how politically unpopular a veto of FOIA revisions would be with the American public. In a post-Watergate political climate, better to be against "motherhood," one quipped, than against the concept of "freedom of information." Nevertheless, they advised Ford to veto the "obnoxious" bill.[31] Nixon's staff, apparently still harboring animosity toward the "liberal" mass media, dismissed the bill as another piece of legislation crafted for special interests. One White House aide allegedly complained, "who gives a damn [about a veto] besides the *Washington Post* and the *New York Times*?" But this was precisely the point. As one *Post* editorial explained, FOIA revisions would be a powerful tool for a democratic government. The new FOIA bill, the paper wrote, "goes to the heart of what a free society is all about." If it was special interest legislation, the editors wrote sarcastically, it was intended to "assist the very special interest of the American people in being informed about the processes and practices of their government."[32] The new administration seemed oblivious to this important point.

On Capitol Hill, liberals and conservatives united to support the new legislation. Ted Kennedy managed the bill in the Senate and with his counterpart in the House, William Moorhead, gave the new president time to consider the bill and to recommend any necessary changes before they put it to a vote.[33] Ford assured Kennedy and Moorhead that he supported the "spirit" of the bill, but he urged them to compromise with the White House on a few key provisions. The administration objected to the burden, in both time and dollars, the new rules would impose on executive agencies. Forcing agencies to defend their classification of documents in a court of law—paragraph by paragraph—would compel civil servants to scour thousands of pages of documents. "More flexible criteria" should dictate agency responses, Ford urged, so as "not to dilute the primary responsibilities of these law enforcement activities." The president considered the imposed agency response times unrealistic for an expansive bureaucracy.[34]

In addition to imposing unrealistic burdens on the bureaucracy, Ford insisted that compliance with the new law would endanger the nation's security. The president trotted out old tropes, warning that "military or intelligence secrets and diplomatic relations could be adversely affected" by FOIA revisions. The president opposed judicial review of top-secret classified documents. This provision, he claimed, afforded judges the opportunity to make a judgment in "sensitive and complex areas where they have no particular expertise." Declaring the bill "unconstitutional and unworkable" in its current form, the president vetoed it on October 17, 1974.[35]

Following as it did on the heels of Ford's most controversial decision as president—the full pardon of his predecessor Richard Nixon for crimes he may have committed as president—the president had not endeared himself to the American public.[36] Juxtaposed with the pardon, the presidential veto suggested to Americans that Ford was not interested in being a different kind of president. The *Post* underscored this sentiment, writing that the president's veto of the FOIA bill undermined the "spirit of the kind of relationship between government and the public that Mr. Ford assured the Congress he wanted" when he took office. Ford's opposition to the legislation, wrote the editors at the *Los Angeles Times*, was based on the "alarmist view" that the courts would use the bill to reveal national secrets and endanger national security. The president seemed ignorant of congressional intent: "to stop the abuse of classifying information that by any rational standard cannot be remotely connected to national security."[37] As Congress mulled over the president's veto, Attorney General William Saxbe publicly acknowledged the FBI's top-secret domestic spying operation, COINTELPRO. It could not have come at a worse time for the beleaguered president.

The attorney general was the victim of events beyond his control. Following the Media, Pennsylvania, break-in by the Citizens' Commission to Investigate the FBI, NBC television news journalist Carl Stern had filed an FOIA request for documents relating to the FBI's COINTELPRO–New Left program.[38] Started in the 1960s by Director Hoover, the program was, according to historian Richard Gid Powers, the "Bureau's covert war" against the New Left radical student movement. The program broke with bureau guidelines that had until then required all domestic targets to have a connection with an international movement. Before the burglary in Media, according to Powers, the agency had never been subject to public scrutiny, and this "luxury" had allowed Director Hoover to develop programs that clearly abused the power of the agency. The burglary opened up these secret programs for public scrutiny and enabled investigative journalists like Stern to file FOIA requests and publicly expose the programs.

Then attorney general Richard Kleindienst denied Stern's request, and the journalist sued the Department of Justice in federal district court under the original FOIA. The court ordered the Justice Department to release documents to Stern in December 1973. Receiving only some of the documents he requested, Stern filed a followup request with FBI Director Clarence Kelley in 1974. Kelley denied it, and Stern appealed to his boss, Attorney General William Saxbe. Considering Stern's request, Saxbe came across some COINTELPRO materials that concerned him. He ordered his assistant attorney general, Henry Petersen, to conduct an internal review. When he read Petersen's report months later, Saxbe decided to preempt a sensational news story by going public and emphasizing the positive, rather than negative, aspects of FBI domestic surveillance activity under Director J. Edgar Hoover. On November 18, 1974, Saxbe released the report, underscoring that only 1 percent of the COINTELPRO programs had been illegal.[39]

Unfortunately for the Ford administration, which was battling Congress over the finer points of the proposed FOIA revisions, Saxbe's attempt to spin unlawful FBI activities failed miserably. Rather than congratulate the attorney general for his candor, FOIA supporters used the episode to rally support to override the presidential veto of FOIA revisions. Stern's three-year odyssey to obtain records of extralegal FBI activity helped firm congressional resolve to provide the media and other interested parties with better tools to investigate the executive branch. Three days after Saxbe disclosed the Petersen report, on November 21, 1974, Congress overrode the president's veto and the Freedom of Information Act revisions became law.[40]

Ford and his staff learned the hard way that the American public and Congress were increasingly skeptical of the executive branch's claims of secrecy in the name of national security. Columnist Joseph Kraft bemoaned the declining respect that many Americans held for the concept of "national security." Only years before, Kraft observed, the term "national security" had "conferred a kind of grace" on those "conscientious Americans" who "labored diligently in thankless tasks all over the world." Political leaders who pursued the nation's national security interests "were almost automatically deemed 'responsible.'" Watergate and Vietnam, Kraft concluded, had broken that sacred trust. Now, Kraft lamented, "national security has become a term of scorn and secret operations an object of automatic suspicion."[41] As former State Department and CIA staffer Arthur Cox put it, Watergate and Vietnam had revealed the "myths" of national security—too often used as a cover to deceive the American people. The public had learned that "countless lies [had been] perpetrated under cover of a vast system of executive secrecy, justified on grounds of protecting our national security."[42]

President Ford hoped that affixing his signature to the Privacy Act on New Years' Eve, 1974, would help him shore up flagging public support. And though he did not believe privacy was a constitutionally guaranteed right, he sympathized with citizens concerned about privacy violations at the hands of big institutions. "People feel threatened by big information systems just as they are troubled by the growth of big government, big business, big unions, and by big institutions generally," he stated. "Anxiety is experienced because big systems and big organizations seem inhuman in that they appear not to respect a person as an individual but treat him as just another unit in a broad category of persons."[43] Berkeley Free Speech radical Mario Savio could not have said it better.

With the passage of FOIA revisions and the Privacy Act, the Ford administration hoped that Congress had exorcised the ghosts of Watergate and that the constitutional crisis between the legislative and executive branches had been averted. Indeed, elected officials like Moss, Moorhead, and Ervin and their public interest group allies such as the ACLU, the American Bar Association, and Common Cause, for whom these laws represented years of investigation, public relations work, and advocacy, had reason to celebrate. Together the revised FOIA rules and Privacy Act offered a new legal framework for the collection and exchange of information in a postmodern democracy.

Despite such legislative achievements, top brass at the ACLU remained unsatisfied. Many within the organization believed that the presidential scandal had introduced constitutional issues, especially the executive branch's use of the national security agencies for political purposes that had yet to be adequately investigated. To consider these issues, the ACLU Foundation, with financial assistance from the Fund for Peace, founded the Center for National Security Studies (CNSS) to focus exclusively on the problems of extrademocratic agencies, specifically the national security state. The ACLU chose a Washington attorney formerly with the Institute for Policy Studies, Robert Borosage, to lead the organization. In a statement to the press Borosage explained that CNSS would investigate the national security state to ensure that its capacities are not "employed to subvert our democracy at home." CNSS conferences would explore "the ominous growth of state power which has developed, both at home and abroad, under the banner of 'national security.'" For a quarter century Americans "witnessed the alarming growth of the national security state, and the expansion of Executive power and prerogative." Through public forums, CNSS hoped to promote "a public re-appraisal of the purposes and policies of our national security institutions" including the CIA, NSC, military establishment, FBI, and Law Enforcement Assistance Administration. CNSS projects would fight the assumption that "matters of 'national security' are above the limits of the law, and beyond the control of the Congress or the people." In the aftermath of the twin crises of Watergate and Vietnam, the powers of the executive branch and the national security institutions remained unchecked. CNSS pledged to "help foster public consideration of national security issues" by working with citizens and other groups to "expose policies decided in secret to public discussion and questioning. Only if citizens demand a restructuring of these institutions" can Americans be certain "that these institutions do not become a permanent threat to the liberties and security they claim to protect."[44]

CNSS attracted former security insiders like Morton Halperin, as well as attorneys and journalists. In addition to its own research interests, the center sponsored independent projects, including journalist Neil Sheehan's study of America's involvement in Vietnam. CNSS had ten full-time staffers who believed that the Vietnam War and Watergate stood as "shameful monuments to the widely shared assumption that matters of 'national security' are above the limits of the law, and beyond the control of the Congress or the people." They drew upon their connections in the establishment and the media to "provide a constant voice against a military definition of security" and redefine security needs with greater attention to constitutionally protected civil liberties. In the post-Watergate crisis atmosphere, many staff members saw endless legislative possibilities. The CNSS office in Washington, D.C., attracted a growing network of professional critics who could "contribute to a public re-appraisal of the purposes and policies of our national security institutions." Through conference sponsorship, assemblies, and public meetings, CNSS staff strove to foster "broad public debate" on national security issues and to develop alternative policy proposals so that institutions might be more accountable to Congress and the people. The CNSS was funded by grants from the Abelard Foundation, Field Foundation, and Stern Foundation and was sponsored by the Fund for Peace. Halperin served as director of the Project on National Security and Civil Liberties, a joint project of the ACLU and CNSS, which allowed him to join his experience working in the national security apparatus with his desire to protect civil liberties.[45]

In September 1974, while President Ford and Congress locked horns over revisions of the Freedom of Information Act, CNSS sponsored its first conference on "The CIA and Covert Action." Senator Philip Hart, and Senator Edward Brooke, a Republican from Massachusetts and the Senate's only African American member, hosted the event at the new Senate Office Building (now called the Dirksen Senate Office Building). Present and former CIA staff, national security intellectuals, scholars, and elected officials gathered to debate the purpose and future of the CIA. Panels included discussion of the agency's efforts to destabilize Chile and surreptitious and covert operations both in the United States and abroad. Participants questioned the legal and political implications of the CIA's existence, underscoring the problems of a secret agency within a democratic society.[46] Most participants were critical of the agency and its power. CIA Director William Colby was a lone voice in the wilderness, defending the agency and its actions and debating security policy in a public forum. No CIA director had ever before participated in a freewheeling public debate about the nature of the nation's most powerful intelligence agency and a cornerstone of the national security state.[47]

Colby's defense of the agency rested on the basic proposition, opposed by many in attendance, that secrecy was not incompatible with democratic practice. Using the analogy of the military, Colby argued that though the armed forces operated within the contexts of a democratic society, "the public does not demand that our war plans be published." Similarly, Colby reasoned, "judicial conferences and grand-jury proceedings are not conducted in public," yet the American public remains relatively assured that justice is being delivered. To his congressional critics, Colby noted that even Congress "conduct[s] some of its business in executive session, while remaining accountable to the voters for the legislation it passes." In other words, American democratic institutions had always shielded themselves from the prying eyes of the polity. Colby conceded that the CIA could be more transparent to the American public, but that a compromise must be found that respected "legitimate public inquiry" and protected "the necessary secrecy of the sources and methods of our intelligence, which would dry up if publicized." Rather than making the CIA's practices more transparent to the greater public, the director proposed that Congress exercise greater oversight of the agency. Recent disclosures of the agency's "bad secrets" by journalists and scholars were "an essential part" of the democratic process, and Colby himself had been involved in declassifying materials. But he cautioned that some secrets needed to be maintained and proposed new laws to criminalize the publication of "good secrets." Who should determine what constitutes legitimately classified materials, asked one conference attendee. Judges should determine the appropriateness of classification, Colby answered.[48] Few in the audience missed the significance of this statement. The sitting director of the nation's most powerful secret agency had just acknowledged the need for oversight of the nation's security state.

Just a week after the conference, Seymour Hersh, a Pulitzer Prize–winning journalist, published a carefully researched account of CIA efforts to depose Chile's democratically elected president, Salvadore Allende, in the early 1970s.[49] Hersh's front-page story suggested that the Nixon administration had lied repeatedly to Congress about its role in destabilizing the Allende government. Senate Majority Leader Mike Mansfield recognized an opportunity to exert greater congressional control over the CIA, which he had been trying to do for a decade. Congress had maintained an uneasy relationship with the secret intelligence agency. What drove Mansfield and his allies to demand greater oversight in the 1970s was not a belief that the CIA did not function properly, but a prevalent belief that the activities of the agency were incompatible with the tenets of modern democratic government. The Watergate revelations had emboldened Congress to strengthen oversight, particularly of the CIA. Liberals in the House and Senate introduced legislation to ban all covert activity. Though the bills did not pass, they suggested an increase in congressional sensitivity to intelligence abuses. Congress did pass the Hughes-Ryan amendment to the Foreign Assistance Act, increasing congressional oversight of the CIA by requiring the agency to report to six congressional committees (up from four), including Mansfield's own Senate Committee on Foreign Relations, and the House Foreign Affairs Committee. Hughes-Ryan also required the president to brief these committees when covert action was required (generally thought to be within forty-eight hours).[50] Mansfield proposed a Senate resolution to create a special investigatory committee to look into allegations made by Hersh and others.

En route to the family's annual holiday ski vacation in Vail, Colorado, President Ford opened his Sunday *Times* to find a shocking front-page exposé about the CIA by Seymour Hersh. According to anonymous government insiders, the CIA had "conducted a massive, illegal domestic intelligence operation during the Nixon administration against the antiwar movement and other dissident groups" in violation of the agency charter. The 1947 National Security Act strictly forbade the agency from any "police, subpoena, law enforcement powers or internal security functions" on American soil. Hersh contended that the agency maintained some 10,000 files on American citizens.[51]

From Vail Ford telephoned Colby, who had known about Hersh's story for a few days. Was it true, the president wanted to know? Colby assured him that the agency was not currently involved in any "improper activity." Though some officers had participated in "improper actions" in the past, they were the exception rather than the rule. The director assured Ford that all questionable programs had been terminated. Later, in a personal briefing to the president, Colby showed Ford "the Family Jewels," a report detailing all CIA illegal activities, many on domestic soil. Colby acknowledged that some officers were "recruited or inserted" into dissident groups in the United States "to establish their credentials to collect foreign intelligence overseas." Any information that these officers collected in the course of their training ("by-product information" as Colby called it) had been passed on to the FBI.[52]

Ford's aides, especially Chief of Staff Donald Rumsfeld and press secretary Ron Nessen, worried that Hersh's account had the potential to become a second Watergate. The president, they concluded, did not seem to appreciate the gravity of the situation. But Ford's aides misread him. Ford had long been an ardent defender of the CIA and its covert and intelligence analysis activities. He had served on the House Intelligence Oversight Subcommittee of the House Appropriations Committee, where he had, at times, questioned the agency's representatives in executive session and public hearings. But Ford also had a history of ardently defending the agency and had denounced those who tried to publicize CIA activities.[53] The president was not an intellectual; he did not ponder the constitutional issues related to the secret activities of the domestic and international security state. Any congressional investigations, he believed, would be inherently political and driven by overzealous staff members, rather than a desire to get at the truth. In Ford's mind one did not question those agencies that served to protect the national security—period.[54]

At the urging of Deputy Chief of Staff Richard Cheney, however, the president appointed a blue-ribbon commission on January 4, 1975, to investigate CIA domestic intelligence abuses. Headed by Vice President Nelson Rockefeller, the Commission on CIA Activities within the United States was widely denounced as a not-so-subtle effort to stymie congressional inquiry. The ACLU spoke for the administration's critics when it declared that the commission seemed designed to "avoid a full public review [rather] than to facilitate one." In the wake of Watergate the American public, the media, and Congress were not willing to be duped again. An inside job would not suffice.[55] Critics argued that the executive branch had proven incapable of investigating and regulating itself.

Americans were right to be skeptical of the executive branch's ability to police itself. On January 10, 1975, the army announced that had it had "found" dossiers on political dissenters that were supposed to have been destroyed in the wake of Senator Ervin's investigation into domestic spying by the U.S. Army four years earlier. Many on Capitol Hill agreed that if Congress wanted to know the extent of CIA impropriety, it would have to investigate the national security agency itself. The Senate approved a resolution to establish the Select Committee to Study Governmental Operations with Respect to Intelligence Activities on January 27, 1975, and the House established its own committee a few weeks later.

With Congress focused on intelligence investigations, public advocacy groups began the herculean task of forcing government transparency by using the new FOIA law. When Congress passed the FOIA revisions in 1974, the national media praised the act but noted that to be effective the media would have to use it. The original FOIA, commented *Post* editors, was "useful to those with the perseverance to keep pushing" for information. As the Stern case demonstrated, the most tenacious reporters faced years of litigation and missed deadlines. The new law solved many of these problems, but only civil society would determine its success: "Learning how government business is done is the business of the media, and [FOIA revisions] could help," observed the *Post*.[56] Advocacy groups sponsored educational workshops to teach members of the press and the general public how to use the new FOIA law to investigate secret government.

The CNSS pooled resources to jump-start the effort to make FOIA a practical tool. Teaming up with ACLU attorneys, CNSS staffers created the Project on Freedom of Information and the National Security, a program to educate the American public about their rights as citizens in the context of new transparency laws. The project aimed "to secure the release of information needed for an informed public debate on matters of national defense and foreign policy." Using educational tools, like a published pamphlet explaining how FOIA revisions worked, the project held public meetings in the northeast corridor advising scholars, journalists, and interested citizens how to properly request information from the government. Meeting topics included practical information such as where to mail FOIA requests (including the addresses of agencies such as the Department of Defense, State Department, CIA, and NSC) and guidance on who might be expected to pay the attorney fees if the request goes to court (the agency that refused the request must pay, if the court decides in favor of the plaintiff). The project even offered requestors a sample FOIA request letter to use as a template.[57]

The project's training sessions bore fruit, and FOIA requests poured into federal agencies. In 1973 the FBI received an average of five requests per week. The total number of requests in 1974 rose to 447 total requests. Following the FOIA revisions, the Bureau received 705 requests in the first three months of 1975. Meeting these requests, Attorney General Edward Levi complained, meant dispersing some 700,000 pages of agency files. This estimate did not include one request that would compel the disclosure of some 3 million pages on the Communist Party. Levi personally thought complaints that FOIA did not go far enough and that the government still maintained too much secrecy disingenuous.[58]

Levi had good reason to be displeased by the new law. The Department of Justice bore the brunt of the administrative burden created by the FOIA revisions. The attorney general thought Congress had largely overreacted to the crimes of Watergate. Levi believed rightly that power had been a corruptive force in the White House long before Richard Nixon moved in. Congress had oversimplified the transparency issues, Levi believed, by pitting the "people's right to know" against the "President's personal prerogative." The issue, as Levi saw it, was far more complicated. The problem was striking a balance between "a real need for confidentiality and its limitations in the public interest for the protection of the people of our country." The nation's top law enforcement officer did not believe that democracy or the First Amendment offered every citizen the right of access to all government information, and he worried that the "complete disclosure" compelled by FOIA "would render impossible the effective operation of government." "Some confidentiality is a matter of practical necessity," Levi argued. "Successful democracies" must "achieve an accommodation among competing values."[59]

Much like Colby's defense of the CIA to the CNSS conference, Levi's defense of some level of secrecy rested on the fact that all branches of government maintained some degree of secrecy in conducting their affairs. Just as Supreme Court justices confer in private, some aspects of executive branch decision making could not be effectively framed in the context of open public debate. Levi's defense of secrecy was the basis for claims of executive privilege that had been used for decades: "much as we are used to regarding government as an automaton—a faceless, mechanical creature—government is composed of human beings acting in concert, and much of its effectiveness depends upon the candor, courage and compassion of those individual citizens who compose it."[60]

At Levi's direction, Assistant Attorney General Antonin Scalia (later nominated to the Supreme Court by President Ronald Reagan) formulated a legal defense to exempt the Justice Department from the terms of the FOIA revisions. He explained to the White House counsel's office, "generally speaking the components of the White House Office, in the traditional or budgetary sense, are not 'agencies.'" The White House was most eager to exempt the foreign and domestic policy bodies that reported to the president—the NSC and Domestic Council—from FOIA. Since the new law did not clearly define which executive-level agencies were subject to its terms, Scalia recommended that the "concept of a separate 'White House Office' should be fostered and strengthened in as many ways as possible," even down to organizational charts that indicate the existence of such a unit separate and apart from the rest of the Executive Office. He concluded, "Judicial acceptance of such a functional division can greatly simplify our FOIA problems with respect to the Executive Office."[61] The renewed interest in transparency concerned the White House on a number of levels, not the least of which was the ongoing House and Senate investigations into intelligence abuses.

In June 1975 the Rockefeller Commission released its report on the CIA's domestic intelligence programs. Rockefeller promised to deliver a comprehensive report to the public. But in the end, the commission decided to withhold the section about a CIA program to assassinate foreign leaders. President Ford delayed publication until he could determine if it was fit for public consumption. To a cynical public, the president seemed to have something to hide. The public and the media roundly denounced the delay, forcing the president to publish the report (though without the section on assassinations). Two weeks later, the Commission on the Organization of the Government for the Conduct of Foreign Policy released its report. Known as the Murphy Commission for its chairperson, Robert Murphy, the commission studied many activities related to the conduct of foreign policy, including the intelligence agencies. It identified three flaws within the intelligence community: agencies with different missions and lines of command contributed to the overzealous collection of intelligence, an overreliance on technology not because it was useful, but because it was permissible, and operations that went outside the bounds of the Constitution. The final report suggested that there was room for improvement in the intelligence communities, but noted agencies' opposition to it. The report detailed twenty-eight years of activities by the CIA, some of which, the commission concluded, were "plainly unlawful and constituted improper invasions upon the rights of Americans." Some of the most controversial of the activities detailed including letter-opening programs; giving narcotics to unsuspecting people to test the effectiveness for intelligence purposes; Operation CHAOS, a program in the late 1960s and early 1970s that gathered intelligence on law-abiding citizens exercising their First Amendment right to protest; and wiretapping, breaking and entering, and tax record inspection.[62] The press praised the commission's work, citing the candor and thoroughness of the report.[63]

House and Senate investigators undoubtedly referenced the Rockefeller report as they launched their own investigations. No congressional inquiry of this scale had ever been attempted in the nearly thirty years since Congress passed the National Security Act. In the Senate, Majority Leader Mike Mansfield wanted Philip Hart to chair the committee, but the Senator's failing health forced him to decline the offer. Mansfield then offered the chair to Frank Church of Idaho, who had made public his interest in leading the investigation. The House process of selecting a chairman proved to be more complicated. House leadership appointed Lucien Nedzi, a proponent of greater intelligence oversight who had chaired the House Armed Services Committee since 1971. But when Nedzi blocked efforts by more radical members of the committee to publicize CIA scandals and ban covert actions, they called for his resignation. Ultimately, Nedzi resigned. The investigations had always had less support in the House, and the committee languished for months as House leadership tried to work out a compromise. Finally, it settled on the reconstitution of the committee with new membership under chairman Otis Pike and became known as the Pike committee.[64]

Among the Senate Church committee staff, a fundamental disagreement surfaced in the planning stages on how to best approach the investigation. Taking cues from Senator Ervin's successful investigation of the army's surveillance program in the early 1970s (on which a few members of the Church committee staff had worked), some proposed making the Church committee's first priority "to document and analyze the legislative and organizational history and practice of the CIA." After a thorough review of the organization's structure, the committee would then be well positioned to draft legislation designed to address the known issues. Others insisted that only by highlighting intelligence abuses could Congress "achieve fundamental, statutory improvements." It's possible that Senator Church's presidential ambitions made him more inclined to support the latter argument. In any case, the committee did focus the majority of its investigative resources on unearthing the more sensational, "newsworthy," accounts. This approach, as one staff member remembered it, was "less historical than abuse oriented." As one scholar observed, the focus on the sensational may have diverted valuable time and resources from "more systemic analyses of the intelligence community."[65]

Lurid accounts of CIA operations abroad at once captivated and revolted the American public. The CIA had participated in covert operations in countries around the world. It had directly interfered in internal politics of foreign countries to ensure the ascendancy of leaders more suitable to American interests. The agency had concocted elaborate (and occasionally ridiculous) schemes to assassinate foreign leaders like Cuban President Fidel Castro. Senator Church made the most of these sensational stories to achieve maximum media coverage.[66]

Americans were fascinated by the intelligence hearings. They revealed stories of previously unknown abuses. The National Security Agency (NSA) operated completely outside of congressional oversight for decades. Famously, the NSA refused to cooperate with Church committee investigators until the *Times* broke a story alleging that the NSA eavesdropped on the electronic conversations of American citizens. The agency decided it needed to respond to the charges and offered to meet with Church committee investigators. The committee discovered that the agency had, with the full cooperation of telecommunication companies, monitored international telegrams since 1947. The agency terminated Operation SHAMROCK in 1975, probably to avoid its discovery by the Church committee. Under Operation MINARET, begun in the late 1960s, the agency compiled a watch list of dissenters, deserters, and anyone participating in civil disturbances, including notable individuals like Joan Baez, Dr. Martin Luther King, Jr., and Jane Fonda, which it distributed to the army and other government agencies.[67]

For all the new abuses uncovered, the hearings and investigations also filled in details about abuses that had been publicized years earlier by radicals, whistle-blowers, and investigative journalists. The FBI's COINTELPRO programs had first been reported by the *Washington Post* in 1971 after the burglary by radical activists at the Media, Pennsylvania, field office. FBI Director J. Edgar Hoover's program to discredit Dr. Martin Luther King, Jr., had been revealed in the late 1960s, reported in the *New York Times*, and covered in detail at a conference sponsored by the Committee for Public Justice in 1971.[68] The hearings offered proof that claims made and documented by radicals, dissidents, scholars, and journalists since the late 1960s were valid.

The ACLU demanded that the White House contact all Americans who had been targets of national surveillance programs "now admitted to be unconstitutional, illegal, or, at the least, violations of the charters of the intelligence organizations." Americans should be reminded, the organizations urged, that they can request their dossiers through FOIA and privacy laws and that "possible violation of their constitutional rights might entitle them to civil remedies in the federal court system." The ACLU prodded the administration to contact all victims of domestic intelligence abuse and warrantless wiretapping.[69] The White House had no intention, however, of soliciting FOIA requests.

As 1975 came to a close, congressional committees wrapped up their investigations and began the long and arduous task of writing final reports and making legislative recommendations. Staff at CNSS worried that, as with past investigations, the American public and the mass media's interest in the topic would decline precipitously in the aftermath of the hearings. Decades of abuse spoke to the fundamental problems of the state—power and secrecy had proven very good friends to Republican and Democratic presidents alike. The administration was likely to propose in-house reform. If Congress failed to act quickly with legislation, the moment for policy reform would pass, and the agencies would maintain the status quo.

CNSS endeavored to maintain momentum for legislative reform with a conference and publications to promote public debate. Cosponsored by the ACLU Foundation, Americans for Democratic Action, the Committee for Public Justice, Common Cause, the Institute for Policy Studies, and the United Automobile Workers of America, CNSS aimed to go beyond the media sound bytes of "rogue elephants" and exploding cigars to spur conversations about "the conflicts that are inherent in trying to maintain both a democratic government and powerful secret intelligence agencies." Conference attendees debated methods for preventing further abuses by the national intelligence agencies in early November 1975. CNSS intended the conference to serve as a forum for legislating intelligence reform, and panelists were invited to answer questions to that end. Should the United States retain a bureaucracy for covert action? What guidelines should be placed upon the CIA in the United States? What is the role of domestic intelligence? What is the proper mix of legislation and executive directives for reforming the intelligence agencies? What can legislative oversight accomplish? These were the fundamental questions that formed the basis for discussion, and supporters and critics of the intelligence agencies were invited to propose a statutory framework for national security policy. The event proceeded on the basic assumption that "the system of secrecy which surrounds intelligence agencies has been used to protect abuses of power and illegal actions as effectively and with as much conviction as it protects the small amount of information which is actually vital to the national security."[70]

Critics and supporters of the U.S. intelligence agencies were often far apart in their approaches to reform. The panel exploring the role of domestic intelligence was typical. Former attorney general Ramsey Clark believed that reform legislation must first aim to protect constitutional rights of American citizens. Clark cautioned that past legislation—such as the Safe Streets and Crime Control Act of 1968—had failed to protect civil liberties. No judge had denied a government application for a wiretap warrant. New legislation, Clark urged, must outline permissible investigative procedures. Clark proposed establishing a review board, comprised of members of traditionally targeted communities, to review cases where domestic intelligence practices are contested. Mary Lawton, the deputy assistant attorney general and chairperson of the Justice Department Task Force on the FBI, fervently disagreed with Clark's recommendations. She cautioned the nation against overreacting to past mistakes by outlawing the use of legitimate procedures to protect national security. Any legislation, according to Lawton, must first protect the needs of the domestic intelligence agencies.[71]

Most representatives of the intelligence agencies, like former CIA general counsel Lawrence Houston, expressed their satisfaction with the status quo. They fell back on a frequently used defense that the past was the past, the agencies had changed, and that further inquiry or reform would hinder the ability of officers and institutions to protect the country. The so-called "abuses of the intelligence agencies," Houston observed, were once seen as justifiable actions in the context of the times. The cultural climate of the nation had changed, and Houston believed that agencies would respond adequately with some in-house cleaning. In congressional testimony, FBI officials had similarly denied the culpability of agencies and officials in promulgating illegal programs.[72]

The chairman of the Church committee's Domestic Intelligence Task Force, Senator Walter Mondale (D-MN), listened incredulously to these statements. From the lowest-level officers to the top of the intelligence hierarchy, those in the intelligence field had systematically ignored the

Constitution and violated the civil liberties of the American people. In some cases, the agencies themselves had shaped public opinion to justify and legitimize misdeeds.[73] Intelligence officials seemed to suggest that unconstitutional programs represented the will of the people. "When popular opinion brands a group un-American and subversive merely because of its political views," Mondale warned, "all too often the FBI has responded to public expectations." As he knew only too well, Congress did not have the political will to fight popular opinion. Congress had allowed these programs to develop without oversight because elected officials had only a limited interest in protecting constitutional rights. They much more readily responded to voter fears. Mondale called for charter legislation to protect intelligence agencies from "political pressures and hysteria."[74]

In 1973 when CIA chief James Schlesinger asked employees of the CIA to apprise him of programs that might be illegal or in violation of the agency's charter, he received hundreds of leads. Schlesinger compiled these programs in a report known as the "the Family Jewels," evidence that agency staff understood that they sometimes operated outside legal channels and recognized that some agency programs were, if not unconstitutional, certainly questionable. Despite overwhelming evidence that agencies had conceived of and carried out programs of questionable constitutionality for decades, these supporters continued to caution against legislative overreach. As their appearance at the CNSS conference suggested, supporters of the intelligence agencies would fight to maintain the autonomy and extralegality of national security institutions. Morton Halperin believed that a well-informed public would pressure their elected officials to reform the national security state. He wanted to flood the public domain with information that would catalyze a latent public movement for massive intelligence reform.

Dissatisfied with congressional investigations' focus on the sensational at the expense of a broad and succinct review of abuses, CNSS published a short report in late 1975. Relying on evidence gathered from the public record, including records and documents from court proceedings, newspapers, and FOIA requests, the report (185 pages including bibliography) offered a "background and framework for public understanding of how our intelligence agencies have operated beyond the law and the Constitution and contributes to the debate about the need for fundamental reform of the intelligence agencies." The report had none of the political considerations or limitations that the Church and Pike congressional committees faced in compiling their final reports. A case in point: the

THINGS YOUR GOVERNMENT SAID WOULD BE DANGEROUS FOR YOU TO SEE:
A 1975 Herblock Cartoon, copyright by *The Herb Block Foundation*

Ford administration tried to suppress the Church committee's assassination report. The Church committee members seemed willing to allow Ford to decide on this issue, and Church threatened to resign. When the committee turned the issue over to the Senate to decide, the august body seemed reticent to approve the publication, even as they were not committed to blocking it. This was largely due to political considerations.[75]

Much of this information offered by CNSS had been part of the public domain since the Ervin committee hearings into army surveillance practices in 1971.[76] In the mid-1970s, on the issue of national security reform, organizations like the ACLU and CNSS played a central role both in working with and pressuring congressional investigators. These organizations had the resources, staff, and professional skills to make informed contributions to the national debate. The final battle for reform would be waged on the floor of the House and Senate. But public debates, such as the CNSS conference, offered nonpartisan forums where complex issues could be debated and dissenting voices heard. In these subtle ways, public interest groups, working alongside congressional investigators, provided elected officials with substantive resources and information needed for legislative reform. They also worked to keep public interest in policy issues alive. Scholarly works offer detailed accounts of the "Year of Intelligence" from the perspective of congressional committee insiders and the media. However, these accounts overlook the significant contributions to public policy development made by public interest groups in the late twentieth century.[77]

The ACLU's carefully cultivated policy network had become a powerful force on Capitol Hill by the mid-1970s. The work of organizations like the CNSS operated on many levels, and contributed to the development of capstone legislative reforms that will be examined in detail in the next chapter. The committee reports spawned dozens of civil lawsuits for First Amendment violations, many of which were litigated by ACLU attorneys. These initiatives offer a more complex picture of policy reform than examinations of congressional hearings alone would allow. National security reform would be one of the centerpieces of the 1976 presidential contest. Public interest groups demanded that the lessons of the past be remembered when institutionalizing a new national security policy. From 1976 to 1978 reformers institutionalized the final pieces of this new policy regime with the establishment of permanent congressional oversight committees and the Foreign Intelligence Surveillance Act.

CHAPTER SEVEN

"Tempers Change, Times Change, Public Attitudes Change"
Passing FISA

The room buzzed with excitement. After years of suspecting that state and local police infiltrated groups and disrupted peaceful meetings, reformers finally had the evidence to support their suspicions. The Information Digest, *a super-secret intelligence newsletter distributed nationally to an underground red squad network, offered hard proof that Michigan state and local police had infiltrated antiwar, civil rights, and New Left groups for years, spying on individuals and organizations and then distributing their "intelligence" through a national network.*

The newly formed Michigan Coalition to End Government Spying got the word out through an emerging network of concerned citizens that these files would now be available through Freedom of Information Act requests. The news sparked a new FOIA movement. Former participants of the 1960s movement met regularly, organizing seminars to discuss political surveillance and protesting to local officials about these extra-legal activities. Using the Freedom of Information Act, they read their own files. At monthly meetings they all agreed: never again.[1]

In 1976 the Center for National Security Studies (CNSS) insisted that the programs perpetrated on citizens in the name of national security were "not isolated incidents of zealous officers exceeding their authority in the field," but instead "ongoing, bureaucratic programs, often continuing over decades, and ordered and approved at the highest level of the executive branch of government." Former NSC staffer Morton Halperin declared these extralegal programs the "deformed offspring of the modern presidency, an expression of the powers claimed by presidents in the area of national security."[2] ACLU Executive Director Aryeh Neier predicted that revelations of gross constitutional violations by intelligence agencies could mark "the beginning of the end for the national security state." He predicted, "Now that Americans are informed of the shabby things done in the name of national security, perhaps they will put an end to them. Perhaps."[3] Neier's healthy skepticism about the prospects of broad-based domestic security reform reflected the harsh economic reality of the nation's bicentennial year. Salacious details of extra-illegal acts had riveted the nation during the year of intelligence, but as the committees turned to the quiet work of report writing, Americans focused attention on their economic woes. A *New York Times* front-page feature about the state of the union at the beginning of its third century offered grim prognostics for the year.[4]

Worried that the sinking economy would doom the movement for intelligence reform by stalling legislative momentum, ACLU and CNSS staff ratcheted up their rhetoric and redoubled their efforts to focus public debate on national security policy reform. They developed new capacities to reach the public and its leaders. The CNSS launched a monthly publication, *First Principles,* in September 1975. Pledging to focus on the "conflict between expansive claims of national security and civil liberties," CNSS hoped to "contribute to a return to First Principles—the necessary and vital right of a full and informed public participation in government—by increasing public awareness of continuing threats and of opportunities to improve the situation." The newsletter-style format of only sixteen pages would be packed with national security related-issues including conferences, pending court cases, publications, and opinion.[5] At the ACLU, Neier continued to pressure congressional allies to pass legislation restricting warrantless surveillance and to reform national intelligence agencies. He believed that the publication of the Pike and Church committees' final reports would further catalyze a legislative commitment to rein in the state.

CNSS and ACLU plans hinged on their ability to maintain bipartisan, and more specifically conservative, support for legislative reform. Liberals overwhelmingly supported greater congressional oversight of intelligence agencies. Reformers like Neier were reassured by Republican statements that suggested the party favored further reform. The Republican Policy Committee publicly declared that the greatest challenge to reform was "not *whether* Congress should intensify its until now somewhat relaxed oversight of government intelligence, but rather *how* this task should be accomplished."[6] Democrats and Republicans split along party lines when it came to the question of how statutory reform of national intelligence agencies ought to be implemented. Liberals called for statutes restricting domestic surveillance and supported agency charters to define the legal parameters of intelligence activities and programs. Ardent civil libertarians called for the total abolition of intelligence agencies, arguing that covert agencies were incompatible with democratic practice. Republicans pointed to the failures of the congressional committees to prevent leaks and suggested that reforms, if taken too far, could weaken the agencies and undermine the ability of officers to do the important work of protecting the national interest, both at home and abroad. Republicans and Democrats could agree with a *Los Angeles Times* assessment that "the United States has to have a Central Intelligence Agency." The challenge lay in constructing a statutory framework that would allow institutions like the CIA to function within the parameters of a democratic, constitutional government. Clearly, wrote the *LA Times*, the "intelligence community is too secret" and needs to be "brought under closer control by both the President and Congress."[7] Many in Congress agreed and were determined to institute real reform in the coming year.

From 1976 to 1978 activists labored arduously to realize legislative reform. Political opportunities they had so successfully exploited in the past were few and far between. The drama of clandestine intelligence activities was fading from the public's collective memory, overcome by stories of economic hardship, corporations shedding jobs, and spiraling inflation. In the last months of 1975 congressional committees wrapped up their investigations and began the arduous task of compiling reports and making legislative recommendations.

The twin shocks of a CIA officer's assassination and "leaks" from the House intelligence inquiry gave ammunition to a small coterie in Washington who opposed domestic security reform. In his State of the Union address on January 19, 1976, President Ford blamed Congress for "crippling" American intelligence agencies and encouraging adversaries "to attempt new adventures while our own ability to monitor events and to influence events short of military action is undermined."[8] The president's rhetoric in a presidential election year spoke to the increasingly partisan nature of the debate over intelligence reform. All these factors frustrated the work of reformers. In 1976 their policy agenda included the creation of permanent congressional intelligence oversight committees, a statute to restrict the executive's domestic wiretapping and surveillance authority, and charters for the intelligence agencies. Reformers realized two of these legislative goals by the close of the 95th Congress in 1978.

The founders might have appreciated the irony. Amid national, state, and local celebrations commemorating the nation's bicentennial, the legislative and executive branches fought determinedly to protect their

"UH—THESE ARE SORT-OF SECRET ORGANIZATIONS THAT OUR GOVERNMENT
HIRES TO SEE THAT WE ENJOY THE RIGHT KIND OF—UH—LIBERTY": A 1976
Herblock Cartoon, copyright by *The Herb Block Foundation*

respective turf. The congressional inquiry into the nation's intelligence
agencies generated endless clashes between the White House and Congress over access to classified information. In the shadow of the assassination of CIA station chief Richard Welch in Athens in December 1975, the
committees hunkered down to draft final reports and write policy recommendations before their mandates expired in February 1976. Welch
was shot and killed outside his home as he returned from a party. Welch

had not been particularly cautious about concealing his identity—he inhabited the same home as his predecessors even after being warned to find a new residence. Such details were lost in the madness of the media hype. The tragedy of the event prompted some members of Congress to write legislation to criminalize the disclosure of the names of intelligence operatives. The *Post* eulogized Welch as an American hero and claimed his death was the result of critics who were out to permanently damage the agency. Perhaps the *Post* was merely trying to deflect criticism that the media was ultimately to blame for Welch's death. Media stories like Hersh's exposé, these arguments went, contributed to the congressional investigations into the agencies and the exposure of the CIA's dirty laundry.[9]

The politics of a presidential election year further undermined the legitimacy of the final reports. Rumors circulated in the Senate that Church rushed his committee staff to finish and publish the report so that he could launch his presidential campaign. The House faced other political challenges. Demoralized by continuous squabbling with the executive branch, the Pike committee struggled to protect its credibility by issuing a report that didn't pull any punches. Over White House objections, the committee voted to publish the report in its entirety, including material the CIA claimed threatened national security. As a sign of the further deterioration of relations between the executive branch and the legislative branch the CIA protested that portions of the report contained classified information. Publication of such material, it argued, violated prior White House agreements.[10]

As the House readied the report for printing, *Times* journalist John Crewdson, who had briefly been allowed access to a copy of the report, published several articles about it. The White House blasted the committee for "leaking" the report to the *Times*, claiming it violated prior security agreements with the administration. Ford's press secretary declared that the episode underscored the House's cavalier approach to protecting national security and state secrets. The scandal further weakened support for Pike's scandal-ridden committee on Capitol Hill, and the House voted 2–1 not to release the report.[11]

But for an extraordinary course of events, the Pike report might have been permanently relegated to a dusty drawer in the chairman's office. Crewdson wasn't the only journalist with access to the unpublished report; someone leaked a copy to CBS investigative journalist Daniel Schorr. Schorr had earned a reputation for fearlessly challenging authority (much to the chagrin of his employers at CBS news). When he learned of the House decision to suppress the report, realizing he was the only journalist who possessed a copy of it, he concluded that he would not "be the sole person responsible for suppressing it." He offered CBS news the scoop, but his superiors seemed reluctant. Schorr wanted to move fast. Through some connections he located a publisher, the New York *Village Voice*. He decided to keep his own involvement secret and arranged for publication proceeds to go directly to the First Amendment advocacy group, the Reporters' Committee for Freedom of the Press.[12]

Journalists quickly traced the *Village Voice*'s source back to Schorr. The backlash was immediate, and the condemnation from Schorr's colleagues was surprisingly vitriolic. The *Times* accused him of "selling secrets," performing an "offensive element of commercialization wrapped in a mantle of high constitutional purpose," and "laundering" proceeds through the Reporters' Committee. Schorr charged the *Times* with hypocrisy, noting it had profited handsomely from its decision to publish the Pentagon Papers. What the paper objected to, Schorr argued, was that he had not sold "secrets in the customary, or *Times*[,] way."[13] Schorr's tussle with the *Times* suggested a shifting ethos among the nation's top editorial staffs. CBS, exhibiting none of the journalistic bravery that it demonstrated when it weathered the relentless attacks of Vice President Spiro Agnew for its "Selling of the Pentagon" documentary, quietly secured Schorr's resignation. Only a few years before, the *Times* and CBS news had adamantly defended the public's right to know, challenging elected officials and powerful institutions with investigative reports of the highest caliber. Three national reporters, Anthony Lewis, William Safire, and Tom Wicker of the *Times*, were notable exceptions who defended Schorr in print. Lewis's column was typical: "Whatever faults there may have been in the handling of the business, Mr. Schorr violated no visible law, disclosed nothing that in essence is not common in Washington. That he should be pilloried while nothing is done about C.I.A. and F.B.I. officials who grossly abused their power and told flagrant lies indicates the present mood in Washington."[14]

The administration pounced on the "scandal," eager, as Schorr later recalled, to "shift the issue from *what* had gotten out to *how* it had gotten out." The House Ethics Committee launched a seven-month inquiry into the leak. Schorr was subpoenaed and pressed to identify his source.[15] With the media feeding like sharks on one of their own, they paid scant attention to the substance of the Pike report.

The CNSS, frustrated that the Pike committee recommendations were being swamped by a process story, carefully summarized the more than

300-page report for a general audience. The Pike committee report presented a painstakingly detailed account of the CIA's many intelligence blunders. It chastised the agency for "repeated intelligence failures," citing as evidence its inability to predict the 1968 Tet Offensive, the Soviet invasion of Czechoslovakia in 1968, and the 1973 Yom Kippur war. For these failures and other transgressions, most especially the illegal spying on millions of Americans, the Pike report offered a laundry list of recommendations. These ranged from radical demands for total budget disclosure of intelligence agencies, to congressional notification of covert activities, to the abolishment of assassinations and paramilitary activities, to presidential reports on all covert operations in writing to Congress. The Pike committee also recommended limiting the FBI director's term to eight years (no more J. Edgar Hoovers) and replacing the bureau's Internal Security Branch with a new division limited strictly to observing the activities of foreign-directed groups and persons. The final report called for some limitations on covert operations, though it stopped short of recommending charter legislation. Finally, the report recommended creating a permanent intelligence oversight committee with the power to declassify intelligence by a majority vote, transferring the National Security Agency (NSA) to civilian control, and establishing statutory definitions to limit the agency's interception of overseas conversations.[16]

The Schorr scandal lent legitimacy to the less sensational Church committee report. In spite of its more subdued tone, the Senate report issued in May 1976 offered further evidence that intelligence agencies had acted for decades outside the law and in violation of constitutionally protected rights. The committee called for charters outlining the appropriate functions of the agencies and the establishment of a mechanism for controlling and monitoring these activities.[17]

The Welch assassination and the Schorr scandal created political opportunity for opponents of reform to appeal to the public in defense of besieged intelligence agencies. President Ford proposed a bill to criminalize leaks and punish anyone with "authorized access to intelligence secrets" who publicly disclosed that information in order to protect "intelligence sources and methods." To stave off reforms that might severely curtail the power of the executive branch, the president issued an executive order (EO). The order legitimized most extralegal intelligence activities including domestic surveillance of persons "reasonably believed to be acting on behalf of a foreign power or engaging in international terrorist or narcotics activities." The Ford EO allowed the FBI broad counterintelligence authority in the United States, especially regarding "subversive"

The Church committee announcing the release of its final report, 1976 (Boise State University Library, Special Collections and Archives)

people or organizations. It also expanded executive powers to surveil and wiretap with the attorney general's approval—in other words, the status quo. Intelligence collected and retained by the FBI could be disseminated to other intelligence agencies. The order granted the NSA authority to continue its policy of unrestricted eavesdropping on overseas communications. Ford did pursue ostensible reorganization of the intelligence community by creating an intelligence oversight board; enlarging and renaming the 40 Committee (now called the Operations Advisory Group); and developing a National Security Council Committee, chaired by CIA Director George H. W. Bush, responsible for the central coordination of national intelligence. As oversight, the president unrealistically proposed that employees relay "questionable activities" to "appropriate authorities."[18] As was its purpose, the EO kept all reform in-house.

Critics dismissed the president's order as window dressing, a poorly concealed attempt to protect executive prerogative in national security matters, "rather than spreading that responsibility among a number of institutions" including congressional oversight committees. CNSS charged that Ford's EO legitimized "virtually everything which the intelligence investigations had meant to repudiate through disclosure," while parading the new rules as "tough new restrictions." The organization accused the president of "reshuffling" institutions rather than proposing real change. Years of congressional investigations into surveillance practices of various agencies—including the army, the FBI, the IRS, and the CIA—CNSS recalled, offered irrefutable proof that self-regulation was no solution at all. CNSS scoffed at the notion that "an official with knowledge of abuses is told to go through channels within the hierarchy which spawned those abuses." This had proved an ineffective remedy in the past.[19]

CNSS accused the administration of using the order as a ruse for expanding executive powers and legitimizing past extralegal practices. The order allowed for the collection of domestic intelligence on people or groups that "pose a clear threat to intelligence agency facilities or personnel." This was the same rationale, CNSS recalled, that justified the CIA's CHAOS program and led to officers infiltrating antiwar groups in the 1960s. The surveillance of persons "reasonably believed to be acting on behalf of a foreign power" was permitted under the new rules, though this reasoning had led to First Amendment violations by the army's CONUS program, the FBI's COINTELPRO, and the CIA in the 1960s. Past experiences had shown that officers continued domestic surveillance programs even when evidence of foreign influence among targeted groups could not be found. The president's new rules ignored the history of intelligence abuses and effectively "expand[ed] executive branch authority to reflect its broad view of its constitutional mandate whenever it claims overriding 'national security' interests."[20] CNSS's criticism was not unfounded. Presidents often issued executive orders to forestall legislative action. In this case Ford's order was a poorly disguised effort by the administration to appear in favor of reform while actually doing little in the way of pursuing it. Executive orders were subject to the whim of each new administration; real reform must come from the legislative branch. As CNSS persuasively argued, rarely did the executive branch voluntarily "decrease its own powers in order to protect other institutions of the society." Nothing short of "systematic restrictions" on intelligence techniques, urged CNSS, would suffice because "the executive branch has a clear record of expanding any ambiguity or latitude into a broad authorization for executive power; anything less than the strictest reaffirmation of the Bill of Rights will lead to fresh abuses of power by secret agencies."[21]

While CNSS found much in the Pike committee final report to work with, the ACLU believed that congressional recommendations did not do enough to alter the institutional structures of the national security state. Eager to realize substantive reforms after years of carefully coordinating costly litigation and legislative campaigns, the ACLU proposed sweeping legislative reform to drastically reduce secrecy with new classification rules; a statutory definition of all intelligence agencies through new charters; legislation to limit surveillance, wiretapping, and other techniques; and creation of permanent congressional oversight capacities. Appalled by the president's executive order that seemed to legitimate many of the CIA's domestic activities, the ACLU called for the agency to be renamed the Foreign Intelligence Agency and for all domestic intelligence operations and covert action to be forbidden. The ACLU wanted the FBI stripped of its intelligence capacities and restricted to investigating criminal matters. Furthermore, the ACLU proposed that all intelligence procedures violating the Fourth Amendment, including wiretaps and other electronic surveillance, mail covers as well as inquiries into phone and bank records (unless a warrant showing probable cause could be obtained), be strictly forbidden. The ACLU wanted to prohibit the NSA from intercepting any communications by Americans.[22]

Never one to mince words, Morton Halperin offered a harsh critique of the presidential policy, charging that the executive order amounted to a "fraud" that "confirms the authority of the intelligence agencies to conduct surveillance activities directed at lawful activities of American citizens." He accused the administration of excluding "critics" from the "drafting process," and he claimed the order had been effectively written by the agencies themselves. Halperin denounced the order as a presidential "pardon" for the nation's intelligence agencies—not only did the president allow unconstitutional behavior to go unpunished, but the order "granted these very agencies a new license to spy on Americans."[23]

Surely the president hoped the executive order bought the White House some time with Congress. He could do nothing, however, to control the judicial branch. Since the late 1960s the judicial branch had begun slowly to restrain the executive's inherent authority to impinge upon First and Fourth Amendment rights in national security cases. Especially after the Watergate revelations, the courts had grown skeptical of the government's often-employed defense to trust the executive's discretion. For decades presidents and their attorneys general had found legal justification for the use of warrantless wiretaps in national security cases by referring to the executive's constitutional duty to conduct foreign affairs. Though some decisions, like *Keith*, had challenged this claim, the courts had preferred statutory definition to lawmaking from the bench.

Two recent rulings in the federal circuit court advanced a judicial interpretation of the president's constitutional power to wiretap without a warrant. In 1973 the Fifth Circuit granted the executive unfettered power to wiretap in cases related to national security. In *United States v. Brown*, the black radical H. Rap Brown challenged the legality of the Nixon administration's warrantless wiretaps on his home telephone. Reviewing the government's wiretap records *in camera*, the judge ruled that they contained nothing that violated Brown's Fourth Amendment rights and declared the wiretap lawful under the president's "inherent power to protect national security in the context of foreign affairs."[24] The following year the Third Circuit reached a similar conclusion about the power of the executive to conduct warrantless surveillance in the case of national security and foreign intelligence. In *United States v. Butenko* the defendant's conversations had been overheard on a federal wiretap targeting a Soviet citizen suspected of espionage who worked in the Soviet mission to the United Nations. The court found the wiretap did not violate the Constitution based on the 1934 Communications Act, which allowed foreign intelligence gathering as an exception to the warrant rule. In this case, however, the judge noted that warrantless wiretaps were permissible only if one of the targets was directly involved with a foreign government.[25]

These decisions dealt a temporary blow to the ACLU's litigation strategy. But in 1973 a District of Columbia circuit court ruling offered hope for a new strategy. In *Zweibon v. Mitchell* sixteen members of the Jewish Defense League brought a civil action lawsuit against Attorney General John Mitchell and nine FBI officers for installing warrantless wiretaps at its New York headquarters. Mitchell maintained that the wiretaps were vital to protect American national security interests because the league organized anti-Soviet demonstrations and harassed Soviet diplomats. These actions had a direct impact on foreign relations, the attorney general argued, because they made Americans more vulnerable to retaliation from the Soviet Union. Using the legal precedents set by the *Brown* and *Butenko* decisions, Mitchell called the warrantless wiretaps defensible based on the president's constitutional authority to conduct foreign relations.

The court ruled in favor of the Jewish Defense League. Eight judges issued five separate opinions. The plurality opinion (signed by three judges) found the wiretap unconstitutional because the League was neither a foreign government nor a foreign officer. In a second opinion two justices declared the wiretap violated Title III of the Safe States and Crime Control Act of 1968, which restricted the executive's authority to wiretap without a warrant to criminal and national security cases. The judges' failure to reach a consensus on the ruling underscored the weakness of the ACLU's long-term litigation strategy to restrict executive surveillance practices. Such definitions would have to come from Congress.[26]

The Ford administration adamantly opposed legislative efforts to restrict executive power and fought to protect its prerogatives by instituting internal reforms. Attorney General Edward Levi vowed to implement tougher wiretapping and surveillance standards in the Department of Justice. In an address to the American Bar Association he pledged to "develop public guidelines governing electronic surveillance and other activities," especially those of the FBI.[27] Reformers denounced these promises as more of the same. "The public record of abuse places a heavy burden of proof upon the Executive to show that it is both legitimate and necessary to allow the FBI to continue intelligence investigations aimed at American citizens," wrote ACLU counsel Jerry Berman. "Given the intrusions into individual and associational privacy that are inherent in intelligence gathering, this burden of proof is a difficult one to substantiate." Indeed while offering to restrict FBI guidelines, Levi at once proposed to loosen them. In 1976 the attorney general allowed the agency to initiate "preliminary investigations" if a group was thought to be "engaged in activities which involve or will involve the violation of federal law."[28]

Levi's proposals strengthened congressional resolve among a coterie of liberal Democrats to pass legislation restricting surveillance and wiretapping. In 1975 the Senate considered a bill that would require the executive branch to obtain warrants before initiating domestic surveillance in foreign intelligence cases. Additionally, the bill would require the executive branch to report to the Administrative Office of the U.S. Courts and to the Committee on the Judiciary in the House and Senate details of the proceedings and the names and locations of all the intercepted communications. Levi denounced the bill as a bald effort to undermine the president's inherent constitutional duty to protect the nation and conduct its foreign affairs. The Fourth Amendment, the attorney general argued, did not extend to people outside the United States or to foreign powers. He accused civil libertarians of corrupting the original intent of the Fourth Amendment, envisioned by the founders as a means to protect individual privacy, not to "compel exposure of the government." The American public, Levi urged, must trust its leaders to exercise discretion so that "public interest may be served."[29] Levi's statement revealed the administration's inability to comprehend the reality of 1970s American political culture. After years of disclosures of extralegal activities by intelligence agencies, which at the least violated certain constitutional, if not legal rights, the American public was in no mood to trust its leaders.

The administration, however, recognizing the strength of congressional resolve on the issue, introduced its own federal wiretap legislation in 1976 to get ahead of the curve. The *Times* quickly condemned the administration's bill. "Among its more glaring defects," the paper opined, is that the bill "permits electronic surveillance even if no evidence had been presented that a crime has been or is about to be committed." By approving the legislation, the newspaper reported, the Judiciary Committee "gave the intelligence community the benefits of doubt, as if nothing had been learned during the past half-decade."[30] Cosponsors Ted Kennedy and Charles Mathias dismissed the criticism. After more than five years of congressional inquiry into abuses, they proffered, this legislation would be the first to protect Americans from "the unchecked power of the President to engage in foreign intelligence electronic surveillances," a major accomplishment considering that "the personal attitudes of executive-branch officials remain the only governing standard for such operations." Though the bill did not include all that reformers had hoped for, Kennedy and Mathias stressed that it was more important to "adopt legislation that will receive executive assent" than to let another year pass without limiting "the executive's present unfettered freedom to tap and bug in the foreign intelligence area."[31] Congressional overtures to compromise marked a shift in legislative strategy. Years of protracted struggles with the executive branch over the issue had taken a toll. Certain that the public was losing interest in the issues, congressional leaders hoped to ensure legislative success before the window of opportunity closed.

Public interest groups, however, were in no mood for compromise. The ACLU and CNSS virulently opposed the Kennedy-Mathias bill because it rested on the legal assumption that wiretaps were compatible with the protections of the Fourth Amendment. ACLU counsel John Shattuck argued that the courts were still debating this issue, but from the organization's perspective electronic surveillance was an unreasonable search and seizure that should require a warrant. Second, the bill assumed that any cases related to national security offered a legal exception to Fourth Amendment protections and separation of powers, but the Supreme Court had ruled in several cases, *Keith* and more recently *Zweibon*, that there could be no national security exceptions to the Bill of Rights. Speaking on behalf of CNSS, Halperin worried about the loose definitions in the bill. He argued that the administration had intentionally defined "electronic surveillance" narrowly to apply only to wire transmissions. Information passed via transatlantic cable, routed through Canada, or picked up through microwave transmission would not be subject to the new law.[32]

The administration's bill authorized a newly formed secret court, the Foreign Intelligence Surveillance Court or FISA court, to review electronic surveillance warrant applications. The FISA court proved a divisive issue among public interest groups. Halperin supported the FISA court

"DISAGREEING WITH ME, EH? YOU MUST BE SOME KIND OF A NUT": A 1976 Herblock Cartoon, copyright by *The Herb Block Foundation*

because he believed it depoliticized surveillance by taking the authorization out of the hands of the attorney general and the FBI director. Halperin pushed to require attorneys general to sign affidavits certifying that their warrant application was legitimate. Furthermore, he recommended that FISA judges be drawn from the DC circuit where they were likely to be more "sensitive and aware of the considerations that go into both sides of these issues." At Halperin's insistence the Justice Department conceded to adding a civil damages provision to the bill as a penalty to federal officers who violated its provisions.[33] The ACLU and CNSS broke with Halperin, adamantly opposing the court. Though some touted the bill as reform because it required judicial warrants for wiretapping, the organization believed that warrants would rarely be denied. "Instead of providing real reform," wrote the frustrated Washington branch, "liberals and the Administration" conspired to support a "bill that essentially attempted to legitimate the illegitimate."[34] Perhaps because of his experience on the inside of the national intelligence apparatus, Halperin not only supported the bill and its compromises, but thought the legislation a vast improvement over current and past practices.

Former Church committee staff director F. A. O. Schwarz, Jr. cautioned legislators to carefully define the terms in the bill, especially "foreign officer" and "foreign intelligence." Experience showed, Schwartz explained, that "over and over again, people have wrapped themselves in the mantle of national security" in order to violate laws. The wiretapping of Martin Luther King, Jr., would be permissible under current definitions, Schwarz warned, because of the minister's association with former members of the Communist Party. As one justice argued in *Zweibon*, the government can easily define dissidents as foreign officers. Likewise, the bill loosely defined "foreign intelligence" as information "deemed essential . . . to the security" or "to the conduct of the affairs of the United States." Such a definition, cautioned Schwarz, "includes everything under the sun."[35]

Constitutional experts from both sides of the aisle favored the bill. Professor Herbert Wechsler of Columbia University disagreed with Halperin's claims that "foreign intelligence" and "foreign officers" ought to be more carefully defined. To do so, he argued, would effectively tie the hands of government officials who aimed to protect national security. Professor Philip Heymann of Harvard Law School, a longtime advocate for legislation to restrict surveillance, had reservations about this bill. In spite of its weaknesses, however, he called on Congress to take advantage of this opportunity and pass the bill immediately.[36]

The FISA bill proved too complicated and politically divisive for a straight up or down vote. *Times* columnist Tom Wicker predicted that if passed it would "give legislative sanction to intelligence surveillance techniques. And it might well be used as a model for the future—to make intelligence break-ins legal, for example." In an election year most legislators tried to avoid such contentious issues. Civil libertarians, anxious as they were to have this particularly ambiguous area of executive power legally defined, believed that a Jimmy Carter administration would be more sympathetic to their cause, and they were willing to wait until after the election to reconsider the bill. Assuming that Carter would take the White House, John Shattuck encouraged Kennedy and Mathias to postpone action on their bill "in anticipation of an administration more sensitive to civil liberties."[37]

Legislators did agree, however, on the need for better congressional oversight of intelligence agencies. The creation of permanent intelligence oversight committees faced little opposition, either from the administration or on Capitol Hill. Since much opposition to greater oversight typically came from the agencies themselves, congressional hearings on proposed legislation to establish permanent intelligence oversight committees offered a forum for former and current officials to air their concerns. Most elected officials couldn't deny former CIA director John McCone's claim that Congress had at least tacitly approved extralegal intelligence operations. The hearings offered Congress the opportunity to demonstrate its determination to reassert oversight where it had been lacking.

Demoralized by the negative publicity and the rapid turnover at the top, the intelligence community largely supported greater oversight. Former and current intelligence officers seemed eager to avoid embarrassment in the future by spreading responsibility (through disclosure) around a bit, and they urged Congress to pass legislation sooner rather than later. President of the Association of Retired Intelligence Officers David Atlee Phillips, speaking for the members of his organization, supported greater oversight. He adamantly disagreed, however, with claims that recent revelations revealed an unhealthy democracy. Ignoring years of congressional investigations and reports that detailed unconstitutional use of national security capacities both at home and abroad, the former CIA covert operative blamed Nixon's "disposition . . . to use intelligence resources improperly." Watergate and other scandals, Phillips argued, did not seriously threaten "the survival of our form of government nor any of its institutions." Intelligence officers, he declared, supported better congressional oversight because they "want others to share the responsibility, to take some of the heat after the fact, especially when that heat is applied 15 or 20 years later."[38] Phillips's testimony revealed that some members of the intelligence community resented taking the heat for past transgressions that had been explicitly approved by presidents and implicitly approved by Congress. It also suggested an inability on the part of many members of the intelligence community to critically examine the role of a secret community within an open democratic government.

Many senior intelligence officials conceded that programs once approved at the highest levels of government, when examined in a contemporary context, were rightly condemned for violating individual rights. When asked at a Senate hearing if he believed that Congress had failed in its oversight duties, former CIA director Richard Helms replied, "I do not know. You know, Senator, as well as I do, that tempers change, times change, public attitudes change."[39] Helms's reluctance to condemn Congress reflected the unwillingness on the part of many intelligence officials to admit that some intelligence practices had indeed been extralegal. But more than that, his comments implicitly chastised Congress for roundly condemning programs that had been ongoing for decades while suggesting that Congress could have been more assertive in its oversight.

FBI Director Clarence Kelley granted that Congress's renewed interest in oversight was a natural by-product of the Watergate era. He conceded that the "year of intelligence" had revealed "issues" that "needed to be resolved," but he insisted that the bureau had addressed those issues with a thorough internal review. Kelley had approved a plan to reduce the bureau's domestic caseload by 64 percent. He opposed any bill that would allow "direct congressional access to FBI information," proposing instead that all FBI directors be "fully accountable to an oversight committee through sworn testimony." When Republican Illinois Senator Chuck Percy challenged Kelley, insinuating that the FBI's recent caseload reduction was probably due to the realization that "so many programs were illegal," Kelley replied curtly, "I do not recall any [terminated domestic programs] that would meet that classification."[40] Kelley's decision to reduce sharply the bureau's domestic intelligence programs reflected a growing understanding in Washington, following the Church and Pike committee investigations, that extralegal domestic spying programs were products of a political culture that had not only permitted constitutional violations but in some cases also encouraged them. Programs like these would no longer be tolerated by a more assertive Congress.

Clark Clifford, a principal author of the National Security Act of 1947 and an advisor to Truman, Kennedy, and Johnson (and his secretary of defense), testified before the Senate. He urged Congress to rein in executive branch excesses. "The CIA has been badly used. The FBI has been badly used. Their actions in the past were not always in accordance with the laws and the Constitution of the United States." Clifford insisted that the agencies had not been created to violate constitutional rights, though they had been used in that way. "The congressional function must be to prevent that activity," Clifford argued, "because it goes to the heart of our constitutional system."[41]

Public interest groups like the ACLU and CNSS agreed with assessments that tacit congressional approval had encouraged first the development and then the continuation of intelligence abuses. Only intensive legislative oversight, they argued, could rectify this problem. But these organizations refused to support the assessment of former and present intelligence officials that careful examination of extraconstitutional activities of intelligence agencies weakened or endangered national security. Morton Halperin urged elected officials to push for legislation that would require greater transparency. Intelligence abuses, he declared, were the predictable outcome of too much secrecy. "Even when the motive for secrecy is ... that release will harm national security, often no attention is given to the importance of public debate. The executive branch does not balance the public's right to know and the Congress' right to the information against its perception of the national security needs for secrecy." Halperin insisted that three incidents of intelligence failures investigated by the Church committee over White House objections—the assassination report, the report on Chile, and the report on the domestic abuses of the CIA involving COINTELPRO—had revealed nothing that harmed the nation's security. The administration's desire to hide this information from the public was too often a poorly disguised effort "to avoid embarrassment" and "not to have to defend unpopular policies" as opposed to "balanc[ing] the public's right to know against the general requirements of national security."[42] Halperin's argument meshed perfectly with claims made by right to know advocates that top officials too often earlier used secrecy to cover their own mistakes.

The Church and Pike committee investigations had focused on the most controversial of the extralegal programs, most of which were operations conducted by foreign intelligence agencies. Many of the abuses perpetrated by domestic agencies had been "discovered" and examined in some detail before 1975. The unintended consequences of this focus became apparent at the hearings to consider permanent intelligence oversight committees. Testimony reflected the nation's preoccupation with the skullduggery of the CIA and NSC, arguably the agencies least susceptible to democratic pressures. With the exception of FBI Director Clarence Kelley, most witnesses testified on the subject of foreign intelligence abuses. CNSS's Morton Halperin worried that the hearings were moving in the wrong direction, away from a forceful reform of domestic spying by the FBI, the army, and other agencies. Influenced by his association with the ACLU and his own experience as the victim of domestic intelligence abuse, Halperin insisted oversight must include "domestic intelligence" of the FBI, in addition to overseas programs operated by the CIA and the Pentagon. The majority of past abuses, Halperin reminded the committee, had occurred at the overlap between foreign and domestic intelligence.[43]

At least one senator shared Halperin's concerns. Senator Gaylord Nelson, a Democrat from Wisconsin, thought that the Senate had devoted too little time to the problems of domestic intelligence abuses and oversight. Long a proponent of domestic intelligence reform, Nelson had proposed legislation to oversee domestic intelligence operations in 1971, 1973, and 1975. His bills had never been reported successfully out of the Judiciary Committee. Concerned with how this process might translate to oversight when the permanent intelligence oversight committee was formed, Nelson urged his colleagues to establish two committees, one for domestic and another for foreign intelligence. "Domestic surveillance oversight does not involve difficult political, foreign policy, and military security problems," Nelson argued. Domestic intelligence operations must adhere to constitutional protections guaranteed by the Bill of Rights. Nelson believed the First and Fourth Amendments offered "guidelines" for domestic intelligence activities. Domestic intelligence oversight, Nelson urged, was rather simple and did not require the security clearance standards that covert operations do. The Constitution is not enough to protect Americans at home from overzealous officers and institutions. President Nixon had run roughshod over the Fourth Amendment, justifying warrantless wiretaps by claiming they were used for "national security." What Watergate revealed, in full detail, was that a president could abuse that power against "anything that threatened him. For this reason, you cannot have any exceptions at all—either a warrant requirement or to the requirement that surveillance be reported to the oversight committee."[44] Nelson's pleas, however, fell on deaf ears. Government Operations Chairman Abraham Ribicoff, a Democrat from Connecticut, under pressure to send a bill to the Rules Committee in less than one month, dismissed Nelson's proposal as unfeasible.[45]

During Senate hearings about congressional oversight legislation, support for greater reform began to cleave publicly along party lines over the shape that reform should take. Conservatives claimed to support greater oversight but vocally opposed the demands of their liberal colleagues for full public disclosure of intelligence activities. Senator Barry Goldwater conceded that his Senate Armed Services Committee had not exercised effective oversight, but he insisted that most committee members did not want to know about sensitive operations. "Revelation of this information might damage the Nation," Goldwater asserted, and senators "felt the constant danger of ourselves talking about it at inopportune times. Therefore, we would be better serving our country by not hearing it." On principle the senator did not believe the public had a right to know about all programs of the U.S. intelligence agencies, especially covert action. He was concerned that the creation of yet another oversight committee increased the likelihood of national security leaks, like the recent disclosures by the Pike committee in the House.[46]

Republican senators John Tower of Texas and Strom Thurmond of South Carolina opposed the new oversight committee. Tower, who had served as vice chairman of the Church committee, believed agencies needed to be protected from, not subject to, oversight. Though he acknowledged "intelligence excesses," he maintained that the Church committee's recommendations for greater congressional oversight "restrict[ed] Presidential discretion, without enhancing efficiency, control or accountability." Tower supported the president's proposal to criminalize disclosures and argued that any reorganization of the intelligence community should be directed from the executive branch, not imposed by Congress. U.S. intelligence agencies, Tower remarked, performed at a "distinct disadvantage" to their counterparts like the KGB (Soviet internal security force) because they operated in an "open society." He believed that greater congressional oversight would further burden agencies that were the "linchpin" of the national security state. Thurmond worried that greater oversight would inevitably lead to leaks. Intelligence, Thurmond argued, "is a very delicate commodity. If you have a good intelligence force which can keep a secret, it can be most valuable." If intelligence is leaked, Thurmond warned, "it is not worth the time and the effort that it takes to gather it."[47] Conservative opposition to national security reform proved an effective organizing principle for the New Right in the late 1970s and helped bring Ronald Reagan into the White House in 1981.

Conservative opposition in the Senate, however, remained relatively small, and the Senate voted overwhelmingly to establish the Select Senate Committee on Intelligence in May 1976. The House followed in 1977 with the House Permanent Select Committee on Intelligence. *Times* columnist James Reston lauded the committees as irrefutable evidence that Congress and the nation were committed to greater transparency. By acknowledging a legislative role in the conduct of intelligence operations, Reston claimed, Congress challenged the executive branch's long-standing contention that "intelligence operations could not be effective in a disorderly world if they were subjected to the normal constitutional legislative and financial controls of the Congress."[48]

Democratic presidential candidate Jimmy Carter cheered the new committees from the campaign trail. At least some people thought he did. It was hard to pin down Carter on any one issue—conservatives believed the candidate reflected their views, liberals thought he was their candidate. Carter seemed to offer everything to everyone and, therefore, nothing to anyone. One thing all Americans were certain about—this candidate would not be another Nixon. "I will never lie to you," Carter repeated at campaign stops around the country. The relatively obscure former Georgia governor campaigned as the antithesis of "Tricky Dick" Nixon and the man who pardoned him, President Ford. He promised to restore Americans' faith in their government, though exactly how he would do that remained unclear. Untarnished by the scandals of recent years, Carter had a powerful advantage over incumbent Gerald Ford. As historian Bruce Schulman explained, Carter "rode the wave of post-Watergate fears of the imperial presidency" right into the White House.[49]

Carter chose as his running mate the liberal and consummate Washington insider, Senator Walter Mondale of Minnesota, a seemingly unlikely pick for the "outsider" candidate. He was the protégé of Minnesota senator, former vice president, and onetime presidential candidate Hubert Humphrey. As a college student Mondale organized for Humphrey and Truman. He first came to Washington to work for Students for Democratic Action, the student arm of the liberal vanguard, Americans for Democratic Action. He later returned to Minnesota, earned a law degree, married a fellow Macalester alumna, and started a law practice. There he worked on several statewide campaigns and was rewarded for his hard work by being appointed attorney general in 1960 (the youngest state attorney general in the nation) and to a Senate seat in 1964 when Humphrey became President Johnson's vice president.[50]

In the Senate, Mondale quickly became known as a liberal standard-bearer, but even more so, an institutional reformer. During his second term Mondale united with other reform-minded senators such as Jim Pearson, a Republican from Kansas, to change Senate rules to make it easier to break filibusters.[51] He may have been an insider, but for Carter's purposes, he was a proponent of institutional reform, a good fit for Carter's "outsider" run on Washington.

Carter saw in the young senator not only the Washington experience that he lacked but also a fierce commitment to reaffirming checks and balances in constitutional government.[52] The *Times* lauded Carter's vice presidential choice, calling the senator a "major figure from Capitol Hill," who was likely to bring a "healthy Congressional view of the office [of the presidency]" to the administration.[53] In fact, Mondale was a recent convert to the movement for national security reform. Throughout the 1960s he believed, like many other Americans, that the consolidation of power in the executive branch was a necessary development to protect the national interest in a dangerous world. By the early 1970s, however, after the twin disasters of Vietnam and Watergate, Mondale began to see the "imperial presidency" as a threat to democracy. Though he did not wish to see a "weak President," he had come to believe that Congress needed to make the executive branch "act within the constitutional parameters of that power."

Mondale had chaired the Church committee subcommittee on domestic intelligence abuses. This experience turned the young senator into an outspoken critic of the domestic operations perpetrated on the American public in the name of national security. Mondale conceded that proposals to reform the intelligence community would be useless and ineffective if a better system of checks and balances was not implemented. He supported permanent congressional oversight committees in both chambers of Congress. He believed that American citizens should have the right to sue the federal government and elected and appointed officials who violated their constitutional rights. He called for the attorney general to have a stronger role in managing the FBI and other intelligence agencies. He firmly believed that top-level officials should be directly responsible for the conduct of their agencies. This would prevent future abuses from being dismissed as aberrations—no one could again claim that they didn't know what their subordinates were doing. As the Church and Pike committee investigations showed, extraconstitutional activities had often been approved by word of mouth. Mondale called for all new intelligence programs to be approved in writing by a department's legal counsel, firmly stating that such a program would be compatible with constitutional protections. Only a statutory framework, Mondale reckoned, would prevent the emergence of such abuses in the future. He called for charters for the CIA, FBI, and other intelligence agencies to halt constitutional violations.[54]

Carter flip-flopped on the issue of how he would correct intelligence abuses. He supported greater government transparency, except in the case of "narrowly defined national security matters." He would not use the CIA to "overthrow the government or change the policies of other nations," though he supported covert operations in "some circumstances." His vice presidential pick made his support for major intelligence reform known on the campaign trail. Mondale believed that Americans wanted a candidate with a "respect for the law and a willingness to accept defeat if need be rather than break or subvert" it, and a president who maintained a "fundamental respect for the civil liberties of the people guaranteed under the Bill of Rights." Mondale firmly believed the Constitution did not provide any "constitutional authority for the President or any intelligence agency to violate the law," and he was deeply committed to overhauling the intelligence community.[55]

Halperin and the CNSS staff had reason to celebrate in December 1976. Not only had their candidate Carter and the intelligence reformer Mondale won the presidential election, but also the courts and Congress seemed poised to enter a new era of forcing executive accountability for constitutional rights violations and broadening transparency. Only a few months earlier, in September, President Ford signed the Government in the Sunshine Act into law. The law required some fifty federal agencies to give advance notice of scheduled meetings and make the meetings open to the public. The bill also amended FOIA, narrowing the number of agencies that could legally withhold information from the public. The bill was a major coup for transparency advocates.[56]

In December federal district court justice John Lewis held former president Nixon and other top-level officials liable for civil damages for maintaining a nearly two-year-long wiretap on Morton Halperin's home phone. Lewis found that "there can be no serious contention that the Fourth Amendment's independent requirement of reasonableness is suspended in the area of national security searches and seizures." The judge ruled that every citizen, including elected and appointed officials in the nation's highest offices, can be "accountable for personal misconduct." Recent legal precedents, the judge concluded, "indicate that government officials are not immune from suit for alleged illegalities committed in office." The judge ordered the defendants to pay damages to Halperin, in the amount of one dollar each. The case offered many legal firsts. It was the first suit brought against a president for his official conduct while in office to be found in favor of the plaintiff. Nixon was the first president ordered to give a deposition about his activities in office. The lawsuit also made Nixon the first president to be held liable for damages in spite of various immunity defense claims available to high officials. Finally, Nixon was the first president in the nation's history ordered to pay damages to a plaintiff.[57]

With the legislative and judicial branches playing an increasingly assertive role in checking the power of the executive and protecting civil liberties, the ACLU and CNSS believed that Jimmy Carter's inauguration signaled a new era of executive-level restraints on the national security state. Halperin personally believed that CNSS had a friend in the White House and hoped that access to Carter's domestic policy team would lead to much-needed legislative reform. Some of Halperin's former colleagues had joined the new administration, signaling the new president's willingness to maintain open dialogue with public interest groups. Halperin gushed, "The very fact of access [to policymakers] is new. Where Levi refused to even meet with [CNSS] on the national security wiretap bill or the domestic intelligence guidelines, there is now ready access."[58]

If public interest groups were optimistic about the new president, the U.S. intelligence agencies regarded the Carter administration with more than a little trepidation. The recent shake-ups and rapid turnover of top-level appointments left the agencies demoralized and worried over the prospect of more change. Legislative reform, however, required the administration to work closely with congressional allies. Immediately, Carter got off on the wrong foot with the Democratic-controlled Congress. Mondale observed that Carter's self-proclaimed "outsider" status did not sit well with consummate "insiders" on Capitol Hill. Believing he claimed the moral high ground, Carter refused to compromise, lectured leaders on the Hill when they disagreed with him on policy, and refused to consult with his own party on legislative initiatives. His behavior prompted Mondale to proclaim that his boss had the "coldest political nose of any politician I ever met."[59]

Carter's attitude further committed congressional leaders to reasserting their constitutional role of oversight. In one of its first assertions of will, Congress met Carter's nominee for director of Central Intelligence, John Kennedy's former aide Theodore ("Ted") Sorensen, with such fierce opposition that Sorensen withdrew his name. At the heart of the Sorenson debate was the issue of transparency among top-level officials. Liberals like Senator Joseph Biden opposed Sorensen as the nominee because Sorenson had admitted at Daniel Ellsberg's trial to taking several cartons of classified paperwork from the White House (which he later used to help him write his book). Biden called Sorensen "political dynamite" because Sorensen's use of classified information "embodied a philosophy of liberal release of material that ran counter to the views" of members of the new Senate Intelligence Committee. Morton Halperin noted that many rumors circulated about why Sorenson faced such fierce opposition. He believed that the episode reflected how far the movement had to go to defeat the secrecy system. Carter's next choice, retired navy admiral Stansfield Turner, proved much less amicable to reform than Halperin and others hoped. During his confirmation hearings Turner declared further intelligence reform unnecessary. He revived President Ford's effort to punish "leakers," promising to submit legislation to criminalize leaks of intelligence sources and methods. National security reformers might have preferred Sorenson.[60]

Even without the political blunders, Carter faced formidable challenges when he arrived in Washington. Stagflation—slow growth, high unemployment, and roaring inflation—plagued the American economy. When Carter took office nearly 40 percent of all Americans ranked unemployment as the most pressing national concern. Carter's first policy initiatives included welfare reform, energy policy, and combating inflation. Not surprisingly, national security reform did not rank among Carter's top legislative priorities.[61] Halperin denounced the new administration for getting "caught up in the crisis of the day" and for allowing senior staff like NSC advisor Zbigniew Brzezinski, who favored secrecy over transparency, to stymie reform. Halperin fervently believed in the persuasive political abilities of Vice President Walter Mondale: "What is needed is strong leadership from the top to set in motion the mechanism to produce comprehensive legislation to bring the intelligence agencies under the Constitution. The logical man to lead such an effort is the Vice President."[62]

Never content to sit and wait for change to happen, Halperin exerted as much pressure on the Carter administration as possible. In February 1977 he coauthored a careful study of government classification systems. He warned that Carter's campaign commitment to "openness" was likely facing stiff opposition from executive-level agencies. The bureaucracy always has a vested interest in the status quo, Halperin wrote, and "fears the new because of its uncertain impact on power relations." He predicted that institutions would continue to claim "dire consequences" if the executive continued to trend toward transparency and accountability. What Washington needed, urged Halperin, was "nothing less than a radical change in perspective" in order to ensure that "whatever is needed for public debate . . . be made public."[63] But who would lead this radical change in perspective?

The vice president seemed the likely candidate. In the Senate Mondale had helped to draft the original FISA legislation. He was proud of that legislation for its compromises. It didn't "tie the agencies' hands in advance" but would "require that they make their case before a court of law." Mondale began quietly working with members of Congress on a bill to restrict executive-level surveillance and wiretapping. The FISA bill tested Mondale's considerable political skills, not only because Carter's insolence had spurred congressional backlash, but also because congressional leaders were leery of accepting a bill written in conjunction with the administration. Senators Edward Kennedy and Birch Bayh, a Democrat from Indiana, opposed the administration's first bill, tying it up in committee. But Mondale faced stiffer resistance to FISA from within the administration. He recalled that he served frequently as the "main advocate for tough court oversight of the surveillance" among Carter's top advisors. In particular, Zbigniew Brzezinski and CIA Director Stansfield Turner voiced much opposition to the legislation.[64]

The Foreign Intelligence Surveillance Act of 1978 reflected years of compromises between Congress, two presidential administrations, and public interest groups like the ACLU and Common Cause. The bill established a new court, the Foreign Intelligence Surveillance Court, comprised of seven district court judges appointed by the chief justice of the Supreme Court. The statute required the executive branch to submit surveillance requests to the court, and judges had the right to see all evidence supporting the request. Three judges (serving overlapping terms) reviewed requests that were denied. The bill allowed the executive branch broad latitude in special cases. In the event that a request was time-sensitive—if the administration believed court proceedings might compromise intelligence—the attorney general could waive the warrant requirement. No warrants were required for communications between foreign entities. Following a congressional declaration of war, the executive branch could waive the application procedure for the first fifteen days. Most important, the statute excluded wiretapping except through the express authority of the law, denying the executive's legal authority to invoke a broadly construed "inherent power" as justification for warrantless surveillance. In a staff memo on the passage of the bill, White House aide Stu Eizenstat observed that the final bill had the support of the Justice Department and other affected agencies, and even longtime opponent Brzezinski recommended the president's signature.[65]

Close observers noted that the battle to enact FISA had taken a toll on the public and its supporters in Congress. Passing the bill, moaned Senator Bayh, had been "like trying to run in sorghum molasses in January." He wondered gloomily, "How many of our colleagues and how many citizens will have said, well, [Congress has] done enough already" to protect civil liberties? Even as they cheered the passage of FISA, many reformers hoped it was just the "first piece of charter legislation for the intelligence community."[66] Morton Halperin, however, was not so glum. He cheered FISA. "The clearest victory in the [FISA] law is that it lays to rest the claims of inherent presidential power to conduct warrantless national security wiretaps." Even if further reform stalled on Capitol Hill, Halperin thought reformers had much of which to be proud.

If there had once been a broad-based impetus for national security reform among elected officials, it was quickly dissipating. Working closely with a few committed reformers in the House and Senate, CNSS helped draft CIA charter legislation, one of the few remaining items on the legislative "wish list" of national security reformers. In April 1977 the draft charter was making the rounds in the Senate, but reformers were getting little help from the Carter administration.

In fact, Mondale had a change of heart. With the support of CIA Director Turner, Mondale urged the president to consult with the Senate Intelligence Committee and "endorse the principle of intelligence legislation," but ask Congress to delay consideration of the charter until after the administration received internal reviews and recommendations on intelligence activities. Mondale urged Carter to "dispel any suggestions that the Administration is opposed to legislative charters, to assure the Congress that you want to work with it, and to head off premature efforts by the Congress to force the Administration's hand on the substance of such legislation." Carter approved. Mondale recognized the political benefits of supporting charter legislation given Carter's campaign rhetoric but wavered on the real benefits of broad-based intelligence reform. Convinced by the national security team that legislation might tie the hands of the executive branch, Mondale took pains to avoid putting the White House in the "difficult position of seeming to be opposed to intelligence legislation."[67]

Mondale's plan worked brilliantly. The administration successfully stalled the legislation during 1978, going back and forth with Congress over the language and tone of the bill. Liberals, who had once been the lions of security reform, lost their appetite for the fight with one of their own in the White House. Carter's willingness to postpone intelligence charter legislation suggested, according to one scholar, "a level of political sophistication and intelligence unmatched in his performances in other policy initiatives." Carter came to appreciate the institutional perspective of national security and executive prerogative. He had initially supported a legislative charter for the CIA, but faced with foreign policy challenges, he came to favor executive order reforms, and Congress eventually conceded to his demands.[68]

In November 1979 Iranians stormed the American embassy and took sixty-six Americans hostage. Carter quietly asked Congress to postpone consideration of charter legislation until the following year.[69] The next year the Soviets invaded Afghanistan, and the Cold War heated up once again. Facing the reality of these ongoing crises, the impetus for intelligence reform among members of Congress dissolved. The administration convinced Congress to pass a watered-down bill that, as one scholar argued, "legislatively institutionalized a system of lax congressional oversight of the CIA." Congress passed the Intelligence Oversight Act of 1980, which repealed the Hughes-Ryan Amendment of 1974, reducing the number of committees that received intelligence briefings to the two intelligence committees in the House and Senate, allowing the White House to delay notifying Congress of covert operations, and containing virtually none of the charter restrictions envisioned by reformers in the wake of the Church and Pike investigations.[70] The following year, in 1981, the Senate Select Committee on Intelligence, the oversight mechanism of the nation's intelligence agencies, explained in its annual report these shifting priorities. "Events throughout the world portend a future of profound changes" and none more so than in the movement to reform the national security state. The committee identified worldwide events: "The revolution in Iran, the seizure of American diplomats as hostages, the war between Iraq and Iran, the Soviet invasion of Afghanistan," tensions around the world, and "the accelerating proliferation of strategic weapons, the energy crisis, the growing threat of terrorism and assassination, and unparalleled economic and technological developments" as reasons for the nation to have an "intelligence system that is on full alert and responsive."[71] Some believed the movement to reform the national security state had inevitably weakened it. In the changing geopolitical climate, these developments would weaken public and institutional support for reform.

The movement to restrict intelligence abuses of the FBI never received the public support that the CIA charter briefly did. This was an unintended consequence of the Church and Pike committees' overwhelming focus on abuses by the foreign intelligence community. People attributed the abuses of the Bureau to the perverse proclivities of its longtime director J. Edgar Hoover. One *Times* journalist who specialized in intelligence matters penned an opinion that was widely shared on Capitol Hill: "A lot of what is now labeled wrong about the bureau's methods was an outgrowth of the personality and attitude of J. Edgar Hoover. . . . It was Hoover who urged his officers to discredit Dr. King and who authorized the tricks and turns of cointel[pro]."[72] Following nearly a decade of airing the agency's dirty laundry, many felt satisfied that the FBI's ghosts had been sufficiently exorcised. In the aftermath of the Church and Pike investigations, directors like Clarence Kelley worked assiduously to assure the public and Congress that a new atmosphere of accountability governed FBI activities. Congress did manage to pass legislation placing a ten-year term limit on the FBI director. This modest legislation signaled the end of tangible legislative reform in the 1970s era.

Ronald Reagan's election in 1980 marked the end of intelligence reform. The legislative and judicial successes of the reform effort, however, would continue to be felt into the twenty-first century. Activists had achieved success that many would have not thought possible in the mid-1960s. They took advantage of political opportunities. They reformed the state by strengthening checks and balances, not demolishing the apparatus itself. Finally, they took democracy seriously and brought the national debate about these issues to American living rooms across the country. They successfully framed two issues—the "right to know" and the "right to privacy"—to appeal to liberals and conservatives alike. This bipartisan support proved crucial to the legislative success of the movement.

The national security state inherited by the Reagan administration in 1981 looked much like the one that presidents Kennedy and Johnson presided over. In fact, the state itself remained remarkably the same. What had changed, however subtly, was the relationship that average Americans—from across the political spectrum—had with it. The Leviathan of the Eisenhower-Kennedy-Johnson administrations, though still intimidating and immense, seemed no longer impenetrable. Now, citizens had new tools with which to pry into the state's dark recesses and expose its secrets. These tools have played, and will continue to play, vital roles in our democratic process.

Epilogue

For all its accomplishments, the movement to reform the state did not realize some of its goals by the end of the 1970s. The contingencies that had created a window of opportunity for reformers to challenge entrenched state power—revelations of government impropriety, a vibrant investigative journalism, powerful, well-funded public advocacy groups, and reform-minded elected officials—had firmly closed by the end of the decade. Even before the Foreign Intelligence Surveillance Act became law on October 25, 1978, the neo-progressive movement no longer exercised the same degree of influence it once had in Washington. This was largely the result of two developments in American society in the late 1970s. Key players, individuals as well as organizations and institutions, that had been central to the success of the movement lost their ability to influence the debate. Second, a series of unanticipated global events gave fuel to those who opposed further national security reform and strengthened national security institutions that had been weakened by nearly a decade of scandal.

For nearly two decades the American Civil Liberties Union had been the hub of a vigorous knowledge network dedicated to checking the powers of the executive branch through legislative and judicial reform. By the mid-1970s, the ACLU faced a number of public relations challenges that eventually undermined its standing among even its most ardent supporters. The ACLU had drawn public support primarily from liberals, progressives, and civil libertarians. As Aryeh Neier recalled, "the ACLU thrives on adversity." Where presidents Nixon and Ford had been good for the organization's membership drives, the Carter administration, which professed a desire to rein in national security abuses, was bad.[1] The economic crisis led some Americans to let their memberships expire. The organization's robust litigation and legislative strategies had depended, in part, on revenue from annual membership as well as funding from foundations. Fewer annual memberships forced the organization to reprioritize and scale back on some of its programs.

If the ACLU's greatest challenge had been financial, then its decline might only have been temporary. Ronald Reagan's election in 1980 might have encouraged old members to come back to the organization as well as attract new members, but in the late 1970s the ACLU's reputation as a civil liberties bulwark suffered from two public relations disasters. Documents obtained through a standard FOIA request to the FBI revealed that the Bureau had paid informers working within the ACLU throughout the 1950s. This revelation damaged the organization's political position in Washington and disappointed even its most staunch defenders. The ACLU suffered a second blow in 1977 when it decided to defend the rights of Nazis to demonstrate in Skokie, Illinois. Both these episodes and the negative publicity they generated undermined the ACLU's ability to continue to shape public opinion.

In his book *Reforms at Risk*, political scientist Erik Patashnik argued that so-called "coalition leaders" who do the work of writing legislation and defending it, who forge the political compromises necessary to see legislation passed, and who monitor long-term policy implementation are vital to the long-term success of policy agendas.[2] Aryeh Neier had been one such leader in the national security reform movement. In 1978 he left the ACLU to join a fledgling organization, Helsinki Watch (later Human Rights Watch), and advocate for human rights policy at home and abroad. A number of prominent congressional leaders who had worked as allies and defenders of the movement's goals of transparency and greater checks and balances retired in the 1970s. Neo-progressives had relied upon elected officials like Senator Sam Ervin and Representative John Moss to influence the debate, to inform the public and their colleagues, and to forge bipartisan coalitions. Sam Ervin retired in 1974 after realizing his personal goal of enacting right to privacy legislation. Representative John Moss, an early proponent of transparency and accountability and a strong supporter of bills to strengthen checks and balances, retired in 1978, returning to work in the private sector. Ervin's chief counsel on the Senate Constitutional Rights subcommittee, Larry Baskir, accepted a position in 1974 in the Ford White House as director of the Presidential Clemency Board. Christopher Pyle continued to consult with Senate committees through 1976 when he accepted a position as professor of political science at Mt. Holyoke College in Massachusetts.

Without these seasoned reformers, neo-progressives faced considerable challenges on Capitol Hill. Partly as a result of the Watergate scandal, Congress was an institution in transformation. Some of the movement's most stalwart allies either left Washington or lost the power to shape legislative change. When Vice President George H. W. Bush presided over the swearing-in of the Senate of the 97th Congress on January 5, 1981, more than 50 percent of the Senate had served less than a full six-year term. Though some in Congress still remembered the battles to reform the national security state that had consumed Congress at mid-decade, Congress's interest in these issues had dissipated considerably.

Despite its efforts to reaffirm checks and balances, Congress continued to suffer from public distrust for elected officials. One of the many casualties of this new political climate was Senate Republican Clifford Case of New Jersey. A member of the Senate since 1955, Case lost his primary race in 1978 to Jeffrey Bell, a former aide to Ronald Reagan. Case's surprise defeat demonstrated the Republican Party's shift to the right. As ranking member of the Senate Foreign Relations Committee, Case had been a knowledgeable voice in the battles over national security policy. When asked to explain his unexpected primary loss, Case blamed public dissatisfaction with government institutions: "People are unhappy with Congress, the Senate, not with any one person." For Case, public dissatisfaction came from people's sense that Congress had failed to adequately address pocketbook politics. He cautioned: "There is no single solution, like a tax cut for example, that will solve all [the nation's economic] problems."[3] With inflation the public's number one concern, transparency and civil liberties violations took a backseat.[4]

As the example of Senator Case suggests, American politics and political culture were undergoing a sea change in the late 1970s. The watershed election of 1980 offered the Republican Party a resounding victory. With a Republican majority in the Senate for the first time since 1955, the changing of the guard was palpable. Senate Historian Emeritus Richard Baker recalled that "the Democrats had been doing what they had been doing for several decades. . . . 1981 brought lots of hope and optimism."[5] Having been the minority party in the Senate for twenty-six years, Republicans declared that they would run things differently in the majority. New committee chairmen had long lists of legislative priorities. Under the leadership of President Reagan, who favored a strong national security state and a powerful executive, institutions like the CIA, FBI, and NSC would find a climate more favorable to their interests and a Congress less eager to exercise oversight. In the early 1980s Reagan rolled back restrictions on the FBI, instructing Attorney General William French Smith to broaden surveillance of domestic groups who posed a threat to internal security. As justification for relaxing Watergate-era restrictions, Smith cited FBI officers' reluctance to investigate domestic organizations because of concerns over "personal liability."[6]

Given their stalled reform agenda, reformers like John Shattuck devoted institutional resources to the quieter work of educating the public, requesting dossiers via the Freedom of Information Act and Privacy Act, and working on behalf of citizens who believed their rights had been violated by national security institutions. As Shattuck's ACLU speaking tours suggest, the organization did not abandon its efforts to challenge executive power but developed strategies to challenge that power in new ways. CNSS organized community-based workshops to teach citizens how to use FOIA to gain information about surveillance practices from national agencies. In Chicago, the ACLU sponsored a conference to teach local litigators how to sue state and local governments for access to individual dossiers using the examples of successful ACLU lawsuits against municipal red squads. Chicago's Better Government Association published a litigation manual and drew up plans to develop a "library" to hold all the documents that became available as a result of successful litigation.[7]

Their efforts paid off. Americans, with the assistance of public advocacy groups like the ACLU and CNSS, brought civil lawsuits against government agencies and officers and demanded restitution for the violation of their constitutional rights. The government expense for legal representation of government employees soared, from an average of $60,000 in legal fees paid to private attorneys in 1974 and 1975, to more than $448,000 in 1977 and more than $450,000 in 1978.[8]

At the Center for National Security Studies Morton Halperin launched the Campaign to Stop Government Spying in 1977, creating a coalition of more than seventy organizations who battled to exert greater oversight over local, state, and federal intelligence agencies. Taking cues from the Carter administration's attention to human rights issues, the CNSS shifted its focus in the late 1970s from the domestic abuses of the national security state to the broader applications of national security policy under the Reagan administration. During the first Reagan term, the organization leveled much criticism at the president's foreign policies in Latin America and Cambodia, and offered sharp critiques of the administration's human rights record.[9]

The movement for national security reform that ignited public debate in the 1970s did not begin or end then. Two episodes in the 1980s and 1990s illustrate both the retrenchment of the executive branch and a disavowal of the reformist impulse. In 1986 evidence that the Reagan administration had sold weapons to Iran, then under an arms embargo, in order to secure the release of American hostages and to fund the U.S.-backed Contras in Nicaragua, caused a national scandal. Congress assembled a joint committee to investigate, and the hearings were televised live to a curious and, at times, incredulous American audience. The hearings revived public debates about executive power, transparency, and checks and balances. Unlike similar investigations during the 1970s, however, the Joint Committee's final report failed to produce lasting legislative reform. In the 1990s Congress, frustrated with the executive branch's lack of transparency but unwilling to exercise aggressive oversight, created a commission to investigate classification programs and government secrecy—the first in four decades. The Commission on Protecting and Reducing Government Secrecy issued its final report in 1997, which included a number of legislative recommendations. None of the commission's proposals became law.[10]

The relative success in the 1970s of a loose coalition of good government activists, investigative journalists, elected officials, and public interest groups underscores the contingencies that made the reform of the national security state possible. The Freedom of Information Act revisions and the Privacy Act of 1974 created a framework that continues to govern the flow of information between the American public and its government. The establishment of permanent congressional intelligence oversight committees in 1976 and 1977 reinvigorated congressional oversight of the CIA and other federal intelligence agencies, though the exercise of that aggressive and effective oversight has ebbed and flowed as public opinion on issues of transparency and accountability has changed over time. The Foreign Intelligence Surveillance Act of 1978 established a new role for the judiciary in the process of domestic surveillance and wiretapping. This legislative watershed restrained the ability of the president and, more generally, the executive branch of the federal government from operating independently of democratic oversight and running roughshod over the civil liberties of the American citizenry.

Recent revelations that the administration of President George W. Bush circumvented and revised FISA, stonewalled FOIA requests, and demonstrated little regard for the Privacy Act do not undermine the significance of the reform movement of the 1970s. This study puts these contemporary issues into historical context. Contemporary debates eerily echo the past. This much is certainly true. The Bush administration's decision to circumvent the FISA court and wiretap Americans at home without a warrant might have gone undiscovered but for one whistle-blower who grew uneasy about the Justice Department's handling of this special program. Eventually, he called the *New York Times*. The *Times* decided, somewhat cautiously, to publish the story in spite of the administration's contention that to do so would threaten national security.[11]

This recent account reminds us that the legal framework reformers established in the 1970s is important. For this reformers can claim credit and also deserve the gratitude of the American people. Laws are only as good as those citizens and institutions willing to use them, and who demand that government obey them. When the nation feels threatened, as in the years after September 11, that desire and willingness can dissipate— and understandably so. Historians can only offer the lessons of the past as a warning. Certainly, the task remains to bring some of the issues that I have explored here into the twenty-first century.

The right to know movement reinvigorated and modeled a kind of civic activism that demands transparency and accountability from public institutions. Recent advances in technology, such as the personal computer and the internet, have empowered new organizations to defend the public's right to know what its government is doing. The National Freedom of Information Coalition, for example, protects "the public's right to oversee its government." The National Security Archive at the George Washington University maintains a clearinghouse of national security documents obtained through FOIA requests. Through new social media technologies, the citizen's "right to know" has become a global movement, with groups like the Freedom of Information Advocates Network, founded in 2002, serving as an "international information-sharing network" of individuals and organizations who demand access to government information. Media organizations have banded together, forming the Sunshine in Government Initiative to promote "policies that ensure the government is accessible, accountable and open." One of its members is the American Society of News Editors, one of the outspoken advocates for the freedom of information movement in the 1950s. OMB Watch, created in 1983 in response to the Reagan administration's efforts to cut spending in federal human services programs, functions to promote "open government, accountability, and citizen participation."[12] Ironically, computer technology, which spurred the demands for transparency in the 1960s and 1970s, provides greater opportunities to promote freedom of information than ever before. The culture of transparency and accountability has inspired a new generation of online activists. *Time* magazine recently observed that online transparency forums "could become as important a journalist tool as the Freedom of Information Act."[13]

Battles over government transparency and accountability continue to inform our national policy debates and structure our political culture in the early twenty-first century. This is perhaps the most enduring legacy of the reform movement of the Vietnam and Watergate era.

Notes

INTRODUCTION

1 "Political Spying Topic of Seminar," *The Detroit News*, 9 June 1977, 8-B; "Newsletter of the Michigan Coalition to End Government Spying," Winter 1978, MSUSC; author's interview with John Shattuck, 8 November 2007, audio recording (in author's possession).

2 Douglas T. Stuart, *Creating the National Security State: A History of the Law That Transformed America* (Princeton, NJ: Princeton University Press, 2008), 43.

3 David Garrow, *The FBI and Martin Luther King, Jr.: From "Solo" to Memphis* (New York: W. W. Norton, 1981); Kenneth O'Reilly, *Hoover and the Un-Americans: The FBI, HUAC, and the Red Menace* (Philadelphia: Temple University Press, 1983); Richard Gid Powers, *Broken: The Troubled Past and Uncertain Future of the FBI* (New York: Free Press, 2004); Alan Theoharis, *The FBI and American Democracy: A Brief Critical History* (Lawrence: University Press of Kansas, 2004), and *Chasing Spies: How the FBI Failed in Counterintelligence but Promoted the Politics of McCarthyism in the Cold War Years* (Chicago: Ivan R. Dee, 2002); John Elliff, *The Reform of FBI Intelligence Operations* (Princeton, NJ: Princeton University Press, 1979).

4 Arthur M. Schlesinger, *The Imperial Presidency* (Boston: Houghton Mifflin, 1973); Thomas E. Cronin, "A Resurgent Congress and the Imperial Presidency," *Political Science Quarterly* 95, no. 2 (Summer 1980): 209–237; Theodore J. Lowi, "Presidential Power: Restoring the Balance," *Political Science Quarterly* 100, no. 2 (Summer 1985): 185–213; Sidney M. Milkis, "The Presidency, Democratic Reform, and Constitutional Change," *PS: Political Science and Politics* (Summer 1987): 628–636.

5 Theda Skocpol, *Diminished Democracy: From Membership to Management in American Civic Life* (Norman: University of Oklahoma Press, 2003); Robert Putnam, *Bowling Alone: The Collapse and Revival of American Community* (New York: Simon and Schuster, 2000).

6 Steve Fraser and Gary Gerstle, eds., *The Rise and Fall of the New Deal Order, 1930–1980* (Princeton, NJ: Princeton University Press, 1989); Edward Berkowitz, *Something Happened: A Political and Cultural Overview of the Seventies* (New York: Columbia University Press, 2006); Bruce Schulman and Julian Zelizer, eds., *Rightward Bound: Making America Conservative in the 1970s* (Cambridge, MA: Harvard University Press, 2008); Thomas Borstelmann, *The 1970s: A New Global History from Civil Rights to Economic Inequality* (Princeton, NJ: Princeton University Press, 2012); Jefferson Cowie, *Stayin' Alive: The 1970s and the Last Days of the Working Class* (New York: New Press, 2012).

7 As James Morone has observed about American democracy, "the search for more direct democracy builds up the bureaucracy." See *The Democratic Wish: Popular Participation and the Limits of American Government* (New Haven, CT: Yale University Press, 1998), 1.

8 Aryeh Neier, *Only Judgment: The Limits of Litigation in Social Change* (Middletown, CT: Wesleyan University Press, 1982), 154.

CHAPTER 1. "RECRUITING AN ARMY": RUSS WIGGINS DEMANDS TRANSPARENCY

1 This is compiled from a House committee staff report of the incident. "Memorandum for the Record, Subject: Giraffes," 28 October 1957, box 921, Miscellaneous; Records of the U.S. House of Representatives, Committee on Government Operations, Special Subcommittee on Government Information (RG233), NADC. See also Nate Haseltine, "Giraffe Resembles Hypertensive Cow Pinched into G-Suit, Doctor Reports," *Washington Post* (hereafter *WP*), 28 October 1957.

2 "Fort Monmouth Case," *New York Times* (hereafter *NYT*), 14 January 1954, 28.

3 David M. Oshinsky, *A Conspiracy So Immense: The World of Joe McCarthy* (New York: Free Press, 1983), 435–445.

4 Jeff Broadwater, *Eisenhower and the Anti-Communist Crusade* (Chapel Hill: University of North Carolina Press, 1992), 151–157; James Patterson, *Grand Expectations: The United States, 1945–1974* (New York: Oxford University Press, 1996), 267–268; "Unnecessary Suspense," *NYT*, 18 May 1954, 28; Oshinsky, *Conspiracy So Immense*, 442–443.

5 Robert O. Blanchard, "A Watchdog in Decline," *Columbia Journalism Review* 5, no. 2 (Summer 1966): 17.

6 Harry S. Truman, "Executive Order 10290—Prescribing Regulations Establishing Minimum Standards for the Classification, Transmission, and Handling, by Departments and Agencies of the Executive Branch, of Official Information Which Requires Safeguarding in the Interest of the Security of the United States," September 24, 1951. Online by Gerhard Peters and John T. Woolley, *The American Presidency Project*, http://www.presidency.ucsb.edu/ws/?pid=78426.

7 Edward T. Folliard, "Truman Orders Uniform Code for U.S. Secrets; Newsmen Fear It May Mean Clamming Up," *WP*, 26 September, 1951, 3; "AP Editors Hit Truman Order Curbing News," *Los Angeles Times*, 30 September 1951, 1; "Editors Denounce Truman News Ban," *NYT*, 30 September 1951, 39; Robert McCormick, "Freedom of the Press III," *Chicago Daily Tribune*, 4 November 1951, 22.

8 "Security Lid Is Clamped on Federal Departments," *Christian Science Monitor*, 26 September 1951, 17.

9 Paul Alfred Pratte, *Gods within the Machine: A History of the American Society of Newspaper Editors, 1923–1993* (Westport, CT: Praeger Publishers, 1995), 72–103; "Editors Plan Ways to Fight News Gag," *WP*, 21 November, 1954, M6; "Editors Lambaste News Suppression," *WP*, 22 April, 1951, M9.

10. "Editors Urged to Fight 'Tightening Down of News Barriers,'" *Christian Science Monitor*, 27 September 1951, 5; "Editors Map Fight on News Restrictions," *WP*, 27 September 1951, 3; "Editors Lambaste News Suppression," *WP*, 22 April 1951, M9.

11. "Censorship Begins to Get out of Hand," *The Hartford Courant*, 11 January 1951, 8; Drew Pearson, "Democratic Custom Abandoned," *WP*, 16 December 1951, B5; Robert McCormick, "Freedom of the Press III," *Chicago Daily Tribune*, 4 November 1951, 22.

12 "Censorship Begins to Get Out of Hand," 8; "Editors Map Fight," 3.

13 Harold L. Cross, *The People's Right to Know: Legal Access to Public Records and Proceedings* (Morningside Heights, NY: Columbia University Press), 1953, vii–x.

14 John E. Moss, Oral History Interview, conducted in 1989 by Donald B. Seney, California State University, Sacramento, for the California State Archives, State Government Oral History Program, 1–4.

15 Ibid., 7–8.

16 Ibid., 6, 10–11, 29, 39, 47–50.

17 Ibid., 51–54.

18 Ibid., 25, 63–64.

19 Ibid., 99–100.

20 George R. Berdes interview with John E. Moss, 13 April 1965, in Berdes, *Friendly Adversaries: The Press and Government* (Milwaukee: Center for the Study of the American Press, Marquette University, 1969), 61; Ed Creagh, "Reporters Still Fight News Blackout," *WP*, 27 June 1955, 19.

21 William Dawson to John Moss, 9 June 1955, U.S. Congress, House of Representatives, Committee on Government Operations, *Availability of Information from Federal Departments and Agencies, Part 1: Panel Discussion with Editors, et al.: Hearings before a Subcommittee of the Committee on Government Operations, House of Representatives*, 84th Cong., 1st Sess., 1955, 2.

22 See Samuel Archibald and Harold Relyea, "The Present Limits of 'Executive Privilege,'" a study prepared under the guidance of the House Foreign Operations and Government Information Subcommittee by the Library of Congress Congressional Research Service, 20 March 1973, box 518, Presidency, U.S., Executive Privilege, Bella Abzug Papers, Rare Book and Manuscript Library, Columbia University, New York, New York, 2–4.

23 "Questionnaire on Administrative Organization for Public Information Activities," 10 April 1957; box 916, Civil Aeronautics Board; RG233; NADC.

24 U.S. Congress, House, *Availability of Information from Federal Departments and Agencies*, Part 1, 3.

25 "Statement of J. R. Wiggins, Executive Editor, *Washington Post* and *Times Herald*," in U.S. Congress, House, *Availability of Information from Federal Departments and Agencies*, Part 1, 7–9.

26 Ibid.

27 "Statement of Harold L. Cross, Freedom of Information Counsel for American Society of Newspaper Editors," in U.S. Congress, House, *Availability of Information from Federal Departments and Agencies*, Part 1, 9–13.

28 "Statement of V. M. Newton, Jr., Managing Editor, Tampa (FLA) Morning Tribune," in U.S. Congress, House, *Availability of Information from Federal Departments and Agencies*, Part 1, 13–16.

29 "Statement of Guy Easterly, Publisher, La Follette (Tenn.) Press," in U.S. Congress, House, *Availability of Information from Federal Departments and Agencies*, Part 1, 20–21.

30 "Statement of Joseph Alsop, Jr., Washington Columnist and Author," in U.S. Congress, House, *Availability of Information from Federal Departments and Agencies*, Part 1, 21–22.

31 "Statement of James Reston, Washington Correspondent for the *New York Times*," in U.S. Congress, House, *Availability of Information from Federal Departments and Agencies*, Part 1, 25–27.

32 "Statement of Theodore F. Koop, Director, Washington News and Public Affairs, Columbia Broadcasting Service," in U.S. Congress, House, *Availability of Information from Federal Departments and Agencies*, Part 1, 28–29.

33 "Statement of Wade H. Nichols, Editor and Publisher, Redbook Magazine," in U.S. Congress, House, *Availability of Information from Federal Departments and Agencies*, Part 1, 29–31.

34 U.S. Congress, House, *Availability of Information from Federal Departments and Agencies*, Part 1, 38–41.

35 Ibid., 45.

36 U.S. Congress, House of Representatives, Committee on Government Operations, *Availability of Information from Federal Departments and Agencies, Twenty-fifth Intermediate Report of the Committee on Government Operations*, 84th Cong., 2d Sess., 1956, 93.

37 Ibid., 2.

38 *Availability of Information from Federal Departments and Agencies*, Part 1, 94–99.

39 Robert McG. Thomas, Jr., "John E. Moss, 84, Is Dead; Father of Anti-Secrecy Law," *NYT* 6 December 1997, D15.

40 James Russell Wiggins, *Freedom or Secrecy* (New York: Oxford University Press), 1956, 225; U.S. Congress, Committee on Government Operations, U.S. House of Representatives, and Committee on the Judiciary, U.S. Senate, *Freedom of Information Act and Amendments of 1974 (P.L. 93-502), Source Book: Legislative History, Texts, and Other Documents*; 94th Cong., 1st Sess., 1975.

41 Walter Trohan, "Report from Washington," *Chicago Daily Tribune*, 25 January 1961, 7.

42 "Secrecy Held Waning: White House Cited on Flow of Government Information," *NYT*, 16 April 1961, 38.

43 "Rowan Attacks Attitude of Press on Protecting National Interest," *WP*, 30 September 1961, A4.

44 "U.S. Continues Ban on Press in Cuban Zone," *Chicago Daily Tribune*, 29 October 1962, 6.

45 Jack Raymond, "Pentagon Imposes Restraints on News Coverage," *NYT*, 1 November 1962, 17.

46 "U.S. Aide Defends Lying to Nation," *NYT*, 7 December 1962, 5.

47 "Managing the News," *Chicago Daily Tribune*, 31 October 1962, 36.

48 John F. Kennedy: "The President's News Conference," November 20, 1962. Online by Gerhard Peters and John T. Woolley, *The American Presidency Project*, http://www.presidency.ucsb.edu/ws/?pid=9020.

49 "U.S. Hiding Viet-Nam Facts, House Unit Says," *Los Angeles Times*, 1 October 1963, 1. U.S. Congress, House, Committee on Government Operations, "U.S. Information Problems in Vietnam," Eleventh Report by the Committee on Government Operations, 88th Cong., 1st Sess., 2–3.

50 "Moss Criticizes Press over A-Test Secrecy," *WP*, 1 July 1962, A10.

51 "News Censorship Hearing Planned," *Los Angeles Times*, 14 January 1963, 2; Blanchard, "Watchdog in Decline."

52 Saul Pett, "Right or Wrong, Government Never Tells All," *Los Angeles Times*, 6 March 1966, 1.

53 Ibid.

54 Wayne Morse, *Congressional Record*, 12 August 1966, 19272.

55 "Statement of Norbert A. Schlei," in U.S. Congress, House of Representatives, Committee on Government Operations, *Federal Public Records Law, Part 1: Hearings before a Subcommittee of the Committee on Government Operations.* 89th Cong., 1st Sess. 1965.

56 Ibid., 16.

57 Ibid., 16–17.

58 Ibid., 18, 31.

59 Ibid., 11, 60; Donald Rumsfeld, *Known and Unknown: A Memoir* (New York: Sentinel, 2011), 100–101.

60 U.S. Congress, House of Representatives, Committee on Government Operations, *Administration of the Freedom of Information Act, Twenty-First Report by the Committee on Government Operations Together with Additional Views*, 92d Cong., 2d Sess., 1972, 2–3.

61 Ibid., 4.

62 Arthur Jaeger to the President, 12 August 1965, LBJ papers, presidential files 1963–1969, box 44, fold. EX LE/FE 14-1; Lyndon B. Johnson Presidential Library (LBJPL), Austin, Texas.

63 Lee C. White to Arthur Jaeger, 14 October 1965; LBJ papers, presidential files 1963–1969, box 44, fold. EX LE/FE 14-1; LBJPL.

64 Benny Kass quoted in Michael Lemov, *People's Warrior: John Moss and the Fight for Freedom of Information and Consumer Rights* (Madison, NJ: Fairleigh Dickinson University Press, 2011), 65–68.

65 "Newsmen Accuse Administration of Attempt to Impose Secrecy," *NYT*, 1 November 1965, 24; Professor Paul Fisher of the Freedom of Information Center at the University of Missouri School of Journalism to Alan Reitman, 4 May 1967, box 749, fold. 6; "Weekly Bulletin 2278" 24 October 1966; American Civil Liberties Union Papers, box 749, fold. 7, PPP, DRBSC, Princeton University Library (PUL), Princeton, New Jersey; Attorney General Ramsey Clark, "Attorney General's Memorandum on the Public Information Section of the Administrative Procedure Act," cited in U.S. Congress, House of Representatives, Committee on Government Operations, *Administration of the Freedom of Information Act*, 64; and Wozencraft testimony cited in ibid.

66 Jerry Ford, "Your Washington Review," 29 June 1966, Ford Congressional Papers, box D2, fold.: Ford Newsletters, June–October 1966, Gerald R. Ford Presidential Library (GRFPL), Ann Arbor, Michigan; "Regarding Freedom of Information Bill," Congressman Gerald Ford News Release, 20 June 1966, Ford Congressional Papers, D6, fold.: Credibility Gap 1966, 1967; GRFPL.

CHAPTER 2. "WHAT'S GOING ON IN THE BLACK COMMUNITY?": RAMSEY CLARK INVESTIGATES CIVIL DISORDER

1 This is adapted from Christopher H. Pyle's article, "CONUS Intelligence: The Army Watches Civilian Politics," *Washington Monthly* 12, no. 1 (January 1970): 7–8.

2 "The Paradox of Power," *Time Magazine*, 5 January 1968, http://www.time.com/time /printout/0,88816,712057,00.html; Republican Coordinating Committee, "G.O.P. Statement on Keeping Order," *NYT*, 25 July 1967, 20; "Final Report of Cyrus R. Vance, Special Assistant to the Secretary of Defense, Concerning the Detroit Riots, July 23 through August 2, 1967," Undated Misc., 49, Series 4 Subject Files (SF), Interdivisional Information Unit and Successor Units (IDIU), General Records of the Department of Justice, Record Group 60 (RG 60), National Archives, College Park, Maryland (NACP).

3 James Reston, "Washington: A Time to Change," *NYT*, 23 December 1966, 24.

4 "Justice Department: The Ramsey Clark Issue," *Time Magazine*, 18 October 1968, http://www.time.com/time/printout/0,88816,902460,00.html.

5 Fred P. Graham, "Clark: Target on the Law and Order Issue," *NYT*, 20 October 1968, E13.

6 U.S. Congress, Senate, Select Committee to Study Governmental Operations with Respect to Intelligence Activities, *Final Report of the Select Committee to Study Governmental Operations with Respect to Intelligence Activities Together with Additional, Supplemental, and Separate Views, Supplementary Detailed Staff Reports on Intelligence Activities and the Rights of Americans, Book 3*, 94th Cong., 2d Sess., 1976, 495.

7 Fred Vinson testimony before the Select Senate Committee to Study Governmental Operations with Respect to Intelligence Activities, ibid., 494.

8 Tom Clark served as attorney general from 1945 to 1949. The elder Clark was a strident anticommunist. He initiated the attorney general's "subversives list," a catalogue of organizations identified as potential threats to national security.

9 Fred Graham, "Low-Key and Liberal," *New York Times Magazine*, 2 April 1967, 234; "A Low Key Legal Chief: William Ramsey Clark," *NYT*, 1 March 1967, 24; Department of Justice memo, undated; Personal Papers of Ramsey Clark (PPRC); box 76, Clark, Ramsey, biographical, LBJPL, 2.

10 The Lands Division in the Justice Department oversees all of the federal government's land acquisitions, as well as any issues related to Native American land claims.

11 "Clark Solid Thinker Who Gets Job Done," *Los Angeles Times*, 26 August 1965, 3. Clark's reputation was well deserved. In three years he reduced the division's backlog by half and saved $1 million in administrative costs and standardization procedures. See Department of Justice memo, undated; PPRC, box 76, Clark, Ramsey, biographical; LBJPL; 2.

12 "Texan on Rights Front: William Ramsey Clark," *NYT*, 23 March 1965, 29; "Clark Heads Study Group," *NYT*, 26 August 1965, 21.

13 Ramsey Clark, Oral History Interview III, 21 March 1969, by Harri Baker, LBJPL, 1.

14 See Norman C. Thomas and Harold L. Wolman, "The Presidency and Policy Formulation: The Task Force Device," *Public Administration Review* 29, no. 5 (September–October 1969): 460, 465.

15 Clark Oral History Interview III, 3–4, 13.

16 See Thomas Sugrue, *The Origins of the Urban Crisis: Race and Inequality in Postwar Detroit* (Princeton, NJ: Princeton University Press, 1996).

17 "Report of the President's Task Force on the Los Angeles Riots, August 11–15, 1965," 17 September 1965; PPRC, box 76, Watts, August 1965; LBJPL, 16–22.

18 Ibid., 2.

19 Michael Flamm, *Law and Order: Street Crime, Civil Unrest, and the Crisis of Liberalism in the 1960s* (New York: Columbia University Press, 2005), 66.

20 Clark Oral History Interview III, 4; "Violence in the City—An End or a Beginning?" Report by the Governor's Commission on the Los Angeles Riots (Los Angeles: State of California, 1965).

21 Clark Oral History Interview III, 5. For a less optimistic assessment of the Justice Department's efforts to litigate employment practices, see Hugh Davis Graham, *The Civil Rights Era: Origins and Development of National Policy* (New York: Oxford University Press, 1990), 236–237. Civil rights historian Graham has argued that the Justice Department always lacked the capacity to handle employment discrimination lawsuits. President Johnson, Graham concludes, assigned top priority to other issues of inequality including "voting rights, school desegregation, local defiance, and intimidation."

22 Ramsey Clark, "D.C. Bar Law Day Speech," 30 April 1965; PPRC, box 76, speech material; LBJPL; 1–7; Ramsey Clark, *Crime in America: Observations on Its Nature, Causes, Prevention and Control* (New York: Simon and Schuster, 1970), 19, 29.

23 "81% in a Poll See Law Breakdown," *NYT* 10 September 1968, 31; Graham, "Clark: Target on the Law and Order Issue," E1; Victor Navasky, "Wrong Guy for the Wrong Post at the Wrong Time?" *Saturday Evening Post*, no. 25 (16 December 1967): 74; "Low Key Legal Chief," 24.

24 For the context of the rise of Black Power in the 1960s, see Terry H. Anderson, *The Movement and the Sixties: Protest in America from Greensboro to Wounded Knee* (New York: Oxford University Press, 1995), 154–158.

25 Gene Roberts, "Why the Cry for Black Power?" *NYT*, 3 July 1966, 89.

26 Garrow, *FBI and Martin Luther King, Jr.,* 212–213.

27 Ibid., 106–107.

28 Ibid., 165.

29 U.S. Congress, Senate, Select Committee to Study Governmental Operations with Respect to Intelligence Activities, *Supplementary Detailed Staff Reports on Intelligence Activities and the Rights of Americans, Book 3*, 476–483; Garrow, *FBI and Martin Luther King, Jr.,* 138, 148.

30 Graham, "Low-Key and Liberal," 234; "Low Key Legal Chief," 24; "Curbing Electronic Snoopers," *NYT*, 28 November 1966, 38; Clark, *Crime in America*, 293.

31 Transcript, Cartha D. "Deke" DeLoach, Oral History Interview I, 11 January 1991, by Michael L. Gillette, Internet Copy, LBJPL, 20; PPRC, box 76, Watts, August 1965; LBJPL; Federal Bureau of Investigation, "Telephone Surveillance Denied by the Attorney General," March 1968; NSF, Agency file, box 29; LBJPL; Garrow, *FBI and Martin Luther King, Jr.,* 184.

32 U.S. Congress, Senate, Select Committee to Study Governmental Operations with Respect to Intelligence Activities, *Supplementary Detailed Staff Reports on Intelligence Activities and the Rights of Americans, Book 3*, 498.

33 Leonard Richards, *Shays's Rebellion: The American Revolution's Final Battle* (Philadelphia: University of Pennsylvania Press, 2002); Joan Jensen, *Army Surveillance in*

America, 1775–1980 (New Haven, CT: Yale University Press, 1991). See also Durwood Ball, *Army Regulars on the Western Frontier, 1848–1861* (Norman: University of Oklahoma Press, 2001); Regin Schmidt, *Red Scare: FBI and the Origins of Anticommunism in the United States, 1919–1943* (Copenhagen: Museum Tusculanum Press, 2000).

34 Martin Campbell-Kelly and William Aspray, *Computer: A History of the Information Machine*, 2d edition (Cambridge, MA: Westview Press, 2004), 95–102, 117, 198.

35 Clark Oral History Interview II, 11 February 1969, 14; Attorney General Ramsey Clark to Assistant Attorney General James P. Turner, 9 November 1967, 1971, Incoming and Outgoing Correspondence (IOC), 1970–1972, IDIU, RG 60, NACP.

36 Assistant Attorney General John Doar to Attorney General Ramsey Clark, "Memorandum for the Attorney General," 27 September 1967, PPRC, box 72, DC Planning for Riots, 1967–1968, LBJPL.

37 Memorandum for the Under Secretary of the Army composed by Robert E. Jordan, III, Acting General Counsel, Department of the Army, 10 January 1968, cited in U.S. Congress, Senate, Committee on the Judiciary, Subcommittee on Constitutional Rights, *Federal Data Banks, Computers and the Bill of Rights: Hearings before the Subcommittee on Constitutional Rights of the Committee on the Judiciary*, 92d Cong., 1st Sess., 1971, 1278.

38 To the Attorney General from Cliff Sessions, Director of Public Information, 20 January 1968, Conference on Prevention and Control of Civil Disorder, "A rough reconstruction of the highlights of your remarks to the police chiefs and mayors at Arlie House January 19th," box 18, Speech Material, PPRC, LBJL, 4.

39 Attorney General Ramsey Clark to Assistant Attorney General J. Walter Yeagley, 18 December 1967, 1971, IOC, 1970–1972, IDIU, RG 60, NACP; Attorney General Ramsey Clark to FBI Director J. Edgar Hoover, 14 September 1967, quoted in U.S. Congress, Senate, Select Committee to Study Governmental Operations with Respect to Intelligence Activities, *Supplementary Detailed Staff Reports on Intelligence Activities and the Rights of Americans, Book 3*, 493; Cathy Perkus, *Cointelpro: The FBI's Secret War on Political Freedom* (New York: Monad Press, 1975); and Kenneth O'Reilly, *Racial Matters: The FBI's Secret File on Black America, 1960–1972* (New York: Free Press, 1989).

40 Assistant Attorney General Will R. Wilson, Criminal Division to Attorney General John N. Mitchell, 4 March 1969, 1969, 1, IOC, 1967–1969, IDIU, RG 60, NACP.

41 Will Wilson, Assistant Attorney General, to Mitchell, 4 March 1969, 1969, 1–4, IOC, 1967–1969, IDIU, RG 60, NACP; U.S. Congress, Senate, Select Committee to Study Governmental Operations with Respect to Intelligence Activities, *Supplementary Detailed Staff Reports on Intelligence Activities and the Rights of Americans, Book 3*, 501; Kevin T. Maroney, Chief, Interdivision Information Unit, Fred Vinson, Jr., Assistant Attorney General, Criminal Division, 6 January 1969, 1969, 1, IOC, 1967–1969, IDIU, RG 60, NACP.

42 U.S. Congress, Senate, Select Committee to Study Governmental Operations with Respect to Intelligence Activities, *Supplementary Detailed Staff Reports on Intelligence Activities and the Rights of Americans, Book 3*, 494.

43 Memo for the Under Secretary of the Army composed by Jordan, 10 January 1968, cited in U.S. Congress, Senate, Committee on the Judiciary, Subcommittee on Constitutional Rights, *Federal Data Banks, Computers and the Bill of Rights*, 1278–1279; James

T. Devine, Chief, Interdivision Information Section to Wilson, 13 March 1969, 1969, 1–5, IOC, 1967–1969, IDIU, RG 60, NACP.

44 Fred P. Graham, "U.S. Reviews Cases in Bugging Quest," *NYT*, 1 December 1966, 1, and "A Sweeping Ban on Wiretapping Set for U.S. Aides," *NYT*, 7 July 1967, 1; "Text of Ramsey Clark Memorandum on Wiretaps," *NYT*, 7 July 1967, 16; Navasky, "Wrong Guy for the Wrong Post," 75; "G.O.P. Scores Clark for Bugging Curb," *NYT*, 28 August 1967, 22.

45 New York District Attorney Frank Hogan, quoted in Tom Wicker, "In the Nation: Is Wiretapping Worth It?" *NYT*, 11 July 1967, 36. On President Johnson's own antipathy to wiretaps and surveillance, see Michael Flamm, "The Politics of 'Law and Order,'" in David Farber and Jeff Roche, eds., *The Conservative Sixties* (New York: Peter Lang, 2003), 137n65.

46 Jerry Ford, "Your Washington Review," 4 October 1967; Ford Congressional Papers, box D2, fold.: Ford Newsletters, July–December 1967; GRFPL.

47 Clark, *Crime in America*, 294–295.

48 Attorney General to the President, 14 June 1968; reports on enrolled legislation box 63, P.L. 90-351 HR 5037 6/19/68; LBJPL. The irony is that Clark himself had encouraged implicitly the extralegal use of such devices by state and local law enforcement when he endorsed the development of so-called "Red Squads."

49 McPherson to the President, 14 June 1968; reports on enrolled legislation box 63, P.L. 90-351 HR 5037 6/19/68; LBJPL; "Safe Streets Act Signing Statement," 19 June 1968; presidential papers, Legislation box 80, LE/JL 3 1/1/68-6/19/68; LBJPL.

50 Fred P. Graham, "Clark against Easing Rules for School Desegregation," *NYT*, 7 January 1969, 1.

51 "Cabinet Meeting notes," 03/13/68; Cabinet Papers, box 13, Cabinet Meeting, 3/13/68; Presidential Papers, LBJPL; Graham, "Clark: Target on the Law and Order Issue," E13.

CHAPTER 3. "A COMMUNIST BEHIND EVERY BUSH": THE ARMY SPIES ON CIVILIANS

1 This account is adapted from a report of military surveillance compiled for congressional hearings in 1971. This story was widely reported by the media, by members of Congress, and by civil libertarians as evidence of the excesses of government surveillance. The ratio of activists to undercover officers varies across several accounts, though it remains clear that the number of officers present was nearly equal to the number of activists. Senator Sam J. Ervin, Jr., "Address before the Philadelphia Bar Association," 26 March 1971; Sam J. Ervin Papers, Subgroup A: Senate Records #3847A (SJEPA), Subject files, box 3847, fold. 13856, Privacy: Army Data Banks, Southern Historical Collection (SHC), Wilson Library (WL), University of North Carolina at Chapel Hill (UNCCH).

2 Reston, "Washington: A Time to Change," 24; Graham, "Low-Key and Liberal," 234.

3 See Flamm, *Law and Order*, 91–92; "Final Report of Cyrus R. Vance, Special Assistant to the Secretary of Defense, Concerning the Detroit Riots, July 23 through August 2, 1967," 49.

4 Linda J. Demaine and Brian Rosen, "Process Dangers of Military Involvement in Civil Law Enforcement: Rectifying the Posse Comitatus Act," *New York University Journal of Legislation and Public Policy* 9, no. 166 (2005–2006): 170n3.

5 See Paul J. Scheips, *The Role of Federal Military Forces in Domestic Disorders, 1945–1992* (Washington, DC: Center for Military History, United States Army, 2005); Statement of Robert F. Froehlke, Assistant Secretary of Defense, *Federal Data Banks, Computers and the Bill of Rights,* 377; Ben A. Franklin, "Field Commanders in Alabama Linked by 'Hot Line' to Pentagon," *NYT,* 22 March 1965, 1; Sheips, *Role of Federal Military Forces,* 102–165.

6 Flamm, *Law and Order,* 115–116; Scheips, *Role of Federal Military Forces,* 217.

7 Paul Nitze, *From Hiroshima to Glasnost: At the Center of Decision—A Memoir* (New York: Grove Weidenfeld, 1989), 269; Department of Defense, *Department of Defense Directive 3025.12,* by Paul H. Nitze, Deputy Secretary of Defense, 8 June 1968, cited in *Federal Data Banks, Computers and the Bill of Rights,* 1272–1278; Scheips, *Role of Federal Military Forces,* 224–229.

8 Army intelligence officers who monitored domestic politics in the late 1960s and 1970s had varied backgrounds. But most of those who blew the whistle on this program in the early 1970s had been officers abroad before serving in the United States. See Ralph Stein testimony and statement in *Federal Data Banks, Computers and the Bill of Rights,* 244–276. Stein, for example, had served with distinction as a counterintelligence officer in Korea before being assigned to the army's domestic Counterintelligence Analysis Branch in 1967.

9 "Message from the Director," *FBI Law Enforcement Bulletin* 37, no. 10 (October 1968): 1; "Message from the Director," *FBI Law Enforcement Bulletin* 37, no 9 (September 1968): 1.

10 Frank Donner, *The Age of Surveillance: The Aims and Methods of America's Political Intelligence System* (New York: Alfred A. Knopf, 1980), 289.

11 John Herbers, "Johnson Accused by G.O.P. in Rioting," *NYT,* 25 July 1967, 20. See also Flamm, *Law and Order,* 88–94.

12 "G.O.P. Statement on Keeping Order," statement approved by the Republican Coordinating Committee, *NYT,* 25 July 1967, 20; Flamm, *Law and Order.*

13 "Secretary of Defense," *NYT,* 14 December 1960, 38; Morrie S. Helitzer, "How Do Business Men Do in Washington?" *NYT,* 7 May 1961, SM37; Damon Stetson, "McNamara Is New as a Millionaire," *NYT,* 14 December 1960, 31; Russell Baker, "Twelve Men Close to Kennedy: Close Because of Important Jobs," *NYT,* 22 January 1961, SM6. Biographical accounts of Robert McNamara include Paul Hendrickson, *The Living and the Dead: Robert McNamara and Five Lives of a Lost War* (New York: Alfred Knopf, 1996); Deborah Shapley, *Promise and Power: The Life and Times of Robert McNamara* (Boston: Little, Brown, 1993). Robert S. McNamara, with Brian VanDeMark, *In Retrospect: The Tragedy and Lessons of Vietnam* (New York: Random House, 1995), 5–13.

14 Baker, "Twelve Men Close to Kennedy," SM6; McNamara, *In Retrospect,* 23; "Text of Speech by McNamara Outlining Changes in Policies on National Defense," *NYT,* 25 April 1961, 29.

15 Jennifer Light, *Warfare to Welfare: Defense Intellectuals and Urban Problems in Cold War America* (Baltimore: Johns Hopkins University Press, 2003), 166–170. For a very thoughtful examination of the strategic planning in the late 1960s and early 1970s re-

lated to urban challenges and military solutions, see especially Part III, "The Urban Crisis as National Security Crisis."

16 Pyle, "CONUS Intelligence," 6. Army intelligence operations in the United States prior to 1965 were primarily focused on issues related to routine security clearances. See Richard Halloran, "Army Spied on 18,000 Civilians in 2-Year Operation," *NYT*, 18 January 1971, 1.

17 Halloran, "Army Spied on 18,000 Civilians," 1.

18 Adam Bernstein, "Lt. Gen. William Yarborough Dies," *WP*, 8 December 2005, B05, quote is Yarborough's own words; Halloran, "Army Spied on 18,000 Civilians," 1; Christopher Pyle, *Military Surveillance of Civilian Politics, 1967–1970* (New York: Garland Publishing, 1986), 36–45.

19 Cited in Pyle, "CONUS Intelligence," 8; Pyle, *Military Surveillance*, 36–45; J. Walter Yeagley, Assistant Attorney General, Internal Security Division, to Ramsey Clark, Attorney General, 27 October 1967, "International Aspects of Pentagon Demonstration," PPRC; box 115, Pentagon Demonstrations, LBJPL.

20 Bobby Seale quoted in Anderson, *The Movement and the Sixties*, 176–177; Flamm, *Law and Order*, 119.

21 Froehlke statement cited in *Federal Data Banks, Computers and the Bill of Rights*, 377; Mobe, "Confront the Warmakers, Oct 21–22: Press Statement Issued Aug. 28" (emphasis in original), cited in Charles DeBenedetti and Charles Chatfield, *An American Ordeal: the Antiwar Movement of the Vietnam Era* (Syracuse, NY: Syracuse University Press, 1990), 188; Halloran, "Army Spied on 18,000 Civilians," 1.

22 Froehlke statement cited in *Federal Data Banks, Computers, and the Bill of Rights*, 2382–2363.

23 Pyle, *Military Surveillance*, 47, 69–70; Halloran, "Army Spied on 18,000 Civilians," 1.

24 Stein testimony cited in *Federal Data Banks, Computers and the Bill of Rights*, 251; Halloran, "Army Spied on 18,000 Civilians," 1. Angleton was the CIA's counterintelligence chief from 1954–1975. See Tom Mangold, *Cold Warrior: James Jesus Angleton, the CIA's Master Spy Hunter* (New York: Touchstone Books, 1992); Michael Holzman, *James Jesus Angleton, the CIA, and the Craft of Counterintelligence* (Amherst: University of Massachusetts Press, 2008).

25 Pyle, *Military Surveillance,* 118–119; "Spying: They've Probably Got You on the List," *NYT*, 27 December 1970, 124.

26 Annex B (Intelligence) to Department of the Army Civil Disturbance Plan (U), 1 Feb 1968, cited in *Federal Data Banks, Computers, and the Bill of Rights*, 1119–1121. For an example of a report see "Counterintelligence Research Project: Student Non-Violent Coordinating Committee," published by Department of the Army, Office of the Assistant Chief of Staff for Intelligence, 10 October 1967; NSF, box 5, civil rights and antiwar personalities, LBJPL.

27 For the proliferation of federal data banks, see U.S. Congress, Senate, Committee on the Judiciary, *Federal Data Banks and Constitutional Rights: A Study of Data Systems on Individuals Maintained by Agencies of the United States Government*, Summary and Conclusions prepared by the Staff of the Subcommittee on Constitutional Rights of the Committee on the Judiciary, 93d Cong., 2d Sess., 1974; Halloran, "Army Spied on 18,000 Civilians," 1; Pyle, *Military Surveillance*, 72–73; Ben A. Franklin, "Surveillance of Citizens Stirs Debate," *NYT*, 27 December 1970, 1; Franklin, "Federal Computers

Amass Files on Suspect Citizens, Many among Hundreds of Thousands Listed Have No Criminal Records—Critics See Invasion of Privacy," *NYT*, 28 June 1970, 1.

28 Vasco J. Fenili, Acting Deputy Assistant Chief of Staff for Intelligence (for William P. Yarborough, Assistant Chief of Staff for Intelligence), "Department of the Army Civil Disturbance Information Collection Plan," 2 May 1968, cited in *Federal Data Banks, Computers and the Bill of Rights*, 1122–1123.

29 Stein testimony cited in *Federal Data Banks, Computers and the Bill of Rights*, 247, 249.

30 Ibid., 251–252, 254, 257.

31 Ibid.

32 *Uncle Sam Is Watching You: Highlights from the Hearings of the Senate Subcommittee on Constitutional Rights* (Washington, DC: Public Affairs Press, 1971), 119–120.

33 Testimony of Oliver A. Peirce cited in *Federal Data Banks, Computers and the Bill of Rights*, 305–307.

34 Ibid., 305–307, 309.

35 Stein testimony cited in ibid., 255.

36 *Report of the National Advisory Commission on Civil Disorders* (New York: Bantam, 1968), 487.

37 Pyle, *Military Surveillance*, 27. Assistant Secretary of Defense Robert F. Froehlke cited the Kerner Commission's findings in testimony before Senator Sam Ervin's Constitutional Rights Subcommittee in 1971 in defense of the army's civilian surveillance program. Specifically he noted the commission's recommendation that the army be prepared to "provide aid to cities" where federal troops were committed for civil disorder. Froehlke also noted the commission's observation that lack of "accurate information" before and after disorders posed problems for law enforcement officers and their response planning. See *Federal Data Banks, Computers and the Bill of Rights*, 379–380.

38 Flamm, "Politics of 'Law and Order,'" 143.

39 See Timothy Conlan, *From New Federalism to Devolution: Twenty-Five Years of Intergovernmental Reform* (Washington, DC: Brookings Institution Press, 1998).

40 James T. Devine, Chief, Interdivision Information Section to Will Wilson, Assistant Attorney General, March 19, 1969, 1969, 1–2, Incoming and Outgoing Correspondence (IOC), 1967–1969, Interdivisional Information Unit (and Successor Units (IDIU); General Records of the Department of Justice, Record Group 60 (RG 60), National Archives, College Park, Maryland (NACP).

41 National Commission on the Causes and Prevention of Violence, *Commission Statement on Group Violence*, December 1969, Commission on Violence and Civil Disturbance, 1–2, Subject Files (SF), IDIU, RG 60, NACP. For a thoughtful biography of Eisenhower's career, see Stephen E. Ambrose and Richard H. Immerman, *Milton S. Eisenhower, Educational Statesman* (Baltimore: Johns Hopkins University Press, 1983).

42 National Commission on the Causes and Prevention of Violence, *Commission Statement on Group Violence*, 11.

43 Ibid.

44 Ibid., 13–14, 16.

45 William Appleman Williams, *The Tragedy of American Diplomacy* (New York: Dell,

1962); Thomas J. McCormick, *America's Half Century: United States Foreign Policy in the Cold War and After* (Baltimore: Johns Hopkins University Press, 1989); Gabriel Kolko, *The Politics of War: The World and United States Foreign Policy, 1943–1945* (New York: Random House, 1968); Gar Alperovitz, *Atomic Diplomacy: Hiroshima and Potsdam: The Use of the Atomic Bomb and American Confrontation with Soviet Power* (New York: Simon and Schuster, 1965); Walter LaFeber, *America, Russia and the Cold War, 1955–1966* (New York: Wiley, 1967). Walter LaFeber's *The American Age* is a notable exception; see *The American Age: United States Foreign Policy at Home and Abroad since 1750* (New York: W. W. Norton, 1989).

CHAPTER 4. SENATOR SAM, OR HOW LIBERALS LEARNED TO STOP WORRYING AND LOVE A SOUTHERN SEGREGATIONIST

1 This account is drawn from the author's interview with former army captain Christopher Pyle, 26 June 2007, audio recording (in author's possession).

2 Flamm, *Politics of Law and Order.*

3 "Most in Poll Favor Limiting Freedoms," *NYT*, 16 April 1970, 37.

4 Paul Potter, "Name the System" speech, 17 April 1965, http://www.sdsrebels.com/potter.htm.

5 Anderson, *The Movement and the Sixties*, preface.

6 Todd Gitlin, *The Sixties: Years of Hope, Days of Rage* (New York: Bantam Books, 1987), 134.

7 Charles Peters, *Tilting at Windmills: An Autobiography* (Reading, MA: Addison-Wesley, 1988); Charles Peters, interview by the author, 16 August 2007, audio recording (in author's possession).

8 Peters, *Tilting at Windmills*, 143; Charles Peters and Timothy J. Adams, eds., *Inside the System: A Washington Monthly Reader* (New York: Praeger Publishers, 1970).

9 Best-selling authors and renowned journalists and editors who got their start at *The Monthly* include: Jonathan Alter, senior editor and columnist at *Newsweek*; Amy Sullivan, senior editor at *Time Magazine*; Joshua Green, senior editor of *The Atlantic Monthly*; Timothy Noah, senior writer for *Slate* magazine; Taylor Branch, Pulitzer Prize–winning author and journalist; Katherine Boo, Pulitzer Prize winner and staff writer for *The New Yorker*; and James Fallows, national correspondent for the *Atlantic Monthly*.

10 "Low-Keyed Muckrakers," *Time Magazine*, 29 March 1971, http://www.time.com/time/magazine/article/0,9171,944315,00.html.

11 Charles Peters and Taylor Branch, *Blowing the Whistle: Dissent in the Public Interest* (New York: Praeger Publishers, 1972).

12 "Op. Ed. Page," *NYT*, 21 September 1970, 42. Of course, the *Times* featured editorials and carried opinion columns and letters to the editor before it formally added the Op-Ed page in 1970.

13 Pyle, "CONUS Intelligence: The Army Watches Civilian Politics," 4–16. Pyle won the Hillman and Polk awards for investigative journalism in 1970 and 1971, respectively.

14 Pyle first proposed his army surveillance article to the *Times*, but the editorial department passed, saying the story rated no more than a sidebar to a "Big Brother" piece. Pyle interview.

15 Senator Charles Mathias, *Congressional Record*, 17 July 1970, 24832.

16 Julian Zelizer, *On Capitol Hill: The Struggle to Reform Congress and Its Consequences, 1948–2000* (New York: Cambridge University Press, 2004), 99–100; Frederik Logevall, "The Vietnam War," in Julian Zelizer, ed., *The American Congress: The Building of Democracy* (Boston: Houghton Mifflin, 2004), 595.

17 Francis R. Valeo, Secretary of the Senate, 1966–1977, Oral History Interviews, Senate Historical Office, Washington, DC, 431; Sam J. Ervin, Jr., "Separation of Powers: Judicial Independence," *Law and Contemporary Problems* 35, no. 1 (Winter 1970): 122n59; Lawrence Baskir, interview by author, 11 September 2007, audio recording (in author's possession). Baskir served as chief counsel on the Separation of Powers Subcommittee from 1966 to 1969, and chief counsel on the Constitutional Rights Subcommittee, 1969–1973.

18 Robert Sherrill, "Big Brother Watching You? See Sam Ervin," *Playboy Magazine*, February 1972, 150.

19 Kurt Andersen, "Not Quite Just a Country Lawyer," *Time*, 6 May 1985; John Herbers, "Senator Ervin Thinks the Constitution Should Be Taken Like Mountain Whisky— Undiluted and Untaxed," *NYT Magazine*, 15 November 1970, 51.

20 Karl Campbell, *Senator Sam Ervin, Last of the Founding Fathers* (Chapel Hill: University of North Carolina Press, 2007), 30–31.

21 Sam Ervin, Jr., *Preserving the Constitution: The Autobiography of Senator Sam J. Ervin, Jr.* (Charlottesville, VA: The Michie Company, 1984), 14–15, 29–30.

22 Dick Dabney, *A Good Man: The Life of Sam J. Ervin* (Boston: Houghton Mifflin, 1976), 83–85; Donald L. Smith, *Zechariah Chafee, Jr.: Defender of Liberty and Law* (Cambridge, MA: Harvard University Press, 1986), 88–89, 95–96; Zechariah Chafee, Jr., "Freedom of Speech in War Time," *Harvard Law Review* 32, no. 8 (June 1919): 934.

23 Herbers, "Senator Ervin," 51; James K. Batten, "Claghorn or Statesman? Sam J. Ervin Just Won't Fit in a Mold," *The Charlotte Observer*, 2 April 1967, 5B; Sam Ervin, Jr., "Speaking Freely," a program of WNBC television (transcript), interviewed by Edwin Newman, taped on 8 December 1970, aired 19 December 1970, SJEPA, box 362, fold. 13913, SHC, WL, UNCCH, 11.

24 See Zelizer, *On Capitol Hill*.

25 Robert Caro, *Master of the Senate: The Years of Lyndon Johnson* (New York: Alfred A. Knopf, 2004), 553–554.

26 Regarding the substance of Ervin's opposition, see Graham, *Civil Rights Era*, 94–95.

27 "A Government Watch on 200 Million Americans?" *U.S. News & World Report*, 16 May 1966, 56.

28 Direct Mail samples, November 1970, Common Cause Records (CCR), box 119, fold. "computer letter B", Public Policy Papers (PPP), Department of Rare Books and Special Collections (DRBSC), PUL. See also Zelizer, *On Capitol Hill*, 100–103.

29 Aryeh Neier, *Taking Liberties: Four Decades in the Struggle for Rights* (New York: Public Affairs, 2003), 113. John de J. Pemberton, Jr., Executive Director, to Dr. Henry Steele Commager, 14 February 1967, American Civil Liberties Union Papers (ACLUP), box 379, fold. 4, PPP, DRBSC, PUL. Originally named the Baldwin Foundation in honor of the ACLU founder, Roger Baldwin, it was renamed in 1970 as the ACLU Foundation. "Summary of Major Activities of ACLU departments, June 30, 1969 to June 30,

1970," ACLUP; box 24, fold. 3; PPP, DRBSC, PUL. Nearly 25,000 of the ACLU's new members—almost one-third—joined during the 1968–1970 period. See also Samuel Walker, *In Defense of American Liberties: A History of the ACLU* (New York: Oxford University Press, 1990), 262.

30 Neier, *Taking Liberties*, xvii–xxi.

31 Ibid., xxi.

32 The ACLU is a decentralized organization; members are affiliated with a local (typically state) chapter and with the national organization. In 1963, ACLU Executive Director John Pemberton hired Neier as field director to assist the state affiliates in expanding their rights programs and to establish affiliates where none existed. Neier excelled at this work; the number of affiliate offices nearly doubled from twenty-nine in 1960 to forty-eight by 1970. See "Summary of Major Activities of ACLU departments, June 30, 1969 to June 30, 1970," ACLUP; PPP; DRBCC; PUL.

33 Neier, *Taking Liberties*, 20–25.

34 "ACLU Activity Report," September–December, 1970; ACLUP, box 24, fold. 4, PPP, DRBSC, PUL, 3–4; To Frank Donner from Eleanor H. Norton, assistant legal director, 17 September 1969; and Eleanor Norton to David Hunter, Executive Director, Stern Family Fund, 31 December 1969; ACLUP, box 382, fold. 8, PPP, DRBSC, PUL. The final product of this research was published by Frank Donner, *The Age of Surveillance: The Aims and Methods of America's Political Intelligence System.*

35 "ACLU Activity Report," September–December, 1970; ACLUP, 3–4.

36 Neier describes this strategy in detail in his book *Only Judgment: The Limits of Litigation in Social Change.*

37 "Frank Donner," *The Nation*, 5 July 1993, 4; Donner, *Age of Surveillance*, xi.

38 "Project for the Protection of Dissent," p. 11, December 1969; ACLUP, box 382, fold. 8; PPP; DRBSC; PUL.

39 Vance Packard, "Don't Tell It to the Computer: 'Bureaucratic Efficiency Could Put Us in Chains of Plastic Tape,'" *NYT Magazine*, 8 January 1967, 236.

40 *The Daily Californian*, quoted in Anderson, *The Movement and the Sixties*, 97; *Federal Data Banks, Computers and the Bill of Rights*, 1.

41 Packard, "Don't Tell It to the Computer"; "To Preserve Privacy," *NYT*, 9 August 1966, 36; "A.C.L.U. Scores Plan for Data Centers," *NYT*, 17 August 1966, 15; "A Government Watch," 56–59.

42 Announcement of hearings on federal data banks, computers, and the Bill of Rights, 8 September, 1970, SJEPA, 3847A, section 1, fold. 9339, SHC, WL, UNCCH.

43 Senator Ervin and his staff included a selection of citizen letters he received on the topic of surveillance in the published hearing records, *Federal Data Banks, Computers and the Bill of Rights*, 2063–2085. I have assumed that Ervin and his staff used a representative selection of favorable and unfavorable letters in this mailing. In general, historians have underutilized constituent mail, and letters to Congress more generally, as primary sources. This is unfortunate, as elected officials typically take this correspondence very seriously. Historian David Thelen's book is an exception; he examines constituent letters to elected officials during the Iran-Contra hearings. See *Becoming Citizens in the Age of Television: How Americans Challenged the Media and Seized Initiative during the Iran-Contra Debate* (Chicago: University of Chicago Press, 1996).

44 Name withheld to Senator Ervin, California, 17 December 1971, cited in *Federal Data Banks, Computers and the Bill of Rights*, 2064.

45 Names withheld to Hon. Sam Ervin, Jr., California, 18 April 1971, cited in *Federal Data Banks, Computers and the Bill of Rights*, 1521–1524.

46 A staffer on Ervin's subcommittee heard about Pyle's story from his English neighbor who was then in the process of applying for American citizenship. When challenged by the Englishman to defend the army's program in terms congruent with the Constitution, the staffer brought the problem to Senator Ervin. See Baskir, "Reflections on the Senate Investigation of Army Surveillance," *Indiana Law Journal*, no. 49 (Summer 1974): 621–622n9.

47 Thaddeus R. Beal, Under Secretary of the Army, to Ervin, 20 March 1970, cited in *Federal Data Banks, Computers and the Bill of Rights*, 1052–1053.

48 Ibid., 1051–1052.

49 Pyle interview; Baskir interview; Baskir, "Reflections on the Senate Hearing of Army Surveillance."

50 Pyle interview. The *Boston Globe*, *Miami Herald*, and the *San Francisco Chronicle* were just a few of the regional newspapers to carry Pyle's article.

51 "ACLU Activity Report, Dec 70–Feb 71," prepared by Aryeh Neier and Alan Reitman; ACLUP; box 25, fold. 1; PPP; DRBSC; PUL.

52 Baskir interview.

53 Ibid.; Walter Mondale with David Hage, *The Good Fight: A Life in Liberal Politics* (New York: Scribner, 2010), 137.

54 Francis E. Rourke, "Congressional Use of Publicity," in Robert O. Blanchard, ed., *Congress and the News Media* (New York: Hastings House, 1974), 128–131.

55 Melvin Wulf, "Military Spying on Civilians," Letters to the Editor, *NYT*, 3 January 1971, E10; Aryeh Neier, "Welfare without Privacy," Letters to the Editor, *NYT*, 20 January 1971, 34. For ACLU public relations strategy leading up to the hearings, see ACLUP; box 1097, fold. 13, PPP, DRBSC, PUL.

56 Baskir, "Reflections on the Senate Hearing of Army Surveillance," 623.

57 *Federal Data Banks, Computers and the Bill of Rights*, 100–102; Ben A. Franklin, "Surveillance of Citizens Stirs Debate," *NYT*, 27 December 1970, 1; Baskir interview; Baskir, "Reflections on the Senate Hearing of Army Surveillance," 623–624. Pyle recalls that O'Brien's story sent up a red flag to Ervin staffers. O'Brien's account did not mesh with the accounts gleaned from dozens of other interviews; Pyle interview.

58 Baskir interview; and Baskir, "Reflections on the Senate Investigation of Army Surveillance."

59 Richard Halloran, "Senators Hear of Threat of a Dossier Dictatorship," *NYT*, 24 February 1971, 1; Baskir interview.

60 Miller testimony cited in *Federal Data Banks, Computers and the Bill of Rights*, 8–40.

61 Rosenberg testimony cited in ibid., 69–84.

62 Ervin cited in ibid., 89.

63 "ACLU Activity Report," September–December 1970; ACLUP, 4.

64 *Federal Data Banks, Computers and the Bill of Rights*.

65 Affidavit of Richard Allen Kasson, *Tatum v. Laird* file, ACLUP, box 1728, fold. Tatum v. Laird 1965–1971, PPP; DRBSC: PUL.

66 Baskir interview and Samuel J. Ervin, Jr., FBI file, copy in the author's possession.

67 Donald Janson, "F.B.I. File Theft Stirs Anger and Joy among Residents of Media, PA," *NYT*, 29 March 1971, 20; see also Richard Gid Powers, *Secrecy and Power: The Life of J. Edgar Hoover* (New York: Free Press, 1986), 464–465.

68 "From the Citizens' Commission to Investigate the F.B.I.," *Win Magazine* 8, nos. 4 and 5 (March 1 and 15, 1972), 8. *Win Magazine* received one of the packets of copied FBI files from the Citizens' Commission and published the bulk of the files in their March 1972 edition.

69 "Mitchell Issues Plea on F.B.I. Files, Asks Press Not to Publish Data on Stolen Papers," *NYT*, 24 March, 1971, 24; "Stolen Documents Describe FBI Surveillance Activities," *WP*, 24 March 1971, A1, A11; "F.B.I. Files Tell of Surveillance of Students, Blacks, War Foes," *NYT*, 25 March 1971, 1, 33.

70 In his memoirs *Post* executive editor Ben Bradlee recalls that *Post* editors got word that the *Times* was working on a "blockbuster" story, an exclusive, in early spring of 1971. This story, of course, was the Pentagon Papers. Though he does not mention his decision to publish the Media, PA, files in his book, Bradlee's desire to compete with the *Times'* then unidentified "blockbuster" story perhaps drove the editors at the *Post* to take editorial risks they would not have otherwise considered. See Ben Bradlee, *A Good Life: Newspapering and Other Adventures* (New York: Simon & Schuster, 1995), 310, 314.

71 "What Is the FBI Up To?" *WP*, 25 March 1971, A20; "Policies of Paranoia," *NYT*, 29 March 1971, 32; Baskir interview.

72 Beth Bailey, "The Army in the Marketplace: Recruiting an All-Volunteer Force," *Journal of American History* 94, no. 1 (June 2007): 71–72; "The Selling of the Pentagon," prod. CBS News, Peter Davis, Perry Wolf, written by Peter Davis, reporter Roger Mudd (CBS, 23 February 1971), transcript in Columbia Broadcast System, Inc., *From Subpoena to Recommittal: An Indexed Collection of Materials and Reprints Dealing with the Case of the Subpoenaing of Outtakes of the CBS News Broadcast, The Selling of the Pentagon* (New York: CBS, 1971).

73 "C.B.S. Is Challenged by Agnew to Admit 'Errors' in 3 TV Films," *NYT*, 21 March 1971, 30; James M. McNaughton, "Agnew Criticizes C.B.S. over a TV documentary," *NYT*, 29 March 1971, 79.

74 Professor Paul Fisher of the Freedom of Information Center at the University of Missouri School of Journalism to Alan Reitman, ACLU, ACLUP, 4 May 1967; box 749, fold. 6; PPP; DRBSC; PUL.

75 David Halberstam, *The Powers That Be* (New York: Alfred Knopf, 1979), 565–570; "Annual Report, July 1970–June 1971," ACLUP; box 1881, fold. 2; PPP; DRBSC; PUL: 18. For the editorial decision to publish the Pentagon Papers, see Halberstam, *Powers That Be*, 565–578; Richard Hudson, "Let's Declassify," *NYT*, 1 July 1971, 47; Max Frankel, "Court Decision: Presses Roll—But the Conflict Remains," *NYT*, 4 July 1971, E1.

76. "ACLU mailings, Sept–Dec 1971," ACLUP, box 25, fold. 3; PPP; DRBSC; PUL.

CHAPTER 5. IT'S "POPPYCOCK": CONGRESS CHALLENGES EXECUTIVE PRIVILEGE

1 This account is adapted from the testimony of Senator William V. Roth, Jr. (R-DE), cited in U.S. Congress, Senate, Committee on the Judiciary, *Executive Privilege: The*

Withholding of Information by the Executive, Hearing before the Subcommittee on the Separation of Powers of the Committee on the Judiciary, 92d Cong., 1st Sess., 27, 28, 29 July, 4, 5 August 1971, 227–240.

2 Despite army pronouncements that its domestic surveillance program had been discontinued and its dossiers destroyed, anonymous sources within CONUS Intel reported that surveillance continued unabated. See "U.S. Held Unable to Destroy All Army Data on Civilians," *NYT*, 29 May 1972, 20; Christopher Pyle, "CONUS Revisited: The Army Covers Up," *Washington Monthly* 2, no. 5 (July 1970): 49–58; and Pyle, "Spies without Masters: The Army Still Watches Civilian Politics," *Civil Liberties Review* (Summer 1974): 38–49.

3 Arthur M. Schlesinger, Jr., *The Imperial Presidency* (Boston: Houghton Mifflin, 1973); see also Bruce Schulman, *The Seventies: The Great Shift in American Culture, Society, and Politics* (New York: Da Capo Press, 2001), and Edward Berkowitz, *Something Happened: A Political and Cultural Overview of the Seventies* (New York: Columbia University Press, 2006).

4 After World War II Schorr covered Eastern Europe for print and radio agencies including the *New York Times, Christian Science Monitor, Time, Newsweek,* and CBS. See Schorr, *Clearing the Air* (Boston: Houghton Mifflin, 1977), 1–9, 91–92.

5 See Schorr, *Clearing the Air,* 66–67, 70–71. On Nixon's development of the "enemies list," see Stanley I. Kutler, *The Wars of Watergate: The Last Crisis of Richard Nixon* (New York: Knopf, 1990), 104.

6 Schorr, *Clearing the Air,* 67, 70–73, and Kutler, *Wars of Watergate,* 180. Schorr was involved in another imbroglio over his reporting in 1976 on issues related to national security that ultimately led to his dismissal from CBS; see chapter 7.

7 See Joanne B. Freeman, "Explaining the Unexplainable: The Cultural Context of the Sedition Act," in Meg Jacobs, William Novak, and Julian Zelizer, eds., *The Democratic Experiment: New Directions in American Political History* (Princeton, NJ: Princeton University Press, 2003), 20–49.

8 On the historic relationship between the news media and presidential administrations in the twentieth century, see Timothy Crouse, *The Boys on the Bus* (New York: Random House, 1973); Halberstam, *Powers That Be*; and Donald Ritchie, *Reporting from Washington: The History of the Washington Press Corps* (New York: Oxford University Press, 2005). On the Nixon administration's relationship with the media, see David Greenberg, *Nixon's Shadow: The History of an Image* (New York: W. W. Norton, 2003); and Kutler, *Wars of Watergate,* 161–184.

9 Neier to Board of Directors, "Priorities for 1972," ACLUP, box 25, fold. 3, PPP, DRBSC, PUL.

10 See Campbell, *Senator Sam Ervin,* 210–220; U.S. Congress, Senate, Committee on the Judiciary, *Freedom of the Press: Hearing before the Subcommittee on Constitutional Rights of the Committee on the Judiciary,* 92d Cong., 1st and 2d Sess., 1971–1972, 1–4.

11 Cronkite testimony in *Freedom of the Press,* 77–106.

12. Testimony of Harding F. Bancroft, Executive Vice President of the New York Times Co., cited in *Freedom of the Press,* 18–22; Wolfgang Saxon, "Harding Bancroft, 81, Executive at The Times and Diplomat, Dies," *NYT,* 7 February 1992, http://query.nytimes.com/gst/fullpage.html?res=9E0CE2D8113AF934A35751C0A964958260.

13 "Text of the presentation of the Paul White Award," by Jim McCulla of the Radio and Television News Directors Association, 1 December 1972, SJEP, 3847A, box 351, fold. 13691, First Amendment Issues, Freedom of the Press, SHC; WL; UNCCH.

14 "Federal Files: Freedom of Information . . . ," *WP*, 20 November 1974, A26.

15 *Administration of the Freedom of Information Act: An Evaluation of Government Information Programs under the Act, 1967–1972* (New York: Praeger Publishers, 1973), 7; the mere announcement of hearings prompted some agencies, including the Environmental Protection Agency, the Department of the Army, and the Department of Health, Education and, Welfare (to name a few), to revise their in-house regulations.

16 U.S. Congress. House of Representatives. Committee on Government Operations. *Administration of the Freedom of Information Act, Twenty-first Report by the Committee on Government Operations Together with Additional Views.* 92d Cong., 2d Sess. 1972, 6, 8; U.S. Congress, Senate, Committee on the Judiciary, Subcommittee on Administrative Practice and Procedure, *Freedom of Information Act Source Book: Legislative Materials, Cases, Articles,* 93d Cong., 2d Sess., 1974, 8, 15, 23, 27.

17 Chairman Moorhead held hearings in 1972 and 1973 to evaluate the 1967 FOIA statute and develop recommendations for reforms. See *Administration of the Freedom of Information Act,* and U.S. Congress, House of Representatives, Committee on Government Operations, *Freedom of Information Act: Hearings before a Subcommittee of the Committee on Government Operations,* 93d Cong., 1st Sess., 1973.

18 Opening statement of Senator Sam Ervin, 1 February 1972, *Freedom of the Press,* 415.

19 U.S. Congress, Senate, Committee on the Judiciary, *Executive Privilege: The Withholding of Information by the Executive,* 4.

20 See John Moss, Chairman, Foreign Operations and Government Information Subcommittee, House of Representatives, to President Lyndon Johnson, 31 March 1965; and Lyndon Johnson to Chairman Moss, 2 April 1965; PPRC; box 88, fold.: Executive Privilege; LBJPL; President Nixon to John E. Moss, House of Representatives, 7 April 1969; Kenneth Lazarus Papers, box 1, fold.: Executive Privilege, Presidential Powers, succession, etc. (2); GRFPL.

21 U.S. Congress, Senate, Committee on the Judiciary, *Executive Privilege: The Withholding of Information by the Executive,* 1.

22 For release to Sunday papers, 19 December 1971, text of letter by Senator Edward M. Kennedy to members of administrative practice subcommittee regarding non–court ordered electronic surveillance; 17 December 1971, ACLUP, box 1092, fold. 7, PPP, DRBSC, PUL.

23 Mardian to Kennedy, 1 March 1971, ACLUP, box 1092, fold. 7, PPP, DRBSC, PUL. When he joined the Justice Department in 1970, Mardian was assigned to revive the Internal Security Division. His division was in charge of wiretapping administration critics, including public officials and members of the media. In 1972 Mardian served as legal counsel for President Nixon's Committee to Reelect the President. He fervently denied any involvement in the Watergate break-in and cover-up. He was convicted of conspiracy though the charges were later dropped and he never served time. See Patricia Sullivan, "Robert Mardian, Attorney Caught up in Watergate Scandal," *WP*, 21 July 2006, B07.

24 Kennedy to Mardian, 12 March 1971; Mardian to Kennedy, 23 March 1971, author's emphasis; ACLUP, box 1092, fold. 7, PPP, DRBSC, PUL.

25 Paul R. Clancy, *Just a Country Lawyer: A Biography of Senator Sam Ervin* (Bloomington: Indiana University Press, 1974), 268.

26 Richard Nixon, "Reorganization Plan No. 2 of 1970," *Public Administration Review* 30, no. 6 (November–December 1970): 611–619. James Reston, "Washington: A 'Small' Staff in an 'Open' Administration?" *NYT* 17 June 1970, 46. See James Reston, "Mr. Nixon's First Whiff of Trouble," *NYT*, 9 February 1969, E12.

27 U.S. Congress, Senate, Committee on the Judiciary, *Executive Privilege: The Withholding of Information by the Executive*, 3, 23, 381–391.

28 Ibid.

29 Campbell, *Senator Sam Ervin*, 210–213.

30 Melvin Wulf, interview by the author, 4 April 2008, audio recording (in author's possession). Marlise James, "Mel Wulf and the New ACLU," in *The People's Lawyers* (New York: Holt, Rinehart and Winston, 1973), 24–31; "Court Asked to Bar Army Dossier Suit," *NYT*, 4 January 1972, 22.

31 *NAACP v. Alabama*, 357 U.S. 449 (1958); *Talley v. California*, 362 U.S. 60 (1960); *Griswold v. Connecticut*, 381 U.S. 479 (1965); *Stanley v. Georgia*, 394 U.S. 557 (1969); *Wisconsin v. Constantineau*, 400 U.S. 433 (1971).

32 Campbell, *Senator Sam Ervin*, 256.

33 "Court Asked to Bar Army Dossier Suit," 22; Baskir interview, Wulf interview, Pyle interview.

34 Neier, *Taking Liberties*, 96; Richard Halloran, "Aide to Mitchell Opposes Any Curb on Surveillance," *NYT*, 10 March 1971, 1.

35 "Justice Rehnquist's Decision to Participate in *Laird v. Tatum*," *Columbia Law Review* 73, no 1 (January 1973): 106–124.

36 Neier, *Taking Liberties*, 97–98. Fred P. Graham, "Court Bars Trial of Army over Civilian Surveillance," *NYT*, 27 June 1972, 1, 24; *Tatum v. Laird*, 408 U.S. 1 (1972).

37 Fred P. Graham, "White House View of Wiretap Right Denied on Appeal," *NYT*, 9 April 1971, 1; John Kifner, "A Chicago Retrial Tied to Wiretaps: U.S. Must Decide Whether to Disclose Secret Data," *NYT*, 23 November 1972, 21.

38 For a brief history of the development of Howard University's prestigious law program, see Richard Kluger, *Simple Justice: The History of* Brown v. Board of Education *and Black America's Struggle for Equality* (New York: Alfred A. Knopf, 2004), 123–131. Agis Salpukas, "The Judge in Wiretapping Case: Damon Jerome Keith," *NYT*, 20 June 1972, 23. In 2002 Keith, in *Detroit Free Press v. Ashcroft*, held that the George W. Bush administration's secret deportation hearings were unconstitutional. See Bob Herbert, "Secrecy Is Our Enemy," *NYT*, 2 September 2002, A15.

39 Keith's ruling cited in "Amicus Curiae filed on behalf of the ACLU to the US court of appeals, 6th circuit," ACLUP, box 1791, fold. *U.S. v. United States District Court for East Michigan*, PPP, DRBSC, PUL; "Decisions," *Time*, 8 February 1971, http://www.time.com/time/magazine/article/0,9171,909822,00.html.

40 "Melvin Wulf to George Meany, President, AFL-CIO, 14 October 1971," ACLUP, box 1791, fold. *U.S. v. United States District Court for East Michigan*, PPP, DRBSC, PUL.

41 See Fred Graham, "A Counterweight to A.C.L.U. Thrives," *NYT*, 22 February 1971, 26.

42 "Amicus Curiae filed on behalf of the ACLU to the US court of appeals, 6th circuit," ACLUP, 1–8.

43 Ibid.

44 Ibid.

45 *Youngstown Sheet & Tube Co. v. Sawyer* (343 U.S. 579) (1952); "Amicus Curiae filed on behalf of the ACLU to the US court of appeals, 6th circuit," ACLUP, 12-23; 343 U.S. 579 (1952).

46 *United States v. United States District Court*, 407 U.S. 297 (1972); "High Court Curbs U.S. Wiretapping Aimed at Radicals," *NYT*, 20 June 1972, 1.

47 John P. MacKenzie, "Court Curbs Wiretapping of Radicals," *WP*, 20 June 1972, A1.

48 "The Restraint of Law," *NYT*, 20 June 1972, 38.

49 "The Court and Electronic Surveillances," *WP*, 20 June 1972, 18.

50 "Transcript of the President's News Conference Emphasizing Domestic Policy," *NYT*, 23 June 1972, 14.

51 See Kutler, *Wars of Watergate*, 201-202. This seems a plausible theory to explain this third break-in. Others claim that White House aides learned that the DNC possessed information related to a call girl operation (with Democratic clientele as well as White House officials).

52 Keith W. Olson, *Watergate: The Presidential Scandal That Shook America* (Lawrence: University Press of Kansas, 2003). Rick Perlstein carefully details the "black bag jobs" and "dirty tricks" and their consequences in *Nixonland: The Rise of a President and the Fracturing of America* (New York: Scribner, 2008), 628-637.

53 Kutler, *Wars of Watergate*, 209-210, 218-222.

54 On CREEP's "dirty tricks," see Perlstein, *Nixonland*, 607-719; and Sam Ervin, Jr., *The Whole Truth: Watergate* (New York: Random House, 1980), 248-252.

55 Kutler, *Wars of Watergate*, 255-257.

56 Ervin, *Whole Truth*, 23; Samuel Dash, Robert Schwartz, and Robert Knowlton, *The Eavesdroppers* (New Brunswick, NJ: Rutgers University Press, 1959), 7.

57 Kutler, *Wars of Watergate*, 346; Campbell, *Last of the Founding Fathers*, 276-277. Campbell persuasively argues that Ervin's hearings on Army surveillance offered a "rehearsal" for his work on the Watergate committee.

58 Kutler, *Wars of Watergate*, 260-262.

59 "Privacy: The Issue and the Agenda," *WP*, 23 January 1974, A24.

60 "Address by the President on the American Right of Privacy," live on nationwide radio, 23 February 1974, Ford Vice Presidential Papers, Office of Legal Counsel, box 83, fold.: DCCRP, March 24-June 14, 1974, GRFPL.

61 Raymond J. Waldmann, "The Domestic Council: Innovation in Presidential Government," *Public Administration Review* 36, no 3 (May-June, 1976): 260.

62 Memorandum from Sharon Biederman to Aryeh Neier, re: "The Privacy Report," undated, ACLUP, box 683, fold. 8; PPP, DRBSC, PUL. "Memorandum: A Program to Safeguard Individual Privacy," Hope Eastman, Associate Director, undated, ACLUP, box 683, fold. 5; PPP, DRBSC, PUL.

63 Lesley Oelsner, "Hart Says Administration Undermines Privacy Right," *NYT*, 3 March 1974, 40.

64 Barry M. Goldwater, Jr., "Bipartisan Privacy," *The Civil Liberties Review* (Summer 1974): 74-78.

65 Kutler, *Wars of Watergate*, 348.

66 Ervin, *Whole Truth*, 66-67; Campbell, *Senator Sam Ervin*, 285.

67 Ervin, *Whole Truth*, 187-218.

68 *United States v. Nixon* (418 U.S. 683) (1974), http://www.law.cornell.edu/supct/html/historics/USSC_CR_0418_0683_ZS.html.

69 Ervin, *Whole Truth,* 229–239.

70 "Draft Statement on Watergate and Civil Liberties," 25 June 1973; ACLUP, box 27, fold. 5; 1–3 PPP, DRBSC, PUL.

71 Ibid., 1–2.

CHAPTER 6. AN "EFFECTIVE SERVANT OF THE PUBLIC'S RIGHT TO KNOW": REPRESENTATIVE MOORHEAD REVISES FOIA

1 ACLU legal counsel John Shattuck deposed former President Nixon in January 1976 regarding his role in authorizing illegal wiretaps of civil servants during his first term. This account is drawn from John Shattuck and Alan Westin, "Second Deposing of Richard Nixon," *Civil Liberties Review* (June/July 1976), and the author's interview with John Shattuck, 8 November 2007, audio recording (in author's possession); Peter Kihss, "Promoted in A.C.L.U.: John Howard Francis Shattuck," *NYT,* 6 September 1976, 7.

2 "New Battles over Secrecy and Privacy," *WP,* 18 August 1974, C6. Thomas Powers, "The American Police State," *NYT,* 9 January 1977, 238.

3 See U.S. Congress, Committee on Government Operations, United States Senate and the Committee on Government Operations, House of Representatives, *Legislative History of the Privacy Act of 1974, S. 3418 (Public Law 93-579): Source Book on Privacy.* 94th Cong., 2d Sess., 1976, Joint Committee Print.

4 *NYT,* 18 September 1975, 40. Notable works by professional critics include Victor Marchetti and John Marks, *The CIA and the Cult of Intelligence* (New York: Knopf, 1974); Robert L. Borosage and John Marks, eds., *The CIA File* (New York: Grossman, 1976); and Morton Halperin, Jerry Berman, Robert Borosage, and Christine Marwick, *The Lawless State: The Crimes of the U.S. Intelligence Agencies,* A Report by the Center for National Security Studies (New York: Penguin Books, 1977).

5 See Loch Johnson, *A Season of Inquiry: The Senate Intelligence Investigation* (Lexington: University Press of Kentucky, 1985), and Rhodri Jeffreys-Jones, *Cloak and Dollar: A History of American Secret Intelligence* (New Haven, CT: Yale University Press, 2003), 225–227.

6 Morton H. Halperin, "Where I'm At," *First Principles, National Security and Civil Liberties* (hereafter *FP*) 1, no. 1 (September 1975): 15–16; John Shattuck and Alan Westin, "The Second Deposing of Richard Nixon," *Civil Liberties Review* (hereafter *CLR*), June/July 1976. See also *Kissinger v. Halperin,* 452 U.S. 713 (1981).

7 William Beecher, "Raids in Cambodia by U.S. Unprotested," 9 May 1969, *NYT,* 1.

8 Halperin, "Where I'm At," 15–16; Shattuck and Westin, "Second Deposing of Richard Nixon." See also *Kissinger v. Halperin,* 452 U.S. 713 (1981).

9 R. W. Apple, Jr., "Kissinger Hints He Saw Results of the Wiretap on Halperin," *NYT,* 13 May 1973, 48. See Powers, *Broken,* 282. The tap remained on Halperin's phone, allegedly, because he became a consultant for Senator Edmund Muskie's presidential bid.

10 Halperin, "Where I'm At," 15–16; Shattuck and Westin, "Second Deposing of Richard Nixon." See also *Kissinger v. Halperin,* 452 U.S. 713 (1981).

11 Norman Dorsen to Edgar Bernhard, Esq., 7 January 1971, ACLUP, box 1981, fold. 19,

PPP, DRBSC, PUL. Members of note included by late 1971: Ramsey Clark, Marlon Brando, Candice Bergen, Art Schlesinger, Jr., James Vorenberg, C. Vann Woodward, Adam Yarmolinsky, Warren Beatty, Hodding Carter III, Roger Wilkins (chairman), and Lillian Hellman.

12 Stephen Gillers, "Secret Government and What to Do about It: Conference Report," *CLR*, Winter/Spring 1974, 69. The Committee for Public Justice published proceedings in an edited volume: Norman Dorsen and Stephen Gillers, eds., *None of Your Business: Government Secrecy in America* (New York: Viking Press, 1974).

13 Morton Halperin, "Covert Intelligence and Operations," in Dorsen and Gillers, eds., *None of Your Business*, 117; Walter Mondale recalls Stennis's retelling of this episode in *Good Fight*, 137.

14 Dorsen and Gillers, eds., *None of Your Business*; Gillers, "Secret Government," 70.

15 See Hazel Erskine, "The Polls: Presidential Power," *Public Opinion Quarterly* 37, no. 3 (Autumn 1973): 488–503; Hazel Erskine, "The Polls: Corruption in Government," *Public Opinion Quarterly* 37, no. 4 (Winter 1973/1974): 628–644.

16 Remarks by Representative William S. Moorhead for the Pittsburgh Federal Executive Board, on the subject of "Government Secrecy and Credibility," Pittsburgh, PA, 28 June 1974; box 20, fold. 267, William S. Moorhead Papers (WSMP) Manuscripts and Archives, Yale University Library (MAYUL).

17 Remarks of William Moorhead before the Department of Justice Freedom of Information Symposium, 29 November 1973, box 20, fold. 264, WSMP, MAYUL.

18 ". . . And the Right to Privacy," *NYT*, 20 November 1974, A26.

19 "W. Moorhead, Congressman for 22 Years," *Pittsburgh Post-Gazette*, 4 August 1987, 16; "Remarks by Representative William S. Moorhead, Chairman, House Foreign Operations and Government Information Subcommittee, at the Annual Conference of Sigma Delta Chi, Region 4, on the subject of 'A Free New Media,'" William Penn Hotel, Pittsburgh, PA, 14 April 1973, 5; box 20, fold. 263, WSMP, MAYUL.

20 *Congress and the Nation*, vol. 4 (Washington, DC: Congressional Quarterly Service, 1974), 805–806.

21 "FOIAA H.R. 12471," Ken Cole to President Nixon, 2 July 1974; William Timmons files; box 4; Freedom of Information Act Veto (1); GRFPL.

22 House Republican Research Committee, "Recommendation of the House Republican Task Force on Privacy," 21 August 1974; Frederick Lynn May files, box 27, fold.: Background (1); 3, 9–10, GRFPL.

23 See U.S. Congress, Committee on Government Operations, United States Senate and the Committee on Government Operations, House of Representatives, *Legislative History of the Privacy Act of 1974*, 297–299.

24 U.S. Congress, Senate, Committee on the Judiciary, *Federal Data Banks and Constitutional Rights: A Study of Data Systems on Individuals Maintained by Agencies of the United States Government*.

25 Board of Directors ACLU Priorities for 1972, ACLUP, box 24, fold. 6, 12–18, PPP, DRBSC, PUL.

26 Barry Goldwater, *The Conscience of a Conservative* (New York: Hillman Books, 1960), 16–17, 88, 114; U.S. Congress, Committee on Government Operations, United States Senate and the Committee on Government Operations, House of Representatives, *Legislative History of the Privacy Act of 1974*.

27 "A.C.L.U. Official Criticizes Ford on Privacy Bills," *NYT*, 8 January 1975, 23.

28 William Moorhead and Edward Kennedy to President Gerald Ford, 13 August 1974, William Timmons files, box 4, Freedom of Information Act Veto (1), GRFPL; William Moorhead and John Erlenborn to President Ford, 13 August 1974, William Timmons files, box 4, fold.: Freedom of Information Act Veto (1), GRFPL; Kutler, *Wars of Watergate*, 514.

29 Jerry Ford, "Your Washington Review," 29 June 1966, Ford Congressional Papers, box D2, fold: Ford Newsletters, June–October 1966, "Regarding Freedom of Information Bill," Congressman Gerald Ford News Release, 20 June 1966; Ford Congressional Papers, D6, fold: Credibility Gap 1966, 1967, GRFPL.

30 "A Selection of Comments Made by Ford on Various Issues and Individuals," *NYT*, 9 August 1974, 9; "Amending the Information Act," *WP*, 5 October 1974, A18; "A Regrettable Veto," *WP*, 21 October 1974, A22; "New Battles over Secrecy and Privacy," *WP*, 18 August 1974, C6.

31 "Reasonable Freedom of Information Bill Needed," Author unknown, Philip Buchen files, box 17; Freedom of Information Legislation (3), GRFPL; William Timmons to Alex Haig, 13 August 1974; William Timmons files; box 4; Freedom of Information Act Veto (1), GRFPL.

32 Martin Arnold, "Ford Vetoes Effort to Improve Access," *NYT*, 18 October 1974, 16; "Federal Files: Freedom of Information," *WP*, 20 November 1974, A26.

33 William Moorhead and Edward Kennedy to President Gerald Ford, 13 August 1974, William Timmons files, box 4, Freedom of Information Act Veto (1), GRFPL; William Moorhead and John Erlenborn to President Ford, 13 August 1974, William Timmons files, box 4, fold.: Freedom of Information Act Veto (1), GRFPL; Kutler, *Wars of Watergate*, 514.

34 President Gerald R. Ford, 17 October 1974, To the House of Representatives, Legislation Case Files 1974–1976, box 9, fold.: H.R. 12471 (1), GRFPL.

35 Ibid.

36 On Ford's pardon, see Joan Hoff, *Nixon Reconsidered* (New York: BasicBooks, 1994), 322–328; and Kutler, *Wars of Watergate*, 553–573.

37 "A Regrettable Veto," *WP*, 21 October 1974, A22; "Ford's Alarmist View on Secrecy," *Los Angeles Times*, 21 October 1974, part 2, 6.

38 See Powers, *Secrecy and Power*, 464–466. For a detailed discussion of the Media, PA, break-in, see chapter 4.

39 Powers, *Broken*, 276–277, 306–309; John M. Crewdson, "Saxbe Says Top Officials Had Some Knowledge of F.B.I.'s Drive to Disrupt Various Political Groups," *NYT*, 19 November 1974, 27.

40 "Federal Files: Freedom of Information . . . ," *WP*, 20 November 1974, A26; Powers, *Broken*, 306–309; Crewdson, "Saxbe Says Top Officials Had Some Knowledge," 27.

41 Joseph Kraft, "Developing a 'Gullibility Gap,'" *WP*, 23 January 1975, A23.

42 Arthur Macy Cox, *The Myths of National Security: The Peril of Secret Government* (Boston: Beacon Press, 1975), 1. Cox worked in the State Department during the Truman Administration and later served in the CIA as a Soviet specialist.

43 Ford speech at the National Computer Conference, 9 May 1974, box 116, fold. speeches national computer conference, Vice Presidential papers, GRFPL.

44 "Conference on the Central Intelligence Agency and Covert Activities," 5 September

1974, ACLUP, box 630, fold. 6; PPP, DRBSC, PUL; "Center for National Security Studies, 1974," ACLU Foundation Project Files 1964–1978, box 630, fold. 6; PPP, DRBSC, PUL. CNSS sponsored a range of projects in 1974 including: Militarism in the Community, Intelligence and Covert Actions, Law Enforcement Assistance Administration, Study on Classification and Secrecy, American Police and Military Aid Abroad, National Security and the Constitution, and Citizen's Project on National Security.

45 "Conference on the Central Intelligence Agency and Covert Activities," 5 September 1974; "Center for National Security Studies, 1974," ACLU Foundation Project Files 1964–1978, box 630, fold. 6; PPP, DRBSC, PUL.

46 On 11 September 1973 the democratically elected socialist government in Chile was overthrown in a coup d'état (opposition forces were armed and funded by the CIA). President Salvador Allende was murdered. The coup brought an abrupt end to the longest democratic government in Latin America and ushered in the regime of totalitarian general Augusto Pinochet. See Lubna Qureshi, *Nixon, Kissinger and Allende: U.S. Involvement in the 1973 Coup in Chile* (Lanham, MD: Lexington Books, 2008).

47 Conference proceedings were published in an edited volume, Robert L. Borosage and John Marks, eds., *The CIA File*. The volume included the text of William Colby's talk as well as the question-and-answer period that followed.

48 William Colby, "The View from Langley: Address to the Fund for Peace Conference on the CIA and Covert Action," in Borosage and Marks, eds., *CIA File*, 181–213.

49 CIA Director William Colby testified before the House Armed Services Committee in April 1974 detailing that the CIA had distributed some $3 million in 1964 to ensure Allende's defeat. "Destabilizing Chile," Borosage and Marks, eds., *CIA File*, 79; Seymour Hersh, "Kissinger Called Chile Strategist," *NYT*, 15 September 1974, 1.

50 See David M. Barrett, *The CIA and Congress: The Untold Story from Truman to Kennedy* (Lawrence: University Press of Kansas, 2005), 459–461. See also Kathryn Olmsted, *Challenging the Secret Government: The Post-Watergate Investigations of the CIA and FBI* (Chapel Hill: University of North Carolina Press, 1996), 45–46; Johnson, *Season of Inquiry*, 10.

51 Seymour Hersh, "Huge C.I.A. Operation Reported in U.S. against Antiwar Forces, Other Dissidents in Nixon Years," *NYT*, 22 December 1974, 1.

52 "Colby Report," William Colby to President, 24 December 1974, James E. Connor files 1974–1977, box 56, fold: Colby Report, GRFPL; Ron Nessen, *It Sure Looks Different from the Inside* (New York: Playboy Press, 1978), 54–57. The whole document is available at the National Security Archives: http://www.gwu.edu/~nsarchiv/NSAEBB /NSAEBB222/index.htm.

53 Olmsted, *Challenging the Secret Government*, 47–49.

54 See Gerald Ford, *A Time to Heal: The Autobiography of Gerald Ford* (New York: Harper and Row, 1979), 265–267.

55 John Herbers, "Ford C.I.A. Panel: Departure from Tradition," *NYT*, 8 January 1975, 25; Olmsted, *Challenging the Secret Government*, 49–58; "Spying Data Retained by Army, Failure to Destroy Files Probed," *WP*, 11 January 1975, A2.

56 "Amending the Information Act," A18.

57 "The Freedom of Information Act and National Security Information," Project on Freedom of Information and the National Security, February 1975, Kenneth A. Lazarus files, 1974–1977, box 25, fol. LE 8 Freedom of Information Act (2), GRFPL [JF05].

58 Address by Edward Levi, Attorney General before the Association of the Bar of the City of New York, 28 April 1975, Philip Buchen files, box 24, fold.: Justice—Levi, Edward: speeches, GRFPL.

59 Ibid.

60 Ibid.

61 Memorandum for Buchen from Antonin Scalia, Assistant Attorney General, "Re: Applicability of the Freedom of Information Act to the White House Office," 26 February 1975, Philip Buchen files, box 17, fold.: Freedom of Information-General (2), GRFPL.

62 Mark Lowenthal, "Intelligence Community: Reform and Reorganization," Issue Brief IB76039, The Library of Congress Congressional Research Service, Major Issues System, updated, 12/10/1980; 2 (copy in author's possession).

63 Cited in Nessen, *It Sure Looks Different*, 64–65; Olmsted, *Challenging the Secret Government*, 83–85; Commission on CIA Activities within the United States, *Report to the President by the Commission on CIA Activities within the United States, June 1975* (Washington, DC: GPO, 1975).

64 Johnson, *Season of Inquiry*, 13–15; Olmsted, *Challenging the Secret Government*, 49–58, 112–117.

65 Olmsted, *Challenging the Secret Government*, 85; Johnson, *Season of Inquiry*, 33–35, 54–56.

66 Johnson, *Season of Inquiry*, 34, 42.

67 James Bamford, *Body of Secrets: Anatomy of the Ultra-Secret National Security Agency* (New York: Doubleday, 2001), 428–429, 435–440.

68 "F.B.I. Says Kennedy Approved Wiretap on Dr. King' s Phone," 19 June 1969, 25; on the Committee for Public Justice, see chapter 4, and Pat Watters and Stephen Gillers, eds., *Investigating the FBI* (Garden City, NY: Doubleday, 1973).

69 Aryeh Neier, Executive Director, ACLU, Robert Borosage, Director, CNSS, David Cohen, President, Common Cause, Stephen Schlossberg, General Counsel, United Automobile Workers, Leon Shull, National Director, Americans for Democratic Action, Ray Calamaro, Executive Director, Committee for Public Justice, Richard Barnet and Marcus Raskin, Co-Directors, Institute for Policy Studies, Morton Halperin, Director, Project on National Security and Civil Liberties to Honorable Gerald R. Ford, Philip Buchen files 1974–1977, box 17, fold.: Freedom of Information—Requests (3), GRFPL.

70 Christine M. Marwick, "Controlling the Intelligence Agencies: A Report on the Conference Held November 3 and 4, 1975," *FP* 1, no. 4 (December 1975): 3.

71 "What Is the Role of Domestic Intelligence?" *FP* 1, no. 4 (December 1975): 9–10.

72 Ibid.

73 On the FBI's public relation efforts, see Richard Gid Powers, *G-Men: Hoover's FBI in American Popular Culture* (Carbondale: Southern Illinois University Press, 1983); on the CIA, see Hugh Wilford, *The Mighty Wurlitzer: How the CIA Played America* (Cambridge, MA: Harvard University Press, 2008).

74 "Statement of Walter Mondale, Wednesday, November 19, 1975, before the Senate Select Committee Hearings on the FBI," box 3, fold. CIA-FBI groups, 6, Minnesota Historical Society (MHS).

75 Olmsted, *Challenging the Secret Government*, 105–106.

76 Jerry J. Berman and Morton H. Halperin, eds., *The Abuses of the Intelligence Agencies*, A Report by the Center for National Security Studies (Washington, DC: The Center for National Security Studies, 1975), preface.

77 Many excellent, thorough accounts chronicle these investigations. See especially Loch Johnson, *A Season of Inquiry*; and Kathryn S. Olmsted, *Challenging the Secret Government*.

CHAPTER 7. "TEMPERS CHANGE, TIMES CHANGE, PUBLIC ATTITUDES CHANGE": PASSING FISA

1 This account is drawn from newsletters, newspaper articles, and various meetings minutes found in the Michigan Coalition to End Government Spying vertical file, Michigan State University Special Collections, American Radicalism Vertical File. See especially Joe Scales, "Secret Newsletter Found in State Files," *The State News: Michigan University's Independent Voice*, 14 February 1977, 1; and "Political Spying Topic of Seminar," *The Detroit News*, 9 June 1977, 8B.

2 Halperin, Berman, Borosage, and Marwick, *Lawless State*, 4.

3 Aryeh Neier, "Annual Report, 1975," Annual report, ACLUP box 1881, fold. 6: 1975, PPP, DRBSC, PUL.

4 "Charting the Course of the Third Century," *NYT*, 4 January 1976, NES27. Of course, the economic decline was relative. Americans still enjoyed one of the highest standards of living in the world. See David Farber, *Taken Hostage: The Iran Hostage Crisis and America's First Encounter with Radical Islam* (Princeton, NJ: Princeton University Press, 2006), 18–22.

5 See the first issue, *FP* 1, no. 1 (September 1975).

6 "Congressional Oversight of Intelligence Agencies, " Statement #3, Republican Policy Committee of the House of Representatives, 17 February 1975, Congressional Relations Office, box 13, Intelligence—General, GRFPL.

7 "Thinking about the CIA," *Los Angeles Times*, 10 August 1975, part 6, 2.

8 Quote from State of the Union address, 1976, cited in "President Ford '76 Factbook," 8 September 1976, Richard Cheney files, 1974–1977, box 18, President Ford '76 Factbook, GRFPL.

9 "Richard S. Welch," *WP*, 29 December 1975, A16.

10 Taylor Branch, "The Trial of the C.I.A.," *NYT*, 12 September 1976, 209; Olmsted, *Challenging the Secret Government*, 157–158.

11 John Crewdson, "Secrecy Is Cited: A Year's Investigation Uncovered a Number of Irregularities," *NYT*, 26 January 1976, 49; Schorr, *Clearing the Air*, 191–194; Olmsted, *Challenging the Secret Government*, 158–161.

12 Schorr, *Clearing the Air*, 179–207.

13 Ibid., 205; "Congress and Mr. Schorr," *NYT*, 22 February 1976, E14; "Selling Secrets," *NYT*, 15 February 1976, E12; "Overkill on the Hill," *NYT*, 25 February 1976, 36; Schorr, "Letters to the Editor," *NYT*, 22 February 1976, E12.

14 "Congress and Mr. Schorr," *NYT*, 22 February 1976, E14; Olmsted, *Challenging the Secret Government*, 161–164; Schorr, *Clearing the Air*, 217–222. See Lewis, "The Politics of Secrecy," *NYT*, 26 February 1976, 30; Safire, "Bill Paley's Big Secret," *NYT*, 1 March 1976, 18; Wicker, "Defending Dan Schorr," *NYT*, 24 February 1976, 35.

15 Schorr, *Clearing the Air*, 237–258.

16 Christine M. Marwick, "Reforming the Intelligence Agencies: Proposals of the Ameri-

can Civil Liberties Union, the Ford Administration, the House Select Committee on Intelligence," *FP* 1, no. 7 (March 1976): 8–9, 12–13; Olmsted, *Challenging the Secret Government*, 163.

17 U.S. Congress, Senate, Select Committee to Study Governmental Operations with Respect to Intelligence Activities, *Final Report of the Select Committee to Study Governmental Operations with Respect to Intelligence Activities Together with Additional, Supplemental, and Separate Views.* Taylor Branch, former editor of the *Washington Monthly*, was curious about the tone of the report. In a fine example of investigative journalism, Branch wrote an insightful account of the CIA's successful effort to "outfox Congressional investigators" and ultimately avoid reform of its most precious covert operations. See Branch, "Trial of the C.I.A.," 209.

18 Ford issued Executive Order 11905 in February; see "Text of Ford Plan on Intelligence Units and Excerpts from His Executive Order," *NYT*, 19 February 1976, 30. Frank Smist, Jr., provides a thoughtful overview of congressional intelligence oversight in the 1970s in *Congress Oversees the United States Intelligence Community, 1947–1989* (Knoxville: University of Tennessee Press, 1990). For more recent treatments of congressional oversight see Loch Johnson, "Ostriches, Cheerleaders, Skeptics, and Guardians: Role Selection by Congressional Intelligence Overseers," *SAIS Review* 28 (Spring 2008): 93–108; Amy Zegart, "The Domestic Politics of Irrational Intelligence Oversight," *Political Science Quarterly* 126, no. 1 (2011): 1–25; Jennifer Kibbe, "Congressional Oversight of Intelligence: Is the Solution Part of the Problem?" *Intelligence and National Security* 25 (February 2010): 24–49; "President Gerald R. Ford's Executive Order 11905: United States Foreign Intelligence Activities," 18 February 1976, http://www.ford.utexas.edu/LIBRARY/speeches/760110e.htm; Johnson, *Season of Inquiry*, 195.

19 Marwick, "Reforming the Intelligence Agencies," 8, 10.

20 Ibid.

21 Ibid., 9, 10. On the political use of executive orders, see Christopher J. Deering and Forrest Maltzman, "The Politics of Executive Orders: Legislative Constraints on Presidential Power," *Political Research Quarterly* 52, no. 4 (December 1999): 767–783; and Kenneth R. Mayer, "Executive Orders and Presidential Power," *Journal of Politics* 61, no. 2 (May 1999): 445–466.

22 "Controlling the Intelligence Agencies," 12 December 1975, ACLUP, box 392, intelligence no 11; PPP, DRBSC, PUL; Marwick, "Reforming the Intelligence Agencies: Proposals of the American Civil Liberties Union, the Ford Administration, the House Select Committee on Intelligence," 12–13.

23 Morton Halperin, "Point of View: The Fraud Plan," *FP* 1, no. 7 (March 1976): 15–16.

24 484 F.2d 418 (5th Cir. 1973), *cert. denied*, 415 U.S. 960 (1974).

25 494 F.2d 593 (3d Cir.) (en banc) (5-4 decision), *cert. denied sub nom. Ivanov v. United States*, 419 U.S. 881 (1974).

26 *Zweibon v. Mitchell*, 363 F. Supp. 936, 942 (D.D.C. 1973); Philip A. Lacovara, "Presidential Power to Gather Intelligence: The Tension between Article II and Amendment IV," *Law and Contemporary Problems* 14, no. 3, Presidential Power: Part 2 (Summer 1976): 106–131.

27 "Mr. Levi's Initiative," *NYT*, 17 August 1975, 166. See Powers, *Broken*, 314.

28 Jerry J. Berman, "The Case for a Legislated FBI Charter," *FP* 1, no. 10 (June 1976): 5–6.

In 1994 Berman founded the Center for Democracy and Technology, where he currently serves as chair of the board.

29 Address by Edward Levi before the Association of the Bar of the City of New York, 28 April 1975, Philip Buchen files, box 24, fold.: Justice—Levi, Edward: speeches, GRFPL.

30 "Burglaries, Lies and Oversight," *NYT*, 2 July 1976, A26.

31 Edward M. Kennedy and Charles Mathias, Jr., "Letters to the Editor, Intelligence: To Check Executive Power," *NYT*, 22 July 1976, 30.

32 Statement of Mr. John Shattuck, American Civil Liberties Union, and Mr. Morton Halperin, American Civil Liberties Union, cited in U.S. Congress, Senate, Committee on the Judiciary, *Foreign Intelligence Surveillance Act of 1976, Hearing before the Subcommittee on Criminal Laws and Procedures of the Committee on the Judiciary*, 94 Cong., 2d Sess., on S. 743, S. 1888 and S. 3197, 29, 30 March 1976 (Washington, DC: GPO, 1976), 27–41.

33 Statement of Mr. John Shattuck, American Civil Liberties Union, and Mr. Morton Halperin, American Civil Liberties Union, U.S. Congress, Senate, Committee on the Judiciary, *Foreign Intelligence Surveillance Act of 1976*, 27–41.

34 "Civil liberties and the 94th congress, Washington Report by the Washington Office Staff," 8 October 1976, ACLUP, box 392, fold. 13, Washington, DC, Office, 1976, PPP, DRBSC, PUL; Pyle interview.

35 Statement of Herman Schwartz, Professor, Law School, State University of New York at Buffalo, U.S. Congress, Senate, Committee on the Judiciary, *Foreign Intelligence Surveillance Act of 1976*, 44–55.

36 Herbert Wechsler to John L. McLellan, 26 March 1976, printed in U.S. Congress, Senate, Committee on the Judiciary, *Foreign Intelligence Surveillance Act of 1976*, 143–144; Statement of Professor Philip Heymann, Harvard Law School, printed in ibid., 55–59.

37 Tom Wicker, "No Rush for New Tap Law," *NYT*, 23 July 1976, 15; John Shattuck to Vice President Walter Mondale, 5 May 1977, Staff Offices Domestic Policy Staff Civil Rights and Justice Gutierrez, box 35; fold. Wiretapping [O/A 7291] 1, Jimmy Carter Presidential Library (JCPL), Atlanta, Georgia.

38 Testimony of David Atlee Phillips, U.S. Congress, Senate, Committee on Government Operations, *Oversight of U.S. Government Intelligence Functions: Hearings before the Committee on Government Operations*, 94th Cong., 2d Sess., 1976, 105–115. The ARIO later became the AFIO, the Association of Former Intelligence Officers. For more about the ARIO, see Jean M. White, "Intelligence Gathering: Insiders Meet on the Outside," *WP*, 18 September 1976, B1. Also see David Atlee Phillips, *The Night Watch: 25 Years of Peculiar Service* (New York: Atheneum, 1977).

39 Testimony of Clark Clifford and testimony of Richard Helms, U.S. Congress, Senate, Committee on Government Operations, *Oversight of U.S. Government Intelligence Functions*, 218, 224.

40 Testimony of Richard Helms and testimony of Clarence Kelley, U.S. Congress, Senate, Committee on Government Operations, *Oversight of U.S. Government Intelligence Functions*, 281; 171–187.

41 Testimony of Clark Clifford, U.S. Congress, Senate, Committee on Government Operations, *Oversight of U.S. Government Intelligence Functions*, 224.

42 Halperin, "Point of View," 15–16; Testimony of Morton Halperin, U.S. Congress, Senate, Committee on Government Operations, *Oversight of U.S. Government Intelligence Functions*, 275–277; 322–323.

43 Testimony of Morton Halperin, U.S. Congress, Senate, Committee on Government Operations, *Oversight of U.S. Government Intelligence Functions*, 275–277.

44 Testimony of Gaylord Nelson, U.S. Congress, Senate, Committee on Government Operations, *Oversight of U.S. Government Intelligence Functions*, 279.

45 Abraham Ribicoff, U.S. Congress, Senate, Committee on Government Operations, *Oversight of U.S. Government Intelligence Functions*, 281–282.

46 Testimony of Senator Barry Goldwater, U.S. Congress, Senate, Committee on Government Operations, *Oversight of U.S. Government Intelligence Functions*, 333–346.

47 *Final Report of the Select Committee to Study Governmental Operations with Respect to Intelligence Activities Together with Additional, Supplemental, and Separate Views, Book 1,* 574; Testimony of Senator John Tower, U.S. Congress, Senate, Committee on Government Operations, *Oversight of U.S. Government Intelligence Functions,* 45–48; testimony of Senator Strom Thurmond, *Oversight of U.S. Government Intelligence Functions,* 368–371.

48 James Reston, "Money and Secrecy," *NYT*, 21 May 1976, 22.

49 James T. Wooten, "The Well-Planned Enigma of Jimmy Carter," *NYT*, 6 June 1976, 195; David Rosenbaum, "Carter's Position on Issues Designed for Wide Appeal," *NYT*, 11 June 1976, 45; Schulman, *The Seventies,* 122.

50 Steve Gillon, *The Democrats' Dilemma: Walter F. Mondale and the Liberal Legacy* (New York: Columbia University Press, 1992), 85.

51 Mondale, *Good Fight,* 111–134.

52 For his troubles when he moved to the White House, see James Fallows, "The Passionless Presidency: The Trouble with Jimmy Carter's Administration," *Atlantic Monthly* (May 1979): 33–48, http://www.theatlantic.com/unbound/flashbks/pres/fallpass.htm.

53 "Mr. Carter's Choice," *NYT*, 16 July 1976, 16. In 1974 Mondale briefly entertained the idea of a presidential bid but dropped out the same year, claiming he had neither the desire nor the stamina to run for the nation's highest office.

54 Walter Mondale, *The Accountability of Power: Toward a Responsible Presidency* (New York: David McKay, 1975), vii–xv; Walter Mondale, Dennison College Foreign Policy Symposium, 3 October 1975, Senatorial Files, speech text files, box 7, fold.: Dennison College, WFM papers, MHS; Linda Charlton, "Mondale Says Ford Has Failed to Heed Watergate Lessons," *NYT*, 6 October 1976, 89.

55 Wooten, "The Well-Planned Enigma of Jimmy Carter," 195; Rosenbaum, "Carter's Position on Issues Designed for Wide Appeal," 45; Walter Mondale, "The Presidency," *NYT*, 16 July 1976, 17.

56 See U.S. Congress, Committee on Government Operations, United States Senate and the Committee on Government Operations, U.S. House of Representatives, *Government in the Sunshine Act Source Book: Legislative History, Texts, and Other Documents,* 94th Cong., 2d Sess.

57 *Halperin v. Kissinger* civil action no 1187-73 (D.D.C.), ruling issued on 16 December 1976; "In the Courts," *FP* 2, no. 5 (January 1977): 14. See *United States v. Nixon,* 418 U.S. 683 (1974); Morton Halperin, "'My' Wiretap Lawsuit," *FP* 3, no. 1 (September 1977): 15–16.

58 Morton Halperin, "The Carter Administration: In the Mood for Reform?" *FP* 2, no. 8 (April 1977): 15–16.

59 David Binder, "U.S. Intelligence Officials Apprehensive of New Shake-Ups under Carter," *NYT*, 13 December 1976, 43; Gillon, *Democrats' Dilemma*, 190–193. See Berkowitz, *Something Happened*, 112–114. For an alternate perspective, see Jon R. Bond and Richard Fleisher, "Carter and Congress: Presidential Style, Party Politics, and Legislative Success," in Herbert D. Rosenbaum and Alexej Ugrinsky, eds., *The Presidency and Domestic Policies of Jimmy Carter* (Westport, CT: Greenwood Press, 1994), 287–297.

60 Hedrick Smith, "Assertion of Will by Congress: Republicans Were against Sorensen Ideologically and Democrats Feared Bitter and Divisive Fight," *NYT*, 18 January 1977, 15; James Reston, "The Question of Judgment," *NYT*, 19 January 1977, 23; "Point of View: The Sorensen Debacle," *FP* 2, no. 6 (February 1977): 15–16; Halperin, "Carter Administration," 15–16.

61 James Patterson, *Restless Giant: The United States from Watergate to* Bush v. Gore (New York: Oxford University Press, 2005), 111; W. Carl Biven, *Jimmy Carter's Economy: Policy in an Age of Limits* (Chapel Hill: University of North Carolina Press, 2002), 2; Bruce Schulman, "Slouching toward the Supply Side: Jimmy Carter and the New American Political Economy," in Gary M. Fink and Hugh Davis Graham, eds., *The Carter Presidency: Policy Choices in the Post–New Deal Era* (Lawrence: University Press of Kansas, 1998), 54.

62 Halperin, "Carter Administration," 15–16.

63 Morton Halperin and Daniel Hoffman, *Top Secret: National Security and the Right to Know* (Washington, DC: New Republic Books, 1977), 103, 104, 106.

64 Mondale, *Good Fight*, 151–152.

65 U.S. Congress, Senate, Select Committee on Intelligence, *Foreign Intelligence Surveillance Act of 1978: Hearings before the Subcommittee on Intelligence and the Rights of Americans of the Select Committee on Intelligence of the United States Senate*, 95th Cong., 2d Sess. (Washington, DC: GPO, 1978), 2–3; Anthony Lewis, "On Bills to Control Wiretapping, the Infighting Goes On and On," *NYT*, 8 May 1977, 130; "The Foreign Intelligence Surveillance Act: Legislating a Judicial Role in National Security Surveillance," *Michigan Law Review* 78, no. 7 (June 1980): 1129–1135; Memorandum for the President from Stu Eizenstat and Frank White, "Enrolled Bill S. 1566—Foreign Intelligence Surveillance Act of 1978," Staff Office Domestic Policy Government Reform, Neustadt, box 59; fold. Privacy—Statements by Jimmy Carter; JCPL.

66 Senator Walter Huddleston and Senator Birch Bayh, U.S. Congress, Senate, Select Committee on Intelligence, *Foreign Intelligence Surveillance Act of 1978*, 4, 19.

67 Vice President and Director of Central Intelligence to President, "Foreign Intelligence Strategy with the Congress," 14 April 1977, box 2, fold. Intelligence, WFM papers, Materials received from Carter Library, MHS; Peter Hahn, "Jimmy Carter and the Central Intelligence Agency," in Rosenbaum and Ugrinsky, eds., *Presidency and Domestic Policies of Jimmy Carter*, 337–345.

68 Hahn, "Jimmy Carter and the Central Intelligence Agency," 323–351.

69 For the domestic reaction to the Iranian revolution and the subsequent hostage crisis, see Farber, *Taken Hostage*.

70 Hahn, "Jimmy Carter and the Central Intelligence Agency," 342–344.

71 U.S. Congress, Senate, Select Committee on Intelligence, *Report to the Senate of the*

Select Committee on Intelligence, United States Senate, Covering the Period January 1, 1979–December 31, 1980, 97th Cong., 1st Sess., 9.

72 Nicholas M. Horrock, "Polishing Up the F.B.I.'s Reputation," *NYT*, 23 November 1975, 200.

EPILOGUE

1 Neier, *Taking Liberties*, 121.

2 Eric Patashnik, *Reforms at Risk: What Happens after Major Policy Changes are Enacted* (Princeton, NJ: Princeton University Press, 2008), 156.

3 "Case Lays Loss to Antigovernment Mood," *NYT*, 9 June 1978, B2.

4 Richard J. Levine, "Fight to Curb Inflation, Experts Say, Will Take Years and Risk a Slump," *Wall Street Journal*, 20 June 1979, 1.

5 Richard A. Baker, Historian, U.S. Senate Historical Office, 1975–2009, Oral History Interviews, Senate Historical Office, Washington, DC, 47.

6 Robert Pears, "U.S. Officers Get Wider Latitude in Investigations," *NYT*, 8 March 1983, A1.

7 Morton Halperin, "Point of View," *FP* 4, no. 3 (November 1978): 15–16; "In the News," *FP* 2, no. 6 (February 1977): 14.

8 "U.S. Legal Bills Soar Due to Rights Abuse Cases," *The Sun* 21 June 1978, A6.

9 Morton Halperin, Chairperson, Campaign to Stop Government Spying, to President Bloustein, Rutgers University, 12 September, 1977, in ACLUP box 359, fold. 11, PPP, DRBSC, PUL.

10 U.S. Congress, Senate, Committee on Governmental Affairs, *Report of the Commission on Protecting and Reducing Government Secrecy: Hearing before the Committee on Governmental Affairs*, 105th Cong., 1st Sess., 1997.

11 Thomas Tamm blew the whistle on Bush's warrantless wiretapping program in 2004 and the *Times* printed the story in 2005. Tamm himself has only recently gone "public" as the whistleblower. See Michael Isikoff, "The Fed Who Blew the Whistle," *Newsweek*, 22 December 2008, 40.

12 National Freedom of Information Coalition, http://www.nfoic.org/about; The National Security Archive, http://www.gwu.edu/~nsarchiv/; Freedom of Information Advocates Network, http://www.foiadvocates.net/en/about-foianet; The Sunshine in Government Initiative, http://www.sunshineingovernment.org/index.php?cat=38; OMB Watch, http://www.ombwatch.org/ourhistory.

13 Tracy Samantha Schmidt, "A Wiki for Whistle-Blowers," http://www.time.com/time/nation/article/0,8599,1581189,00.html

Bibliography

MANUSCRIPT COLLECTIONS

American Friends Service Committee Archives, Philadelphia, Pennsylvania
California State Archives (CSA)
    John E. Moss Oral History
Columbia University, New York, New York
    Bella Abzug Papers
Gerald R. Ford Presidential Library (GRFPL), Ann Arbor, Michigan
Jimmy Carter Presidential Library (JCPL), Atlanta, Georgia
Lyndon B. Johnson Presidential Library (LBJPL), Austin, Texas
Michigan State University Special Collections (MSUSC)
    Michigan Coalition to End Government Spying papers
Minnesota Historical Society (MHS), St. Paul, Minnesota
    Walter Mondale Papers
National Archives, College Park, Maryland
    General Records of the Department of Justice
National Archives, Washington, DC (NADC)
    Records of the U.S. House of Representatives, Committee on Government Opera-
        tions, Special Subcommittee on Government Information
Princeton University Library (PUL), Princeton, New Jersey
    American Civil Liberties Union Papers (ACLUP)
    Common Cause Papers (CCP)
University of North Carolina, Chapel Hill (UNCCH)
    Sam J. Ervin Papers
Yale University, New Haven, Connecticut
    William S. Moorhead Papers

ORAL HISTORY INTERVIEWS

Lawrence M. Baskir
Aryeh Neier
Charles Peters
Christopher Pyle
John Shattuck
Mel Wulf

Abzug, Bella, papers. Rare Book and Manuscript Library (RBML), Columbia University (CU), New York, New York.

American Civil Liberty Union papers. Princeton University Library (PUL), Princeton, New Jersey.

American Friends Service Committee papers. American Friends Service Committee Archives (AFSCA). Philadelphia, Pennsylvania.

Archibald, Samuel, and Harold Relyea. "The Present Limits of 'Executive Privilege,'" a study prepared under the guidance of the House Foreign Operations and Government Information Subcommittee by the Library of Congress Congressional Research Service, 20 March 1973, Bella Abzug Papers (BAP), Box 518, Presidency, U.S., Executive Privilege, Rare Book and Manuscript Library, Columbia University.

Baker, Richard A. Historian, U.S. Senate Historical Office, 1975–2009, Oral History Interviews, Senate Historical Office, Washington, D.C.

Baskir, Lawrence, interview by author, 11 September 2007, audio recording (in author's possession).

Carter, Jimmy, papers. Jimmy Carter Presidential Library (JCPL). Atlanta, Georgia.

Clark, Ramsey. Oral History Interview by Harri Baker, Lyndon B. Johnson Presidential Library (LBJPL). Austin, Texas..

Commission on CIA Activities within the United States. *Report to the President by the Commission on CIA Activities within the United States.* Washington, DC: GPO, 1975.

Common Cause papers. Princeton University Library (PUL), Princeton, New Jersey.

DeLoach, Cartha D. "Deke." Oral History Interview by Michael L. Gillette, Internet Copy, Lyndon Baines Johnson Library.

Department of Justice, General Records. National Archives. College Park, Maryland.

Ervin, Sam, Jr., papers. Southern Historical Collection (SHC), University of North Carolina, Chapel Hill (UNCCH). Chapel Hill, North Carolina.

Ford, Gerald, papers. Gerald R. Ford Presidential Library (GRFPL). Ann Arbor, Michigan.

Governor's Commission Report on the Los Angeles Riots. "Violence in the City—An End or a Beginning?" Los Angeles: State of California, 1965.

Johnson, Lyndon, papers, LBJPL.

Lowenthal, Mark. "Intelligence Community: Reform and Reorganization," Issue Brief IB76039, The Library of Congress Congressional Research Service, Major Issues System, updated, 12/10/1980; 2 (copy in author's possession).

Michigan Coalition to End Government Spying papers. Michigan State University Special Collections (MSUSC). East Lansing, Michigan.

Mondale, Walter, papers. Minnesota Historical Society (MHS). St. Paul, Minnesota.

Moorhead, William S., papers. Manuscripts and Archives (MA), Yale University (YU). New Haven, Connecticut.

Moss, John E. Oral History Interview, conducted in 1989 by Donald B. Seney, California State University, Sacramento, for the California State Archives, State Government Oral History Program.

Peters, Charles, interview by the author, 16 August 2007, audio recording (in author's possession).

Pyle, Christopher, interview by the author, 26 June 2007, audio recording (in author's possession).

Report of the National Advisory Commission on Civil Disorders. New York: Bantam, 1968.

Shattuck, John, interview by the author, 8 November 2007, audio recording (in author's possession).

U.S. Congress. Committee on Government Operations, U.S. House of Representatives, and Committee on the Judiciary, U.S. Senate. *Freedom of Information Act and Amendments of 1974 (P.L. 93-502), Source Book: Legislative History, Texts, and Other Documents.* 94th Cong., 1st Sess., 1975.

U.S. Congress. Committee on Government Operations, U.S. Senate and the Committee on Government Operations, U.S. House of Representatives. *Legislative History of the Privacy Act of 1974, S. 3418 (Public Law 93-579): Source Book on Privacy.* 94th Cong., 2d Sess., 1976. Joint Committee Print.

U.S. Congress. Committee on Government Operations, U.S. Senate and the Committee on Government Operations, U.S. House of Representatives. *Government in the Sunshine Act—S. 5 (Public Law 94-409), Source Book: Legislative History, Texts, and Other Documents.* 94th Cong., 2d Sess., 1976.

U.S. Congress. House of Representatives. Committee on Government Operations. *Administration of the Freedom of Information Act, Twenty-First Report by the Committee on Government Operations Together with Additional Views.* 92d Cong., 2d Sess., 1972.

——. *Availability of Information from Federal Departments and Agencies, Part 1: Panel Discussion with Editors, et al.: Hearings before a Subcommittee of the Committee on Government Operations, House of Representatives.* 84th Cong., 1st Sess., 1955.

——. *Availability of Information from Federal Departments and Agencies, Twenty-Fifth Intermediate Report of the Committee on Government Operations.* 84th Cong., 2d Sess., 1956.

——. *Federal Public Records Law, Part 1: Hearings before a Subcommittee of the Committee on Government Operations.* 89th Cong., 1st Sess., 1965.

——. *Freedom of Information Act: Hearings before a Subcommittee of the Committee on Government Operations.* 93d Cong., 1st Sess., 1973.

——. "U.S. Information Problems in Vietnam." Eleventh Report by the Committee on Government Operations. 88th Cong., 1st Sess., 1963.

U.S. Congress. Senate. Committee on Governmental Affairs. *Report of the Commission on Protecting and Reducing Government Secrecy: Hearing before the Committee on Governmental Affairs.* 105th Cong., 1st Sess., 1997.

U.S. Congress. Senate. Committee on Government Operations. *Oversight of U.S. Government Intelligence Functions: Hearings before the Committee on Government Operations,* 94th Cong., 2d Sess., 1976.

U.S. Congress. Senate. Committee on the Judiciary. *Executive Privilege: The Withholding of Information by the Executive. Hearing before the Subcommittee on Separation of Powers of the Committee on the Judiciary.* 92nd Cong, 1st Sess., 1971.

——. *Federal Data Banks and Constitutional Rights: A Study of Data Systems on Individuals Maintained by Agencies of the United States Government,* Summary and Conclusions prepared by the Staff of the Subcommittee on Constitutional Rights of the Committee on the Judiciary. 93d Cong., 2d Sess., 1974.

———. *Federal Data Banks, Computers and the Bill of Rights: Hearings before the Subcommittee on Constitutional Rights of the Committee on the Judiciary*, Part 1 and 2. 92d Cong., 1st Sess., 1971.

———. *Foreign Intelligence Surveillance Act of 1976, Hearing before the Subcommittee on Criminal Laws and Procedures of the Committee on the Judiciary.* 94th Cong., 2d Sess., 1976.

———, Subcommittee on Administrative Practice and Procedure. *Freedom of Information Act Source Book: Legislative Materials, Cases, Articles.* 93d Cong., 2d Sess., 1974.

———. *Freedom of the Press: Hearing before the Subcommittee on Constitutional Rights of the Committee on the Judiciary.* 92d Cong., 1st and 2d Sess., 1971–1972.

U.S. Congress. Senate. Select Committee on Intelligence. *Foreign Intelligence Surveillance Act of 1978: Hearings before the Subcommittee on Intelligence and the Rights of Americans of the Select Committee on Intelligence of the United States Senate.* 95th Cong., 2d Sess., 1978.

———. *Report to the Senate of the Select Committee on Intelligence, United States Senate, Covering the Period January 1, 1979–December 31, 1980.* 97th Cong., 1st Sess., 1981.

U.S. Congress. Senate. Select Committee to Study Governmental Operations with Respect to Intelligence Activities. *Final Report of the Select Committee to Study Governmental Operations with Respect to Intelligence Activities Together with Additional, Supplemental, and Separate Views.* 94th Cong., 2d Sess., 1976.

U.S. House of Representatives, Committee on Government Operations Records. National Archives. Washington, DC.

Valeo, Francis R., Secretary of the Senate, 1966–1977, Oral History Interviews, Senate Historical Office, Washington, DC.

Wulf, Melvin, interview by the author, 4 April 2008, audio recording (in author's possession).

BOOKS AND ARTICLES

Administration of the Freedom of Information Act: An Evaluation of Government Information Programs under the Act, 1967–1972. New York: Praeger Publishers, 1973.

Alperovitz, Gar. *Atomic Diplomacy: Hiroshima and Potsdam: The Use of the Atomic Bomb and American Confrontation with Soviet Power.* New York: Simon and Schuster, 1965.

Ambrose, Stephen E., and Richard H. Immerman. *Milton S. Eisenhower, Educational Statesman.* Baltimore: Johns Hopkins University Press, 1983.

Anderson, Terry H. *The Movement and the Sixties: Protest in American from Greensboro to Wounded Knee.* New York: Oxford University Press, 1995.

Bailey, Beth. "The Army in the Marketplace: Recruiting an All-Volunteer Force." *Journal of American History* 94, no. 1 (June 2007): 47–74.

Ball, Durwood. *Army Regulars on the Western Frontier, 1848–1861.* Norman: University of Oklahoma Press, 2001.

Bamford, James. *Body of Secrets: Anatomy of the Ultra-Secret National Security Agency.* New York: Doubleday, 2001.

Barrett, David M. *The CIA and Congress: The Untold Story from Truman to Kennedy.* Lawrence: University Press of Kansas, 2005.

Baskir, Lawrence. "Reflections on the Senate Investigation of Army Surveillance." *Indiana Law Journal*, no. 49 (Summer 1974): 618–653.

Berdes, George R. *Friendly Adversaries: The Press and Government*. Milwaukee, WI: Center for the Study of the American Press, Marquette University, 1969.

Berkowitz, Edward. *Something Happened: A Political and Cultural Overview of the Seventies*. New York: Columbia University Press, 2006.

Berman, Jerry J., and Morton H. Halperin, eds. *The Abuses of the Intelligence Agencies*. A Report by the Center for National Security Studies. Washington, DC: The Center for National Security Studies, 1975.

Biven, W. Carl. *Jimmy Carter's Economy: Policy in an Age of Limits*. Chapel Hill: University of North Carolina Press, 2002.

Blanchard, Robert O. "A Watchdog in Decline." *Columbia Journalism Review* 5, no. 2 (Summer 1966): 17–21.

———, ed. *Congress and the News Media*. New York: Hastings House, 1974.

Borosage, Robert L., and John Marks, eds. *The CIA File*. New York: Grossman, 1976.

Borstelmann, Thomas. *The 1970s: A New Global History from Civil Rights to Economic Inequality*. Princeton, NJ: Princeton University Press, 2012.

Bradlee, Ben. *A Good Life: Newspapering and Other Adventures*. New York: Simon & Schuster, 1995.

Broadwater, Jeff. *Eisenhower and the Anti-Communist Crusade*. Chapel Hill: University of North Carolina Press, 1992.

Campbell, Karl. *Senator Sam Ervin, Last of the Founding Fathers*. Chapel Hill: University of North Carolina Press, 2007.

Campbell-Kelly, Martin, and William Aspray. *Computer: A History of the Information Machine*. 2d edition. Cambridge, MA: Westview Press, 2004.

Caro, Robert. *Master of the Senate: The Years of Lyndon Johnson*. New York: Alfred A. Knopf, 2004.

Chafee, Zechariah, Jr. "Freedom of Speech in War Time." *Harvard Law Review* 32, no. 8 (June 1919): 932–973.

Clancy, Paul R. *Just a Country Lawyer: A Biography of Senator Sam Ervin*. Bloomington: Indiana University Press, 1974.

Clark, Ramsey. *Crime in America: Observations on Its Nature, Causes, Prevention and Control*. New York: Simon and Schuster, 1970.

Congress and the Nation. Washington: Congressional Quarterly Service, 1974.

Conlan, Timothy. *From New Federalism to Devolution: Twenty-Five Years of Intergovernmental Reform*. Washington, DC: Brookings Institution Press, 1998.

Cowie, Jefferson. *Stayin' Alive: The 1970s and the Last Days of the Working Class*. New York: New Press, 2012.

Cox, Arthur Macy. *The Myths of National Security: The Peril of Secret Government*. Boston: Beacon Press, 1975.

Cronin, Thomas E. "A Resurgent Congress and the Imperial Presidency." *Political Science Quarterly* 95, 2 (Summer 1980): 209–237.

Cross, Harold L. *The People's Right to Know: Legal Access to Public Records and Proceedings*. Morningside Heights, NY: Columbia University Press, 1953.

Crouse, Timothy. *The Boys on the Bus*. New York: Random House, 1973.

Dabney, Dick. *A Good Man: The Life of Sam J. Ervin*. Boston: Houghton Mifflin, 1976.

Dash, Samuel, Robert Schwartz, and Robert Knowlton. *The Eavesdroppers*. New Brunswick, NJ: Rutgers University Press, 1959.

DeBenedetti Charles, and Charles Chatfield. *An American Ordeal: the Antiwar Movement of the Vietnam Era*. Syracuse, NY: Syracuse University Press, 1990.

Deering Christopher J., and Forrest Maltzman. "The Politics of Executive Orders: Legislative Constraints on Presidential Power." *Political Research Quarterly* 52, 4 (December 1999): 767–783.

Demaine, Linda J., and Brian Rosen. "Process Dangers of Military Involvement in Civil Law Enforcement: Rectifying the Posse Comitatus Act." *New York University Journal of Legislation and Public Policy* 9, no. 166 (2005–2006): 167–250.

Donner, Frank. *The Age of Surveillance: The Aims and Methods of America's Political Intelligence System*. New York: Alfred A. Knopf, 1980.

Dorsen, Norman, and Stephen Gillers, eds. *None of Your Business: Government Secrecy in America*. New York: Viking Press, 1974.

Elliff, John. *The Reform of FBI Intelligence Operations*. Princeton, NJ: Princeton University Press, 1979.

Erskine, Hazel. "The Polls: Corruption in Government." *Public Opinion Quarterly* 37, no. 4 (Winter 1973/1974): 628–644.

———. "The Polls: Presidential Power." *Public Opinion Quarterly* 37, no. 3 (Autumn 1973): 488–503.

Ervin, Sam, Jr. *Preserving the Constitution: The Autobiography of Senator Sam J. Ervin, Jr.* Charlottesville, VA: The Michie Company, 1984.

———. "Separation of Powers: Judicial Independence." *Law and Contemporary Problems* 35, no. 1 (Winter 1970): 108–127.

———. *The Whole Truth: Watergate*. New York: Random House, 1980.

Farber, David. *Taken Hostage: The Iran Hostage Crisis and America's First Encounter with Radical Islam*. Princeton, NJ: Princeton University Press, 2006.

Fink, Gary M., and Hugh Davis Graham. *The Carter Presidency: Policy Choices in the Post–New Deal Era*. Lawrence: University Press of Kansas, 1998.

Flamm, Michael. *Law and Order: Street Crime, Civil Unrest, and the Crisis of Liberalism in the 1960s*. New York: Columbia University Press, 2005.

———. "The Politics of 'Law and Order,'" in David Farber and Jeff Roche, eds. *The Conservative Sixties*. New York: Peter Lang, 2003.

Ford, Gerald. *A Time to Heal: The Autobiography of Gerald Ford*. New York: Harper and Row, 1979.

"The Foreign Intelligence Surveillance Act: Legislating a Judicial Role in National Security Surveillance." *Michigan Law Review* 78, no. 7 (June 1980): 1129–1135.

Fraser, Steve, and Gary Gerstle, eds. *The Rise and Fall of the New Deal Order, 1930–1980*. Princeton, NJ: Princeton University Press, 1989.

Garrow, David. *The FBI and Martin Luther King, Jr.: From "Solo" to Memphis*. New York: W. W. Norton, 1981.

Gillon, Steve. *The Democrats' Dilemma: Walter F. Mondale and the Liberal Legacy*. New York: Columbia University Press, 1992.

Gitlin, Todd. *The Sixties: Years of Hope, Days of Rage*. New York: Bantam Books, 1987.

Goldwater, Barry. *The Conscience of a Conservative*. New York: Hillman Books, 1960.

Graham, Hugh Davis. *The Civil Rights Era: Origins and Development of National Policy.* New York: Oxford University Press, 1990.

Greenberg, David. *Nixon's Shadow: The History of an Image.* New York: W. W. Norton, 2003.

Halberstam, David. *The Powers That Be.* New York: Knopf, 1979.

Halperin, Morton, Jerry Berman, Robert Borosage, and Christine Marwick. *The Lawless State: The Crimes of the U.S. Intelligence Agencies.* A Report by the Center for National Security Studies. New York: Penguin Books, 1976.

Halperin, Morton, and Daniel Hoffman. *Top Secret: National Security and the Right to Know.* Washington, DC: New Republic Books, 1977.

Hendrickson, Paul. *The Living and the Dead: Robert McNamara and Five Lives of a Lost War.* New York: Alfred Knopf, 1996.

Hoff, Joan. *Nixon Reconsidered.* New York: BasicBooks, 1994.

Holzman, Michael. *James Jesus Angleton, the CIA, and the Craft of Counterintelligence.* Amherst: University of Massachusetts Press, 2008.

Jacobs, Meg, William Novak, and Julian Zelizer, eds. *The Democratic Experiment: New Directions in American Political History.* Princeton, NJ: Princeton University Press, 2003.

James, Marlise. "Mel Wulf and the New ACLU," in *The People's Lawyers.* New York: Holt, Rinehart and Winston, 1973.

Jeffreys-Jones, Rhodri. *Cloak and Dollar: A History of American Secret Intelligence.* New Haven, CT: Yale University Press, 2003.

Jensen, Joan. *Army Surveillance in America, 1775–1980.* New Haven, CT: Yale University Press, 1991.

Johnson, Loch. "Ostriches, Cheerleaders, Skeptics, and Guardians: Role Selection by Congressional Intelligence Overseers." *SAIS Review* 28 (Spring 2008): 93–108.

———. *A Season of Inquiry: The Senate Intelligence Investigation.* Lexington: University Press of Kentucky, 1985.

"Justice Rehnquist's Decision to Participate in *Laird v. Tatum.*" *Columbia Law Review* 73, no. 1 (January 1973): 106–124.

Kibbe, Jennifer. "Congressional Oversight of Intelligence: Is the Solution Part of the Problem?" *Intelligence and National Security* 25 (February 2010): 24–49.

Kluger, Richard. *Simple Justice: The History of* Brown v. Board of Education *and Black America's Struggle for Equality.* New York: Alfred A. Knopf, 2004.

Kolko, Gabriel. *The Politics of War: The World and United States Foreign Policy, 1943–1945.* New York: Random House, 1968.

Kutler, Stanley I. *The Wars of Watergate: The Last Crisis of Richard Nixon.* New York: Knopf, 1990.

Lacovara, Philip A. "Presidential Power to Gather Intelligence: The Tension between Article II and Amendment I." *Law and Contemporary Problems* 14, no. 3, Presidential Power: Part 2 (Summer 1976): 106–131.

LaFeber, Walter. *America, Russia and the Cold War, 1955–1966.* New York: Wiley, 1967.

———. *The American Age: United States Foreign Policy at Home and Abroad since 1750.* New York: W. W. Norton, 1989.

Lemov, Michael. *People's Warrior: John Moss and the Fight for Freedom of Information and Consumer Rights.* Madison, NJ: Fairleigh Dickinson University Press, 2011.

Light, Jennifer. *Warfare to Welfare: Defense Intellectuals and Urban Problems in Cold War America.* Baltimore: Johns Hopkins University Press, 2003.

Lowi, Theodore J. "Presidential Power: Restoring the Balance." *Political Science Quarterly* 100, no. 2 (Summer 1985): 185–213.

Mangold, Tom. *Cold Warrior: James Jesus Angleton, the CIA's Master Spy Hunter.* New York: Touchstone Books, 1992.

Marchetti, Victor, and John Marks. *The CIA and the Cult of Intelligence.* New York: Knopf, 1974.

Mayer, Kenneth R. "Executive Orders and Presidential Power." *Journal of Politics* 61, no. 2 (May 1999): 445–466.

McCormick, Thomas J. *America's Half Century: United States Foreign Policy in the Cold War and After.* Baltimore: Johns Hopkins University Press, 1989.

McNamara, Robert S with Brian VanDeMark. *In Retrospect: The Tragedy and Lessons of Vietnam.* New York: Random House, 1995.

Milkis, Sidney M. "The Presidency, Democratic Reform, and Constitutional Change," *PS: Political Science and Politics* (Summer 1987): 628–636.

Morone, James. *The Democratic Wish: Popular Participation and the Limits of American Government.* New Haven, CT: Yale University Press, 1998.

Mondale, Walter. *The Accountability of Power: Toward a Responsible Presidency.* New York: David McKay, 1975.

——— with David Hage. *The Good Fight: A Life in Liberal Politics.* New York: Scribner, 2010.

Neier, Aryeh. *Only Judgment: The Limits of Litigation in Social Change.* Middletown, CT: Wesleyan University Press, 1982.

———. *Taking Liberties: Four Decades in the Struggle for Rights.* New York: Public Affairs, 2003.

Nessen, Ron. *It Sure Looks Different from the Inside.* New York: Playboy Press, 1978.

Nitze, Paul. *From Hiroshima to Glasnost: At the Center of Decision—A Memoir.* New York: Grove Weidenfeld, 1989.

Nixon, Richard. "Reorganization Plan No. 2 of 1970." *Public Administration Review* 30, no. 6 (November–December 1970): 611–619.

Olmsted, Kathryn. *Challenging the Secret Government: The Post-Watergate Investigations of the CIA and FBI.* Chapel Hill: University of North Carolina Press, 1996.

Olson, Keith W. *Watergate: The Presidential Scandal That Shook America.* Lawrence: University Press of Kansas, 2003.

O'Reilly, Kenneth. *Hoover and the Un-Americans: The FBI, HUAC, and the Red Menace.* Philadelphia: Temple University Press, 1983.

———. *Racial Matters: The FBI's Secret File on Black America, 1960–1972.* New York: Free Press, 1989.

Oshinsky, David M. *A Conspiracy So Immense: The World of Joe McCarthy.* New York: Free Press, 1983.

Patashnik, Eric. *Reforms at Risk: What Happens after Major Policy Changes Are Enacted.* Princeton, NJ: Princeton University Press, 2008.

Patterson, James. *Grand Expectations: The United States, 1945–1974.* New York: Oxford University Press, 1996.

———. *Restless Giant: The United States from Watergate to Bush v. Gore.* New York: Oxford University Press, 2005.

Perkus, Cathy. *Cointelpro: The FBI's Secret War on Political Freedom.* New York: Monad Press, 1975.

Perlstein, Rick. *Nixonland: The Rise of a President and the Fracturing of America.* New York: Scribner, 2008.

Peters, Charles. *Tilting at Windmills: An Autobiography.* Reading, MA: Addison-Wesley, 1988.

Peters, Charles, and Taylor Branch. *Blowing the Whistle: Dissent in the Public Interest.* New York: Praeger Publishers, 1972.

Peters, Charles, and Timothy J. Adams, eds. *Inside the System: A Washington Monthly Reader.* New York: Praeger Publishers, 1970.

Phillips, David Atlee. *The Night Watch: 25 Years of Peculiar Service.* New York: Atheneum, 1977.

Powers, Richard Gid. *Broken: The Troubled Past and Uncertain Future of the FBI.* New York: Free Press, 2004.

———. *G-Men: Hoover's FBI in American Popular Culture.* Carbondale: Southern Illinois University Press, 1983.

———. *Secrecy and Power: The Life of J. Edgar Hoover.* New York: Free Press, 1987.

Pratte, Paul Alfred. *Gods within the Machine: A History of the American Society of Newspaper Editors, 1923–1993.* Westport, CT: Praeger Publishers, 1995.

Putnam, Robert. *Bowling Alone: The Collapse and Revival of American Community.* New York: Simon and Schuster, 2000.

Pyle, Christopher. *Military Surveillance of Civilian Politics, 1967–1970.* New York: Garland Publishing, 1986.

Qureshi, Lubna. *Nixon, Kissinger and Allende: U.S. Involvement in the 1973 Coup in Chile.* Lanham, MD: Lexington Books, 2008.

Richards, Leonard. *Shays's Rebellion: The American Revolution's Final Battle.* Philadelphia: University of Pennsylvania Press, 2002.

Ritchie, Donald. *Reporting from Washington: The History of the Washington Press Corps.* New York: Oxford University Press, 2005.

Rosenbaum, Herbert D., and Alexej Ugrinsky, eds. *The Presidency and Domestic Policies of Jimmy Carter.* Westport, CT: Greenwood Press, 1994.

Rumsfeld, Donald. *Known and Unknown: A Memoir.* New York: Sentinel, 2011.

Scheips, Paul J. *The Role of Federal Military Forces in Domestic Disorders, 1945–1992.* Washington, DC: Center for Military History, United States Army, 2005.

Schlesinger, Arthur M., Jr. *The Imperial Presidency.* Boston: Houghton Mifflin, 1973.

Schmidt, Regin. *Red Scare: FBI and the Origins of Anticommunism in the United States, 1919–1943.* Copenhagen: Museum Tusculanum Press, 2000.

Schorr, Daniel. *Clearing the Air.* Boston: Houghton Mifflin, 1977.

Schulman, Bruce. *The Seventies: The Great Shift in American Culture, Society, and Politics.* New York: Da Capo Press, 2001.

Schulman, Bruce, and Julian Zelizer, eds. *Rightward Bound: Making America Conservative in the 1970s.* Cambridge, MA: Harvard University Press, 2008.

"The Selling of the Pentagon." Prod. CBS News, Peter Davis, Perry Wolf, written by Peter Davis, reporter Roger Mudd (CBS, 23 February 1971), transcript in Columbia Broadcast System, Inc., *From Subpoena to Recommittal: An Indexed Collection of Materials and Reprints Dealing with the Case of the Subpoenaing of Outtakes of the CBS News Broadcast, The Selling of the Pentagon.* New York: CBS, 1971.

Shapley, Deborah. *Promise and Power: The Life and Times of Robert McNamara.* Boston: Little, Brown, 1993.

Skocpol, Theda. *Diminished Democracy: From Membership to Management in American Civic Life.* Norman: University of Oklahoma Press, 2003.

Smist, Frank, Jr. *Congress Oversees the United States Intelligence Community, 1947–1989.* Knoxville: University of Tennessee Press, 1990.

Smith, Donald L. *Zechariah Chafee, Jr.: Defender of Liberty and Law.* Cambridge, MA: Harvard University Press, 1986.

Stuart, Douglas T. *Creating the National Security State: A History of the Law That Transformed America.* Princeton, NJ: Princeton University Press, 2008.

Sugrue, Thomas. *The Origins of the Urban Crisis: Race and Inequality in Postwar Detroit.* Princeton, NJ: Princeton University Press, 1996.

Thelen, David. *Becoming Citizens in the Age of Television: How Americans Challenged the Media and Seized Initiative during the Iran-Contra Debate.* Chicago: University of Chicago Press, 1996.

Theoharis, Alan. *Chasing Spies: How the FBI Failed in Counterintelligence but Promoted the Politics of McCarthyism in the Cold War Years.* Chicago: Ivan R. Dee, 2002.

———. *The FBI and American Democracy: A Brief Critical History.* Lawrence: University Press of Kansas, 2004.

Thomas, Norman C., and Harold L. Wolman. "The Presidency and Policy Formulation: The Task Force Device." *Public Administration Review* 29, no. 5 (September–October 1969): 459–471.

Uncle Sam Is Watching You: Highlights from the Hearings of the Senate Subcommittee on Constitutional Rights. Washington, DC: Public Affairs Press, 1971.

Waldmann, Raymond J. "The Domestic Council: Innovation in Presidential Government." *Public Administration Review* 36, no. 3 (May–June 1976): 260–268.

Walker, Samuel. *In Defense of American Liberties: A History of the ACLU.* New York: Oxford University Press, 1990.

Watters, Pat, and Stephen Gillers, eds. *Investigating the FBI.* Garden City, NY: Doubleday, 1973.

Wiggins, James Russell. *Freedom or Secrecy.* New York: Oxford University Press, 1956.

Wilford, Hugh. *The Mighty Wurlitzer: How the CIA Played America.* Cambridge, MA: Harvard University Press, 2008.

Williams, William Appleman. *The Tragedy of American Diplomacy.* New York: Dell, 1962.

Zegart, Amy. "The Domestic Politics of Irrational Intelligence Oversight." *Political Science Quarterly* 126, no. 1 (2011): 1–25.

Zelizer, Julian. *On Capitol Hill: The Struggle to Reform Congress and Its Consequences, 1948–2000.* New York: Cambridge University Press, 2004.

———, ed. *The American Congress: The Building of Democracy.* Boston: Houghton Mifflin, 2004.

Index

Abzug, Bella, 130
Agnew, Spiro, 92, 98, 116, 155
Alsop, Joseph, Jr., 22
American Bar Association, 101
American Civil Liberties Union (ACLU),
    77, 78, 79, 164
    and Christopher Pyle, 81, 83–85
    litigation strategy, 79–80, 106–107, 123,
    182
    and right to privacy, 117, 130, 180
    see also Center for National Security
    Studies (CNSS); Ervin, Samuel
    James, Jr.; Federal Bureau of
    Investigation (FBI)
Americans for Democratic Action, 145
American Society of News Editors, 184
American Society of Newspaper Editors
    (ASNE), 4, 12, 15, 16, 17, 20
Associated Press Managing Editors
    Association (APME), 15
Association of Retired Intelligence
    Officers, 165

Baker, Richard, 181
Bancroft, Harding, 99
Baskir, Lawrence, 180
Bayh, Birch, 175
Biden, Joseph, 173
Brookings Institute, 124
Brzezinski, Zbigniew, 174, 175
Buckley, James, 130
Bush, George H. W., 157
Bush, George W., 183–184
Butterfield, Alexander, 118

Campaign to Stop Government Spying, 182
Carter, Jimmy, 165, 182
    and FISA, 174–176

and intelligence reform, 170, 177, 179
    and Morton Halperin, 172–173
    and Walter Mondale, 170–171, 174–175
Case, Clifford, 181
Catledge, Turner, 15
Center for National Security Studies
    (CNSS), 141, 147, 182
    and ACLU, 135, 139, 145, 158, 164, 173
    and CIA, 137–138, 145, 155
    founding of, 135–137
Central Intelligence Agency (CIA), 181
    charter, 176, 177
    and Chile, 138, 139
    and oversight, 137, 138, 139
    and secrecy, 23
Chafee, Zechariah, 74
CHAOS. See Operation CHAOS
Cheney, Richard, 139
Church, Frank, 5
Church Committee. See Senate Select
    Committee to Study Governmental
    Operations with Respect to
    Intelligence Activities (Church
    Committee)
Citizens Commission to Investigate the
    FBI, 90, 91, 133. See also Federal
    Bureau of Investigation (FBI)
Civil disorder, 3, 80
    congressional response, 47–49
    CONUS, 55–57, 59
    Department of Defense response, 3–4,
    51–53, 62–63, 66
    Department of Justice response, 3–4,
    34–35, 45–46
    Ramsey Clark and, 34, 37, 39–40, 43–45,
    47
    Robert McNamara and, 54–55, 57
    William P. Yarborough and, 56, 58–59

Clark, Ramsey, 125
and civil disorder, 35, 37–38, 40
and domestic surveillance, 47–49, 66, 146
and FBI, 40–42
and IDIU, 34, 44–46, 50
Clifford, Clark, 166, 167
COINTELPRO, 45, 158. *See also* Federal Bureau of Investigation (FBI)
Colby, William, 137–139
Commission on CIA Activities within the United States (Rockefeller Commission), 139, 142
Commission on Protecting and Reducing Government Secrecy, 183
Commission on the Organization of the Government for the Conduct of Foreign Policy (Murphy Commission), 142
Committee for Public Justice, 125, 126, 145
Common Cause, 77, 101, 145
Computers, 81
Computer technology, 43
Conyers, John, 1
Cooper, Kent, 15, 16
Crewdson, John, 154
Cronkite, Walter, 99
Cross, Harold, 16, 17, 21
Cuban Missile Crisis, 26–27

Dash, Sam, 114
Dawson, William, 19, 24
Democratic National Convention, 1968, 80
Department of Justice, Interdivisional Information Unit (IDIU), 44, 45, 46. *See also* Clark, Ramsey
Dirksen, Everett, 73
Domestic Council Committee on the Right of Privacy, 116
Donner, Frank, 79–80, 85

Easterly, Guy, 22
Eisenhower, Dwight, 11–12, 19–20, 24
Eizenstat, Stu, 175
Ellsberg, Daniel, 93, 112, 124
Erlenborn, John, 130
Ervin, Samuel James, Jr., 3, 5, 73–74, 180
and Army surveillance hearings, 82–86, 90
and civil rights legislation, 75

and freedom of the press hearings, 99–100
and right to privacy, 76, 117, 129, 130
Executive power, 5

Family Jewels, 139, 147. *See also* Central Intelligence Agency (CIA)
Federal Bureau of Investigation (FBI), 4, 22, 58, 124, 136, 139, 146–147, 163, 171
and ACLU, 158–161, 167–168, 180, 182
and civil rights movement, 40–42, 64
and COINTELPRO, 45, 133–134, 144, 158
and dissemination of intelligence, 60, 141, 157
Hoover, J. Edgar, and, 41–42, 53, 86, 125, 177–178
methods of, 42, 103
and Media, Pennsylvania, burglary, 90–91, 133, 144
transparency of, 6, 8, 83, 122, 128
and Watergate, 113
see also Clarke, Ramsey; civil disorder
Ford, Gerald
and CIA, 139
and FISA, 161
and FOIA (1966), 32
and FOIA (1974), 131, 132, 133, 134, 135
and intelligence oversight, 157
and Privacy Act of 1974, 135
and right to privacy, 116
wiretapping, 47
Foreign Intelligence Surveillance Act (FISA), 161–165, 175–176, 179, 183
Fort Holabird, 72
Freedom of Information Act (FOIA 1966), 28–31, 133–134
Freedom of Information Act (FOIA 1974), 127–129, 131, 134, 140–142, 182, 183
Freedom of Information Advocates Network, 184
Fulbright, J. William, 5, 105

Gardner, John, 77
Gillers, Stephen, 125
Goldwater, Barry, 130, 168–169
Goldwater, Barry, Jr., 5, 117, 130
Government in the Sunshine Act, 172
Graham, Phil, 13
Griffin, Robert, 28, 30
Griswold v. Connecticut, 106
Gude, Gilbert, 130

Halperin, Morton, 3–4, 124, 136, 159, 176
    and ACLU, 125–126
    and Carter administration, 173–174
    and CNSS, 136, 182
Hart, Phil, 130
Helms, Richard, 166
Hersh, Seymour, 4, 138–139
Hoffman, Clare, 23, 25
House Committee on Government
        Operations, 1, 5, 12, 19, 24, 29
House Permanent Select Committee on
        Intelligence, 169
House Select Intelligence Committee
        (Pike Committee), 154–158, 167
House Subcommittee on Foreign
        Operations and Government
        Information, 127
House Subcommittee on Government
        Information, 12, 20–24, 28–30
Hughes-Ryan Amendment, 138
Human Rights Watch, 180
Humphrey, Hubert, 130

Institute for Policy Studies, 145
Intelligence oversight, 167, 168, 171
Intelligence Oversight Act of 1980, 177
Investigative journalism, 4, 5, 71
Iran Hostage Crisis, 177

Jewish Defense League, 160
Johnson, Lyndon, 3–5, 97
    and censorship, 27–30
    and executive privilege, 31, 102
    and law and order, 33–38, 40–43,
        48–50
    and FOIA (1966), 29, 32

Kass, Benny, 31
Katzenbach, Nicholas, 41
Keith, Damon, 108–110
Kelley, Clarence, 166
Kennedy, Edward, 5, 102–103, 132, 162
Kennedy, John, 25, 35, 41
    and censorship, 26–28
    and executive privilege, 102
Kennedy, Robert, 4, 35–36, 41
King, Martin Luther, Jr., 4, 40, 41, 52, 64
Kissinger, Henry, 103, 124–125
Kleindeist, Richard, 134
Koch, Ed, 130
Koop, Theodore, 23

Korean War, 15–16
Kraft, Joseph, 134

Levi, Edward, 141, 142, 160–161
Long, Edward, 30

McCarthy, Joseph, 10–11
McClellan, John, 47
McCormick, Robert, 14
McNamara, Robert, 93
    and CONUS, 54–56
    and military as law enforcement, 51–52
    and responses to civil disorder, 55,
        57–58
Magnuson, Warren, 130
Mansfield, Mike, 5, 73, 114, 138, 143
Mathias, Charles, 162
Media and Army hearings, 87, 88
Michigan Coalition to End Government
        Spying, 1, 150
Miller, Arthur, 89
Mitchell, John, 91, 160
Mondale, Walter, 5, 170–171
    and Carter administration, 174–176
    and Church committee, 146–147
    see also Carter, James
Moorhead, William, 5, 100–101, 127–128
Moss, John, 3, 5, 17–19, 130, 180

NAACP v. Alabama, 106
National Advisory Commission on
        Civil Disorder (the Eisenhower
        Commission), 64–65
National Freedom of Information
        Coalition, 184
National Security Act of 1947, 3, 166
National Security Agency (NSA), 144
National Security Archive, 184
Neier, Aryeh, 3–4, 77–80, 179–180
Nelson, Gaylord, 168
Newton, V. M., 15, 21, 22
New York Times, 49, 71, 72, 93, 144, 151
    and Ervin investigations, 86, 88, 90
    and Nixon administration, 98, 99, 111,
        124
    and Robert McNamara, 51, 54
    and Russ Wiggins, 10, 13
    and transparency, 10, 15, 22–23, 132,
        184
New York Times v. United States, 93
Nichols, Wade, 23

Nixon, Richard, 3
    and censorship, 91
    and executive privilege, 84, 102, 103,
        104, 118
    and FOIA (1974), 128, 129
    and media, 92, 97, 98
    and right to privacy, 115, 116
    and wiretaps, 124, 125, 126
National Security Council (NSC), 181

Oatis, William, 15
O'Brien, John, 88
OMB Watch, 184
Operation CHAOS, 143, 158
Operation SHAMROCK, 144
Organized Crime Act of 1970, 124

Packard, Vance, 81
Pearson, Drew, 16
Pentagon Papers, 93, 98, 105, 124. See also
    American Civil Liberties Union
    (ACLU); Halperin, Morton;
    McNamara, Robert; New York
    Times
Percy, Charles, 5, 130, 166
Permanent intelligence oversight
    committees, 165, 166, 168, 169, 183
Peters, Charles, 4, 68–70, 72, 120
Petersen, Henry, 134
Pett, Saul, 28
Phillips, David Atlee, 165
Pike, Otis, 143
Pike Committee. See House Select
    Intelligence Committee (Pike
    Committee)
Pope, James, 15, 23
Privacy Act, 182, 183
Privacy Act of 1974, 130, 135
Public opinion
    of civil disorder, 39–40
    of Congress, 72
    right to privacy, 82–83
    and Watergate, 127
Pyle, Christopher, 3, 4, 88, 180
    and domestic spying, 67, 72, 89
    and Ervin investigations, 83–85

Reagan, Ronald, 178, 181
Reese, Edward, 18, 19
Reporters' Committee for Freedom of the
    Press, 155

Report of the President's Task Force on
    the Los Angeles Riots, 38. See also
    Clark, Ramsey; Johnson, Lyndon B.
Reston, James, 169, 170
    and censorship, 22, 23
Ribicoff, Abraham, 168
Right to privacy, 81, 106, 107
Rockefeller, Nelson, 139
Roosevelt, Franklin, 4
Rosenberg, Jerry, 89
Roth, William, 95
Rowan, Carl, 26
Rumsfeld, Donald, 5, 28–29, 139

Safe Streets and Crime Control Act of
    1968, 47–49, 102–103, 160
Saxbe, William, 133–134
Scalia, Antonin, 142
Schlesinger, James, 147
Schorr, Daniel, 97, 98, 154, 155
Schwarz, F. A. O., Jr., 164
Selling of the Pentagon, 92, 98
Senate Committee on Foreign Relations,
    105
Senate Permanent Subcommittee on
    Investigations, 11. See also Wiggins,
    Russell J.
Senate Select Committee on Intelligence,
    169, 177
Senate Select Committee on Presidential
    Campaign Activities. See Watergate
    Committee
Senate Select Committee to Study
    Governmental Operations with
    Respect to Intelligence Activities
    (Church Committee), 148, 167
    and CNSS, 140, 141, 145
    discovery of abuses, 144, 146–147
    report of, 154, 156
Senate Subcommittee on Constitutional
    Rights, 68, 114, 180
    and domestic surveillance, 73, 130
    and Nixon administration, 99, 102
Senate Subcommittee on Separation of
    Powers, 73, 102, 114
Shattuck, John, 165
    and ACLU, 1, 122, 182
    and electronic surveillance, 162
    and Morton Halperin, 122, 125
    see also American Civil Liberties Union
    (ACLU); Halperin, Morton

Sigma Delta Chi, 4, 15, 32
Smith, William French, 181
Sorenson, Theodore, 173
Soviet invasion of Afghanistan, 177
Stanley v. Georgia, 106
Stanton, Frank, 92
Stein, Ralph, 85
Stennis, John, 126
Stern, Carl, 133, 134
Sylvester, Arthur, 26

Talley v. California, 106
Tatum, Arlo, 106
Tatum v. Laird, 106–107
Thone, Charles, 130
Thurmond, Strom, 169
Tower, John, 169
Truman, Harry
    and censorship, 13
    and executive privilege, 110
Turner, Stansfield, 174

United Automobile Workers of America,
    145
United States v. Brown, 159
United States v. Butenko, 160
United States v. Nixon, 119, 131
*United States v. United States District
    Court* (Keith decision), 108–111

Vance, Cyrus, 46, 52
Vietnam War, 34, 40, 61
    and freedom of information, 30, 32, 68,
        102, 120
    and journalism, 27–28, 92, 136
    see also Freedom of Information Act
        (FOIA 1966); Moss, John

Village Voice, 155

The Washington Monthly, 69–70, 72.
        See also Peters, Charles; Pyle,
        Christopher
The Washington Post, 2, 10, 13, 90144
    and Russ Wiggins, 2, 10, 13
    and transparency, 91, 92, 122, 132
    and Watergate, 112, 125
    see also Wiggins, Russell J.
Watergate committee, 73, 114–115, 118
Watergate scandal
    and CREEP, 112–113
    and Nixon trial, 112, 118–119, 120
    and "plumbers," 112–114, 115
    see also Ervin, Samuel James, Jr.;
        Nixon, Richard, *United States. v.
        Nixon*
Welch, Richard, 153, 154
Westin, Alan, 72
White House correspondents, 14
Wicker, Tom, 164
Wiggins, Russell J., 2, 4
    and censorship, 15
    and freedom of information, 20–21, 25,
        31
    and *Washington Post*, 10–13, 15, 31
Wisconsin v. Constantineau, 106
Wulf, Mel, 79, 84, 87. *See also* American
        Civil Liberties Union (ACLU)

Yarborough, William P., 56, 57. *See also*
        McNamara, Robert
Youngstown Sheet & Tube Co. v. Sawyer, 110

Zweibon v. Mitchell, 160